EVERYDAY SAINTS

EVERYDAY SAINTS

By: Fr Luke Sidarous

ST SHENOUDA PRESS
SYDNEY, AUSTRALIA
2025

Everyday Saints

By: Fr Luke Sidarous

COPYRIGHT © 2025
St. Shenouda Press

All rights reserved. Except for brief quotations in critical publications or reviews, no part of this book may be reproduced in any manner without prior written permission from the publisher.

ST SHENOUDA PRESS
8419 Putty Rd,
Putty, NSW, 2330
Sydney, Australia

www.stshenoudapress.com

ISBN 13: 978-1-7638415-7-4

All scripture quotations, unless otherwise indicated, are taken from the New King James Version®. Copyright © 1982 by Thomas Nelson, Inc. Used by permission. All rights reserved.

Contents

Introduction 1

Preface 3

PART 1

1. Papa Sadek 7
2. Mr. Abdel Malek Twadros 19
3. A Rare Epitome for Repentance 25
4. Blessed Is the Giving 31
5. Ascended into Heaven 35
6. After Five Days 39
7. Your Prayer Is Heard 41
8. The Service of the Angels 45
9. Poor, Yet Making Many Rich 47
10. The Blessing of the Lord Makes One Rich and Adds No Sorrow with It 51
11. Fruit According to Its Kind 57
12. The Deacon Youssef Habeeb 61
13. George from Rome 67
14. Let Me Die the Death of the Righteous 71
15. Jesus Helps the Tempted 75

PART 2

16. Illuminated the Insight..87
17. Chosen Vessel...91
18. The Word of God Is Living and Powerful.................................95
19. They Shall Be Taught by God..97
20. Saint George and the Quick Help..99
21. Peace, Peace, to Him Who Is Far and to Him Who Is Near.............103
22. Saint Mark the Evangelist..107
23. The Guardian Angel 109
24. Hail to Mari Mina 113
25. The Lady "Mother of Mourad" A Friend of the Angels 121
26. Overcoming Death...129
27. The Angel of the Lord Encamps All Around Those Who Fear Him and Delivers Them 133
28. The Chastity of Joseph..141
29. The Lord Answers You in the Day of Trouble 147
30. Mikhaeel the Simple..151
31. The Cross Is the Power of God..155
32. Poor, Yet Rich in Faith..161
33. Drink of the Spirit..167
34. A Ceremonial Reception in Heaven 171
35. "Epitome" of the Christian Family..175

PART 3

36. The Wonder Worker 183
37. St. George Abolished the Trouble 187
38. In the Last Watch 191
39. Perfect Patristic Conduct 195
40. From All Social Classes 199
41. Faithfulness in What Is Least 203
42. Impossible with Men 209
43. Courage of the Martyrs 215
44. Astounding Faith 219
45. Simplicity and Faith 223
46. The Christian Epitome 225
47. Do Not Let the Sun Go Down on Your Wrath 229
48. The Holy Baptism 233
49. The Perpetual Prayer 237
50. A Physician Lives the Life of Prayer 241
51. The Lord Shall Give You the Desires of Your Heart 245

PART 4

52. Let Me Die the Death of the Righteous 249

53. Only Let Your Conduct Be Worthy of the Gospel of Christ 251

54. Meekness of the Lambs and Bravery of the Martyrs 253

55. Whom I Have in Heaven .... Psalm 73 257

56. Prayer Is Better than Life 261

57. In the Name of Jesus 265

58. The Sermon on the Mount 269

59. The Feast of Nayrouz 271

60. Not by "Measure" God Gives the Spirit 275

61. January 11th 279

62. Angelic Glimmer 283

63. Just Believe 289

64. Examples of Loyalty 293

65. Account of a True Repentance 299

66. Alive Conscience 301

67. Examples of Thanks Giving in Illness 305

68. Beautiful Icon 309

69. The Litany of the Travelers 311

PART 5

70. Practical Faith Overcomes the Enemy.......................................315
71. The Faithful Witness..319
72. Friendship in Christ..337
73. How Beautiful Forgiveness Is!..343
74. Memory That Was Engraved so Profoundly 349
75. The Fervent Prayer..353
76. The Zeal for Your House Has Eaten Me Up..........................357
77. Your Word Is a Lamp to My Feet..361
78. The Ministry of Prayer..367
79. Mothers Sowing Faith...369
80. Always Ought to Pray and Not Lose Heart...........................375
81. Testimony of Faith..379
82. If Anyone Wants to Take Away Your Tunic,
    Let Him Your Cloak Also 385
83. Rejoice in the Lord Always 389
84. Harmless as Doves..393
85. Examples of "Giving" with Liberality...................................397
86. Confess to the Last Breath...401

   Epilogue..405

Introduction

In a world where holiness often feels distant and spiritual life appears to move slowly beneath the weight of daily struggles, The Sweet Fragrance of Christ in the Lives of Contemporary Righteous – Volume One offers a gentle yet profound call to rediscover the presence of God among us. Are you longing to witness the living work of the Holy Spirit today? Are you seeking examples of righteousness that inspire and uplift? This book invites you into a spiritual journey where every life, every struggle, and every quiet act of faith becomes a testimony to the sweet aroma of Christ.

Drawing from the timeless Orthodox understanding of holiness, this volume illuminates the lives of contemporary righteous individuals—men and women whose daily walk with God reflected humility, purity, and a heartfelt devotion to Christ. Their stories reveal how the Holy Spirit continues to work powerfully in every generation, shaping souls and guiding hearts toward the path of holiness.

In each account, Hegumen Loka Sidaros offers a window into the spiritual depth of those who lived among us—those whose presence radiated peace, whose words carried grace, and whose actions testified to the quiet work of God within them. These examples challenge us to see holiness not as something distant or reserved for monastics alone, but as a living reality available to all who seek God sincerely.

As the saints throughout the ages remind us, holiness is a journey that requires perseverance, humility, and love. These lives bear witness to the truth that sanctity grows gradually—nourished by prayer, strengthened by the Holy Spirit, and shaped within the hidden struggles of the heart.

Join us in this contemplative journey. Allow the fragrance of these righteous lives to inspire your own walk with Christ, to awaken in you a deeper longing for spiritual growth, and to remind you that holiness still blossoms beautifully in our time.

Preface

The life accounts of the saints were linked, in the minds of some, to separation from the world and further disattachment from the flesh. It has settled, in the minds of some, that the "Way of Holiness" or the "Life with God" in its perfect depiction requires an exodus to a monastery or a cave. The cause that helped enhance the spread of such ideology, perhaps unintentionally, is certain writings that manifested, in totality, examples of the lives of the saintly fathers in monastic life. Also, some of the "Servants of the Word" contributed to anchoring this ideology through their sermons and teachings, which were not void of manifesting only the "Aspects of Holiness" of the saintly fathers of the monks. To the point that the hearer, once he hears the word "Saint," his thoughts are directed to the synonym embedded in his mind… That is "The Devout Monk in the Wilderness."

It reached a point that some people started teaching, with ease and simplicity, in such a manner saying; "Once upon a time, a righteous monk……. Etc." Or "There was this certain saintly monk…. Etc." Thus, it was almost eradicated from our teachings and Tradition, which is recorded through the written or the heard word; the fact that our Church is full of countless righteous people and witnesses to the Lord from all sorts of people in every generation, under all aspects of the social life, and from the poor and the rich alike.

We don't intend to underestimate the monastic life or the holiness of the fathers who had trodden the world and loved Christ more than life. We don't deny the grace and holiness of our saintly fathers, the monks, throughout all the epochs of the Church, whether from the vintage times, those whose reputation reached the ends of the inhabited world, or the modern generations.

We only desire to enhance another meaningful aspect that ought to be vividly clear which that is the saint, according to the orthodox concept, is not only the wonderworker. But he is the one who is walking and striving in the "Way of Holiness." The Church, since her birth, was guided and supported by the Holy Spirit with miracles and wonders that were performed by the hands of the Apostles. For the Lord was testifying to the grace of His Word with signs according to His promise, "And these signs will follow those who believe1"[1].

However, even though this authority over healing the sick, casting out demons, and performing miracles was given to the Church, those who were bestowed as assistance from God and support of the Holy Spirit. Yet, let it be known that the Church, from the beginning, was characterized by holiness. The believers were called "Saints." The Apostle Paul addresses the Church, in numerous places, as saints:

- "Paul and Timothy, bondservants of Jesus Christ, to all the saints in Christ Jesus." Philippians 1

- "Paul, an apostle of Jesus Christ by the will of God, to the saints who are in Ephesus, and faithful in Christ Jesus." Ephesians 1

- "Paul, an apostle of Jesus Christ by the will of God, and Timothy our brother, to the church of God which is at Corinth, with all the saints." II Corinthians 1

Therefore, we wanted to knock on the door concerning the talk about the "Contemporary Righteous." Those whom we had seen with our eyes closely encountered them, and the traits of holiness and its aroma permeated their lives.

We present some examples, with brief words, that reveal the depth and richness of the Spirit in the lives of those who walked by the Spirit according to Scripture's commandment. We hope, in the Lord, that they become the first fruits of an abundant recording of the "Lives of Contemporary Righteous."

---

[1] Mark 16:17

PART 1

1

Papa Sadek

That Pious man lived, amongst us, the last part of his life on earth after leaving Cairo in 1960. He departed, at Alexandria, in 1969 around the age of 68 years.

While residing in Cairo, he was known to many loved ones. Especially from the Church of the Lady Virgin of Rod El Farag[2] in Shobra[3], at which he spent many years.

The life of Mr. Sadek Raphael was distinguished by simplicity and depth at the same time.

While residing in Cairo, he was known to many loved ones. Especially from the Church of the Lady Virgin of Rod El Farag[2]in Shobra[3] , at which he spent many years.

---

[2] A district in the Northern Area of Cairo.
[3] A major city of Cairo Governorate, Egypt.

The life of Mr. Sadek Raphael was distinguished by simplicity and depth at the same time.

He, during his youth, did not know the "Fun of the Youth. On the contrary, his profound fellowship with Christ was the source of purity and sanctification for his mind[4]. Hence, he kept a child's pure heart at twenty-one years of age.

His elder brother departed to the Heavenly places in the prime of youth. He left behind a wife and a young daughter.

As for "Sadek" …. He proposed in his heart, from an early age, a specific type of life. He shall live it while consecrating it entirely for the One that loved him and sacrificed His life for him[5] He was determined, wholeheartedly, to enter one of the monasteries, but the sudden departure of his brother faced him with an inevitable responsibility. Hence, he decided to wait until his brother's widow married or settle down. While he was choosing to do as such, his mother, whom he dearly loved, fell sick. During her last moments, she endowed him, saying, "Do not go to the monastery until you are fully assured about your brother's widow and daughter." He promised her. Afterwards, she departed on that same day. Since then, "Sadek" has cared for his brother's widow and her daughter. He became the sole supporter of her. Many had proposed to her for marriage. However, she, influenced by the life of prayer, Bible satiety, and relinquishing all that is of the world. For she acknowledged that joyfully depicted in the life of Mr. Sadek, adamantly refused to marry another man. She decided to live for Christ as well……. And so, it was.

Mr. Sadek continued to look after his brother's widow, raising her daughter while working for the Ministry of Justice until his retirement. Afterward, he left Cairo and resided in Alexandria. In every field that pious man was present in, all people testified that he was a "Man of God." In the field of work, he gained the trust of his leaders and the respect of his subordinates. He was light and salt, according to the Gospel.

The rest of his time was devoted to the Spiritual life. The Grace had bestowed him with an outpouring of condolences and depth in Spirit. So that when he opens his mouth to speak, words flow out copiously like a flowing river. So that everyone who hears him is inflamed with joy, repentance, and inexpressible spiritual emotions.

---

[4] Thoughts.
[5] The Lord Jesus Christ.

He informed that once he was visiting a devout Christian family, and during the evening, the day of the visit, they were being comforted by the "Word of Grace." Time passed without them realizing it, and they were surprised to hear the milkman outside announcing his presence[6.] It has become morning while they were in the trance of the Spirit. They prayed, and he left and headed to his workplace.

The comfort of the brother's widow was acquired by her encounter with, next to her residence in Cairo, the Church's orphanage of Saint Mary that the departed Hegumen Dawood El-Makary founded. He was a pious man and a close, beloved friend to Mr. Sadek. Thus, she began to preoccupy herself with the children and showered them with love and tenderness.

During one of Kiahk's vigil nights, as they were assembled in the Church every Saturday as usual reciting praises, the brother's widow was sitting down embracing and comforting some of the children. And since she possessed a simple and naive heart, she whispered in Mr. Sadek's ear, "O my brother Sadek! Why doesn't the Virgin come to us now as we are vigil around her?" Upon uttering the words in her mouth, the Holy Virgin appeared before them in complete form, walking inside the altar. Mr. Sadek prostrated to the ground, and she leaped while rejoicing, offering peace and blessings upon the pure saint.

Astonishingly, none of the present people enjoyed that revelation except some little children.

His Life in Alexandria:

Mr. Sadek escaped Cairo because he realized he had become known to many people. He preferred to live a quiet life far from people's attention, so while he lived in Alexandria, he kept to himself and didn't mingle with people.

He resided next to Saint George's Church of Sporting. He was acquainted with our departed father, Bishoy Kamel, since the beginning of his service. When Abouna Bishoy wanted to obtain some rest from the troubles of the service, he would enter Mr. Sadek's home. They both were comforted by the overflowing words of Grace.

Mr. Sadek was surrounded by a small group of youth, primarily expats, and he was a fountain of doctrine and great blessings for them.

---

[6] It was customary during that time in Egypt for the milkman to go into apartment buildings and announce his presence with a loud voice. It was one of the methods of selling dairy products.

Mr. Sadek didn't accept to deliver sermons at the Church or her assemblies, saying, "The Holy Spirit is the One who appointed in the Church Apostles first, then teachers second. As for me, The Holy Spirit didn't appoint me a teacher, but I receive comfort along with my brethren who share the faith with me. And all that I receive from God, I don't withhold it from anyone."

The Liturgy Prayer:

An image will linger in my mind for as long as I live: the image of Mr. Sadek at the Church during the Liturgy. I bear witness by the truth that I never witnessed ever before as such ....He enters the Church, walks in humility towards the East Altar, prostrates with the utmost respect, then enters into the men's chamber, prostrates, and stands, as if his feet were nailed down, without moving throughout the Liturgy till its conclusion. From the moment he entered the Church and stood before the Altar, his eyes overflowed with tears as if they were the "Running Waters" of Jeremiah the Prophet.

Thus, we perceived Mr. Sadek at all the Liturgies he attended at the Church. His eyes didn't cease crying even during only one single Liturgy. Where do those profuse tears come from? Only from a pure, tender heart. From sensitive spiritual emotions and by absolute acknowledgment of Christ's presence.

Self-Denial:

During my conversion with the departed Pope Kirollos on the 6th in 1967, we were inside the altar of St. Mark's Cathedral in Alexandria; he asked me to bring him, Mr. Sadek. So, that same day, I went to Mr. Sadek and informed him of His Holiness the Pope wanted to see him. The words came down like a thunderbolt on the man .... He was crying with an audible sound and saying, "God forgives you; you ought to shield me till I pass through ...... I, the despicable one, what does the Pope want of me?" I calmed him, saying, "The situation should not go beyond just a mere meeting and an introduction."..... Finally, he said, "I will go to him and obey his word. But I will greet him and take his blessing amid the people without introducing myself to him." He asked Christ, Glory be to Him, with prayers and pleas to conceal his identity from the Pope so he would not know him. Because he was aware that the Lord bestowed Pope Kirollos the 6th with the Grace and the talent of knowing the secrets……. And so it was, he went to the Pope while in disguise…. And the Pope didn't know him as he was among the people. Thus, that pious man manifested humility and meekness of spirit that is rare to encounter in our present time.

The Grace:

The teachings of Papa Sadek, which flowed from his conduct and his words full of wisdom and spiritual depth, he attributed, entirely, to the Grace. He was denying himself as a doer or as a speaker. So, it was …. When he signs himself, by the sign of the life-giving Cross, at the start of his talk, he says, "The Grace says……" and he goes on with his speech. He confessed numerous times that he placed himself ahead of the hearers and benefited from the word himself before teaching the others by it.

Stranger than Fiction:

I was praying the Divine Liturgy, at the start of my priesthood life, and Mr. Sadek was standing, as he usually did, in the chorus of the Eucharist partakers since the beginning of the service …… I had to deliver the sermon that day and interpret the Liturgy Gospel …… And so it happened: I visited Mr. Sadek at his residence the evening of that day. I found him rejoicing by the Spirit and his face overflowing with joy. He immediately said to me, "Blessed is the name of the Lord ……. I am surprised by God's love and his unbelievable work." I asked him, "What happened so that you say as such?" He answered me as a confession, "During the sermon, of today's liturgy, I was receiving transcendent comforting thoughts and I realized that it was good for the congregation to benefit from them. So, I asked Christ to let you utter those thoughts. And amazingly, you instantly uttered not only the thoughts themselves but also expressed them word by word. So, I was prostrating in the altar, kissing the Lord's feet, thanking His Grace that works in us and the Spirit who supports us and answers our prayers."

In Sickness:

When a respiratory allergic disease hit Mr. Sadek[7] It prevented him from leaving his house even to go to Church. However, he was present with us, even from home, at the Church by the spirit. He followed the liturgy step by step and word by word. And even though he was absent by the flesh, his spirit was enjoying the Church's fellowship and worship.

When he had to partake of the Holy Mysteries while at home …. O the fear, the awe, and O the sweeping love that he was offering while saying to Christ with eyes full of tears, "O You, my beloved, You come to this despicable home and to Your poor servant?!"

Yet, despite his weak body and severe illness, he prostrates to the ground, merely trying to catch his breath. But the spirit is indeed willing. He doesn't cease to offer worship, sacrifice, and love to Him, who loved us to the end[8].

The Word of God is living:

He was suffering, during his last days, from a severe allergic condition. He was breathing with difficulty. Yet, astonishingly, when one of his pupils visited him, he opened his mouth to share the word of eternal life wholeheartedly…. His breathing becomes steady as if he were without illness. His brother's wife (He always addressed her as 'My Sister.') would always say to him, "My brother, truly I am amazed at your situation, a few minutes ago you were dying. Now you are talking. Stay quiet for a little bit so that you can rest." He would answer her with a pleasant smile, "My sister, don't you know the word of God is living and gives life? When I utter it with my mouth, it keeps me alive."

The Last Days:

During his final days, he was concerned with a single thought that occupied his life and was imprinted on all his talk and contemplations. That was the end of the world, "Little children, it is the last hour[9]." It was as if it had been

---

[7] Asthma. There wasn't any medicine available during that time to manage the condition
[8] John 13:1
[9] 1 John 2:18

revealed to him previously, his departure from this world and, shortly after that, the putting off of his tent.[10] Thus, he was exhilarating his children[11]. To stay vigilant and ready to meet the bridegroom. There is no substantial proof of that[12]. Except for a deeply spiritual statement he penned as a preface for one of his letters sent to one of his children abroad. And we, here, present it as an example through which we get acquainted with that giant spiritual figure. Listen to him say:

"My beloved son……

When the days of the Great Lent approach …. The Grace, then, has already furnished before my soul a rich table. So that I partake, for my soul, sustenance sufficient for running to meet the "Beloved13 ." Because of my weakness and negligence, I miss so much. Therefore, Grace compensates me during the New Year for what I have missed to enjoy in the past. And I entreated Christ, for the sake of His love within my heart, to seat your beloved soul next to the soul of your poor old father. So that you, my son, may obtain energy sufficient for running the spiritual road to meet the blessed Christ."

Excerpts from one of his letters to his Children.

My beloved son in the Lord Jesus ………

1. The life of Christ, glory to Him, is for you and revealed in the Holy Scripture and the lives of the Saints. Therefore, study it. But not from the perspective of Christ according to His own person, but about Him in your own self. For you are putting on Christ …… All His actions, feelings, and sayings are issued by Him within you or by Him through you…... Study them in the lives of the Saints, knowing that all that is theirs is yours so that you follow their footsteps in trouncing your will and training it in the same manner they had trained theirs. Hence, it merges into the will of Christ till He is revealed in you just as He was revealed in them.

2. If you sit down to study the Bible, then you are in the presence of Christ Himself. All that you read, personally, is about Him and concerns Him.

---

[10] 2 Peter 1:14
[11] Spiritual Children.
[12] His ideology.
[13] The Lord Jesus Christ.

Therefore, don't be a reader, but be submissive to the work of Grace in your person …... Subsequently, read a little and meditate spiritually a lot, untill you transform what you read into practical life within. And till you acknowledge that you are practicing what you read, believing that God's words are Spirit and life. This is the divine spiritual power born through the interaction of your soul with life, the life of the beloved Savior within you.

3. Don't you dare read or hear anyone except to the Holy Spirit through the teachers and the saints, and them being the spiritual children of your Church. You won't be able to do so unless you establish a Spiritual Life.

4. Let your life be an unceasing perpetual life of prayer by the spirit of love and thanksgiving. For your prayer is your life, and your life is prayer. This means your spiritual fellowship in Christ involves all you read, say, or do, or whatever reaches your senses from outward or inward sources. Let all elements of your prayer be a glorification, praising, thanksgiving, and love wave for Christ the King, responding and interacting with His Salvific works for you and all humans.

5. Train your soul to receive the signals of the Holy Spirit, who is working in you, in all things, in everyone, in every situation, at every time and place, and in every condition, by allowing your perpetual prayer to be a reciprocal relationship between your soul and Christ by the Holy Spirit. As long as you deal with Him according to His own will, by abolishing your own will so that His will be all in all, then you must receive his spiritual invocations, blazing with the fire of love for you, in exchange for your supplications to Him.

6. Always oppose your desires and resist, by the blazing zealous power of the Holy Spirit, your own will, and every other will that pertains to you. Ignite a vigorous war against the flesh and the world by observing Christ's, the king, commandments, and them being His Divine Spirit, which you ought to live by discordant with the "Spirit of the World" and with everything that relates to the "Flesh and its Inclinations." Let them have nothing at all in you so that every physical and worldly loss is a

gain for the sake of Christ. Therefore, you can easily convert everything and every condition to a thanksgiving prayer and glorification in the name of the beloved Savior.

7. Beware of talking unless it expresses the acts and testimonies of the Grace concerning you, someone else, or any other matter.

8. Beware of your contact with the people or the people's contact with you unless it is through Christ, he who abides in you and them and for the benefit of His Salvation, for He is to the wicked... patience, mercy, and love. And to the righteous... purification for their souls and discipline.

9. Let Prayer precede everything and every move that is to be initiated by you so that your faith gets fulfilled by meeting with Christ in every matter you seek and in every situation you encounter. Then, it all ends with the goodness of thanksgiving and glorifying the Lord's name with joy that cannot be taken from you.

10. Beware of human standards, for the wisdom of this world is foolishness[14] .... Beware of self-satisfaction, for it is derived from your own will by the spirit of darkness. But you ought to acknowledge the act of the Holy Spirit alone so that you may please Christ in you and complete your shortcomings.

11. Know, my beloved son, that the children of God are manifested by their spiritual life, which is liberated from all that is bodily, earthly, or secular. And that it is not in their nature to survive by any means of the world. In fact, It is worthless for them because they are aversion to it due to their antithetical nature to all that is secular. More importantly, they consider Christ, alone, the source of their lives as he abides in them. On the contrary, the children of the world. Those who believe the worldly and the earthly provide them with all the essentials for their physical life. Hence, this is the reason behind their lack of interaction

---

[14] 1 Corinthians 3:19

with the word of God. Their souls, through carnal life, are dead. On the other hand, the reason behind the children of God's unresponsiveness to all the temptations of the world and the flesh is that their bodies, through spiritual life, are dead. Therefore, faith is the life, and the life declares the faith. It is either the worship of God or the worship of the world.

These are the instructions of Grace for you, my beloved son … You won't be able to benefit from them, nor would you be able to accomplish any of them unless you stripped off the authority of your flesh and the spirit of the world by intention, conscience, and action, with all the authority of the Holy Spirit, he who diminishes your own will.

If you did, and you could do this immediately if you wished, you would ignite, instantly, your inner self with the love of Christ in correspondence to your perception of His abundant love for you …. Such love that the entire creation constantly declares. Thus, all that pertains to the flesh and the world will bear no effect or carry any value within yourself. Making it easy for you to get rid of their authority and to dash, not by your power but by the power of the Holy Spirit dwelling in you, in the road of the "Divine Glories" of Christ's, who is abiding in you, while being in the bosom of the Grace. Drawn towards the "Heavenly Glories" to be with the "Beloved." So that you may quench your thirst with the grace of your "Father" and His blessings. Glory be to Him forever, Amen.

His Departure:

Finally, after he finished his good race while spending the days of his pilgrimage in prayers… Fasts … Vigil …. Tears …. Love …. Chastity …. Keeping His master's commandments and staying faithful in the least talents, the Lord permitted his departure from this tiresome world. That was on November 6th in the year 1969 (28 Babah). Those who were present at that time testified that a pleasant aroma was smelt from his deathbed and comforted everyone.

And thus, he departed in the same manner as the righteous …. Blessed by all.

His Burial:

We set the time and date of the funeral…… And it happened that the Lord had permitted us to begin construction of a new Church, "The Church of St. Takla Haymanout in El Ibrahemia." Which was close to Mr. Sadek's house. So, we decided to pray on his body there. Since we had never prayed on anyone there prior, he became the "First Fruit" for those who would proceed with him.

We prayed on him as a deacon and according to his rank. We were delayed for some time because the Church was not fully equipped yet, and we couldn't locate the service book. So Abouna Bishoy Kamel had to go and bring a service book from our Church in Sporting. Then, after the prayer, Abouna Bishoy Kamel delivered to the congregation a spiritual sermon that was very powerful and profound. Suitable for the status of that righteous man who lived amongst us. Afterward…. A procession of the pure body transpired in the church and then was carried to the cemetery. We preceded the body to the cemetery and waited. And we waited for a long time, and no one arrived. We were surprised by such a delay. Then, one of the servants said the body was returned to the Church. How could that be? He proceeded to inform us that his relatives who arrived from Cairo asked the hearse driver to return, saying, "It is our privilege to take the body with us, and it is impossible to bury him in Alexandria." He explained that the presence of his body in Cairo would be a blessing for them all since they knew the magnitude of his holiness. Those who were present tried to dissuade them but to no avail. So, they returned and placed the coffin in the Church. It was sunset. So, it was not feasible to take the body to Cairo on that same day. They were forced to keep the body in the Church all night till the morning. That was a great comfort for his children, who gathered around the body praying the psalms and praises till the morning. And so it was, without the intention of any person but by Divine economy…. That Pious man was celebrated in a manner similar to the Patriarchs and the Bishops. That is by prayers, praises, and the presence in the Church the entire night.

In the morning …. We officiated the liturgy; then they took the body to Cairo. There, the body rested at its final destination till it heard the last trumpet. Then the dead will be raised in Christ first, and the corruptible must be put on incorruption. And death is swallowed up by life when the Lord transforms our lowly body so that it may be conformed to His glorious body, according to working by which He can even subdue all things to Himself. The blessings of that pious man be with us all, Amen.

2

Mr. Abdel Malek Twadros

That Pious man lived among us in Alexandria for many years. Before that, he lived and worked in Sudan. When Father Bishoy Kamal got ordained, he resided with his own family for some time. Then, he lived in a small apartment at Mr. Abdel Malek's apartment building. Thus, he got to know him closely, became acquainted with him, and attested to his righteousness and the virtuous life he was living.

Mr. Abdel Malek was married to a virtuous woman and did not have children. They both lived in holiness and the fear of God. Mr. Abdel Malek had two virgin sisters who resided with him. Hence, that household was the epitome of the Christian life by its love and humility. They depicted the verse that says, "Behold, how good and how pleasant it is for brethren to dwell together[15]." It was Mr. Abdel Malek himself who was the mystery behind that house's blessing, for he was extremely close to God and perfect in his generation.

Mr. Abdel Malek was a very organized man. Subsequently, his spirituality was marked by that precise order, for he was praying the Agpya prayers regularly and memorizing its Psalms. He was consistently reading the Holy Bible in the morning and evening. He read the entire Bible twice every year. He read it over a hundred times, to the point of reciting many of its chapters verbatim. He was continuously occupied by the gospel in his talk, in his seclusion, and among people. The Gospel prevailed in his entire life. How was it possible for such a man, and him being responsible for a household and its finances, to obtain all that time? This question is presented by those who seek excuses. But the one

---
[15] Psalm 133:1

who tasted the sweetness of God's word, his time is abundantly blessed. And for him, the Gospel has priority above all obligations.

St. Mark Cathedral:

The Divine Liturgy was officiated daily at Saint Mark's Cathedral, and Mr. Abdel Malek realized his desire was to attend the Liturgies. So, he attended them daily from the beginning of the fifty's decade. He acquired, from his life of discipline and commitment, the strength to participate in the liturgy daily, even though it ended around eight o'clock in the morning[16]. And despite the distance between his house and the Church, he diligently sought the Lord and loved Him according to His promise[17].

Vicar of the Patriarchate:

The patriarchs used to appoint a vicar to take care of the Diocese of Alexandria in the event of the Pope's absence, the bishop of the great city of Alexandria. Most often, that vicar was chosen from amongst the monks. And since Mr. Abdel Malek used to come to Saint Mark's Cathedral every day, he purposed to present an offering to that monk, the vicar of the Patriarchate. Thus, he would arrive early every morning at the patriarchate carrying a handbasket full of prepared food. Then he places it, with all discretion, in front of the cell of the Vicar, during the stillness of dawn, without anyone seeing him. He instructed the patriarchate's intendant to bring back the empty basket daily and stressed to him not to let anyone know anything about that matter and that he ought to keep it secret. The intendant was obedient to him. Some of the patriarchate's vicars didn't know the man either by name or in person. In 1954, one of the monks arrived at Alexandria to be the vicar for the departed Pope Yousab the Second[18]. Every day, he opened the cell's door and found the food basket. He marveled. He tried to find out who was responsible for such a task. He asked the patriarchate's employees and the intendant who brought back the empty basket about its owner. He answered him, saying, "An individual from the congregation." It was the statement that Mr. Abdel Malek instructed him to say when asked.

---

[16] He had to wake up around 3 Am.
[17] Proverbs 8:17
[18] Patriarch of the See of St. Mark (115).

The Vicar had no choice but to wake up very early, around three o'clock in the morning, open his cell's door slightly, and wait for that pious man. The vicar's heart was moved by that secret task and wanted to know the responsible person. At the appointed time, Mr. Abdel Malek arrived carrying his basket, tiptoeing calmly.

When Pope Yousab departed, and Pope Kirollos the 6th succeeded him to sit on the See of St. Mark, he loved Alexandria and spent much time there. Mr. Abdel Malek continued to attend the liturgies as customary. The Pope was delighted with him, for he perceived the man's purity, righteousness, and spirituality. Thus, he drew him close with great affection. Numerous times, the pope invited him to his cell at the patriarchate after the liturgy for coffee and to enjoy his company.

Mr. Abdel Malek continued to offer provisions to the monks who came to Alexandria in complete secrecy and without acknowledgment from anyone in the congregation.

Those who have opposing opinions:

Mr. Abdel Malek spoke abundantly with God and about God, but he spoke minimally with the people or about the people. He lived in the company of the Pope, who was dear to his heart. He was loved by all the Fathers[19] .In the Papal residence.

And so it happened, during the days of Pope Kirollos the 6th, that disagreements in opinion arose between some of the bishops and the monks. How many of those issues have been discussed among people??!!.... And quarrels abounded .... So that the assemblies within the ecclesiastical surrounding were not void of the multitude of words in which sin was not lacking. The people were divided. Some sided with one group, and some with the other. However, Mr. Abdel Malek was indeed a perfect man; he did not get involved in such matters. Rather, he remained loved by all. Obtaining everyone's blessing and not taking sides with any ideological torrents. His heart was capable of accommodating everyone. The Pope was aware that Mr. Abdel Malek was friends with those who disagreed with him[20]. , yet he never discussed the issue or brought it up. On the contrary, the Pope complained about them to Mr. Abdel Malek, to which he always responded

---

[19] Bishops, Priests, and Monks.
[20] The Pope.

with a meek smile, saying to the Pope, "You are their father, and they are your children. All of them seek the peace for the Church." He was a man of peace who kept, in the midst of the torrents, a pure heart uncontaminated by hypocrisy nor polarized by politics. But he, by his simple wise heart, stayed free amongst all while enslaving himself for all.

And thus, Mr. Abdel Malek was the cause of blessing to many people who differed in points of view and ideologies. For he was neither unbiased nor sycophantic to rulers, but pure Christian love for everyone without purpose filled his heart. So, he was adored, without hypocrisy, by all people. And he became trusted by the Pope and by all people. He led many, through his conduct, to a life of peace. The life of that pious man, from this aspect, is suitable to be a lesson for many.

The work of Satan:

Mr. Abdel Malek happened to be present at his friend's house in Sudan. There were also, at that night, several mates seated as they chatted. Among those seated was a bearded man whom Satan had recruited for his works. He was dazzling those who were present by preternatural works. Among the tricks he made was his saying to the spectators, "I am ready now to bring to each of you an item from your home." He asked one by one, and he indeed brought to everyone what he had requested from his home. That happened while Mr. Abdel Malek kept his serenity as the others laughed and screamed. Then, it was Mr. Abdel Malek's turn; the man asked him, "What do you ask of me to bring from your home? And I will bring it immediately and place it on this table like the rest." Mr. Abdel Malek responded, "Thank you. I don't need anything." The man insisted, encouraged by Satan, as he wanted to mortify Mr. Abdel Malek, "You have to ask." Mr. Abdel Malek said, "There is no need for embarrassment." So, the man became clingier and adamant. And when he became increasingly persistent, Mr. Abdel Malek said calmly, "If you can, bring me the small book under my pillow."

That book is The Agpya[21]. It took the man a long time, more than usual, while everyone present was in anticipation like before. The waiting period was long, and the eyes were fixed. Why did he fail this time?!! The man came out of a trance to say, "I cannot bring you this item, but ask of something else." All were amazed and seized by fear. What was it that Satan Couldn't draw near to? They

---

[21] The book of hours (A prayer book).

asked Mr. Abdel Malek, and he answered them in meekness and humility. It was the room where he prayed, and the item was the book of prayers. Demons fear the prayers and flee from the sign of the Cross.

A valid account concerning the Mystagogies:

Mr. Abdel Malek informed me about an elderly priest from the countryside who was saintly and filled with the fruit of the Spirit. Mr. Abdel Malek attested that during the Epiclesis, someone approached that priest, informing him that one of the Church fathers was traveling to Jerusalem. The priest asked him, "What for my son." He answered, "To see the light of Christ." The priest asked a deacon to hand him an unlit candle; he lifted the veil of the chalice and brought the candle close to the chalice. The candle was lit. He returned it to the deacon, saying, "This is the light of Christ, He who is present with us every day at the Altar."

Mr. Abdel Malek retained, in his memory, the commemorations of numerous righteous people, such as that priest, whom he got to know and cherish. He lived his life in holiness, far from banter and worldly talk. He was never seen in the seat of the scornful, and it was never heard of him slandering any person in his life. His life was adorned with many virtues confirmed by those who knew him.

Finally, after finishing his good endeavor, he fell asleep, in the Lord, at righteous old age without sickness. He departed, as such, in peace, serenity, and tranquility. He entered into the fatherly bosoms to enjoy eternity.

3

A Rare Epitome for Repentance

He was an ordinary man all his life; nothing distinguished him from the rest of the men in his generation in his work or his style of living. He was a schoolteacher, and such work dictated that he traveled to many cities until he settled, after getting married and having offspring, in one of Upper Egypt's cities overlooking the Nile. They did not have, in that small city, any means for recreation except one Movie Theater. However, the man didn't frequent it much. He preferred to ride a boat in the Nile along with his children and some of his friends. The man was not of those religious people who frequented the Church in the well-known sense of the people. In his confessions, he didn't know, then, the meaning of repentance. He made a lot of mistakes and fell a lot into sin. However, he was very kindhearted and possessed the utmost delicate emotions.

One day, during school mid-year break, a man and a big group of people were in the midst of the Nile on one of the boats. All were in great pleasure, and as the youth were having fun and frolicsome, they rushed to one side of the small boat. Hence, it lost its balance and flipped at the deepest area of the Nile. The man cried out a resounding cry to the Lord from the bottom of his heart, for he didn't know how to swim. His only son was with him on that boat, for the mother and the daughters didn't want to go along that day, so they remained home. The man embraced his son and realized that everything was over in a moment, for there wasn't time to think or act. Man is helpless in such circumstances.

The man expressed his feelings at that moment, saying, "I have never felt that I cried out, in my entire life, to God, from the depth of my heart, like

I cried that moment." At that moment, the man felt two tender hands carry him; he truly felt them physically. Those two hands brought him to the shore while he was embracing his only son. No one escaped death that day except that man and his son. And it was the beginning of a life of sanctification and prayers that he had never tasted before—total renunciation of the world's false ornaments and despising its vanities. The world lost its appeal in his sight as an immeasurable new domain opened up before him. He realized that God granted him a new life and new days. The man was genuinely kind-hearted and loyal. Thus, he transformed those new days into a treasure in heaven.

The man would return for his work in the afternoon, enter his bedroom, and pray the Psalms of the ninth hour; then he breaks his fast, for he had vowed fasting for repentance and for the return to God as a thanksgiving sacrifice; he would then rest a little then enters into his home office, which he dedicated to prayer since the day of the accident, and keeps his eyes fixed towards heaven while praying from the bottom of his heart and enjoying the Psalms, the praises, and reading his Holy Bible, eating from its sweetness, and receiving discipleship at the feet of its saints. The man continued, as such in his heavenly life and enjoyment, as a thirsty man who anxiously drinks the water of life while his spirituality was in equilibrium and increasing daily.

One night of the nights of prayer, while he was looking up towards heaven, behold, the room's ceiling disappeared, and heaven was opened. The man's mind was perplexed due to the abundance of the Divine benevolence. His heart became heavy with inexpressible feelings of humility and unworthiness. Yet, the man kept all these things in his heart and didn't reveal them to anyone on the face of the earth.

The Liturgies:

The man has been attending Church regularly since the boat accident. Attending the liturgies, the vespers, and the spiritual assembles in all serenity, stillness, and humility. Many people reasoned that the man's behavior was due to his affection by accident, and it was only a matter of time before he returned to his old habits and previous life. Similar to those people who get affected momentarily by incidents or like a person seeing his face in a mirror briefly, according to the saying of the apostle[22]. However, the change that occurred in the man's heart was not temporal, for

---

[22] 1 Corinthians 13:12

he experienced the truth about the demise of the world and also experienced the truth of life, spiritual joy, and the perpetual presence of God, not through preaching or speech but by the experience of living.

The Divine Liturgy was the most favorite for him on the face of the earth. Contrary to the past, it was a dull, heavy burden, and he couldn't bear to stay in the Church. But now, the Church has become a paradise, and the Eucharist is like partaking from the Tree of Life.

And so, after the passage of years, those who knew him attested that the man became an epitome of the Christian life and an embodiment of the Biblical commandments. He was sweet to everyone, meek without affectation, and affectionate towards everyone. His daily life was permeated with the spirit of prayer, humility, and sacrificial service. Thus, the Grace comforted him with Divine revelations and Spiritual views.

One day, he came to the church, as usual, to pray the Liturgy. He raised his eyes towards the altar while the priest was praying the "Commemoration of the Saints." He saw all the saints inside the altar one by one. Whenever the priest mentioned the name of a saint, he appeared to join the "Chorus of the Luminaries." The man's tears ran like a river while standing beside the Altar. Thus, the phrase that we always pray became a reality, "Whenever we stand in Your holy sanctuary, we are considered standing in heaven." Indeed, how fearful is this place? What is this place but the house of the Lord, which is the gate of heaven!!

Those revelations enhanced the man in humility and the acknowledgment of his sins and unworthiness. Thus, he was advancing in virtue and the enjoyment of prayer.

Wiles of Satan:

"Be sober, be vigilant; because your adversary the devil walks about like a roaring lion, seeking whom he may devour. Resist him, steadfast in the faith." (1 Peter 5:8, 9)

The enemy[23] was gnashing his teeth whenever he saw that man increase in virtues. As he, the man, was not seasoned in spiritual warfare, nor was he apprenticed by the hands of a wise father at the monastery, or an insightful counselor in the Church. Rather, he was a simple man supported by Grace as he ran the spiritual way with all effort and love. And if the accuser of our race

---
[23] Satan

tempted the saints and was given authority, as a ruler of this world, to face and fight patriarchs .... Who was that simple man?!!!Satan began to spread his nets and his malicious tricks around him.Hence, he started complaining about the flesh manifested by sickness symptoms, weakness, and need for rest and provisions.Those were the initial steps for a life of laziness, followed by lukewarmness in prayer.The world began to flow little by little into his life ...... Just as the water flows into a large boat through a small hole.Time took it course .... Satan succeeded in his wiles, and the man returned to his old ways of living.

He was reviving now and then, remembering the glory of the days of repentance and the life with God.Thus, he pushes himself to stand for prayer. However, the prayer words were lukewarm and weak.He was praying as if it was an undesired duty.The prayer was tasteless, and the liturgy and the gospel were without effect.He felt sorry within, regretting and mourning the days of glory.Yet, day after day, everything was lost, even the regret and the mourning. It was as if his conscience had died.Ultimately, he fell into his previous sins and returned to his wicked friends.

Is there a return?

God, the rich in His mercy and the sympathetic toward his loved ones does not leave the righteous in their weakness or troubles.He does not allow Satan to overcome His children till the end, but he leads His children in triumph in Christ Jesus. He was restoring the years that the swarming locust had eaten. The Grace returned to visit that lost man. Thus, he returned to the fountains of tears and the room of prayer, saying to God, as he was getting advanced in age, nearing the age of sixty, in his prayer of supplication with a broken spirit, "Is there an acceptance for me?"

As such, life began to run its course, raising the man from the dead.The days of endeavor in the way of eternal life had returned.And just as it was in the days of our father Isaac, as he dug the old wells that were destroyed by the enemy. The wells of the spirit, one by one, till Beersheba, which is the well of satiety[24]. That man, the dignified elder, came and sat next to me to confess.He started talking as his tears ran profusely in a way I had never seen.The man said, "Now I believe that the Lord is good, merciful, and accepts the sinners.And I realized that no matter the magnitude of our sins, the blood of Jesus purifies

---
[24] Genesis 26

us from every sin. And where sin abounded, grace abounded much more. I thought that there was no return, for me, to my first estate and the days of my first repentance. But that which I don't deserve, because of my many sins, the grace had prepared for me." I asked him, "How so?" He said, "I entered the church yesterday and was no longer seeing the Divine depictions and revelations due to my many sins and lukewarmness. I believed there was no return to my status and first estate. But surprisingly enough, my insight was opened once more, and I saw the altar filled with the spirits of the saints and the angels at the hour of sanctification in an indescribable manner. My soul returned to its original humility, humbleness, and joy. I became assured that God balances the abundance of our sins with His copious love and that the door of repentance is open before the utmost wicked sinner."

Joyful end:

The Lord adorned that man's life with suffering towards the end of his days. He was glorified before the Lord every day in much patience, thanksgiving, contentment, and unceasing praises until he joined the "Chorus of Luminaries" to enjoy the full token he had tasted while he was in the flesh.

4

Blessed Is the Giving

Mr. Farid …. A dignified man …… A father of many children. The man was distinguished by extraordinary goodness of heart; his entire life was covered by the virtue of Christian love derived from the heart. He was friends with everyone …. There was no enmity between him and any man throughout his entire life; on the contrary, he lived as a peacemaker—a disciple of his master, the King of peace, and the author of peace. Thus, for every family, he was a healing balm for all wounds. Every place at which he was present, he radiated peace and love. Everyone attested that his presence amongst them caused them to love one another tremendously with a pure heart.

Thus, truly, they are God's children of God …. Once they live the commandment and enjoy the grace, they spread it in simplicity and abundance through works and practical living more than words. And thus was the man, few in his words but influential by his presence.

The man embedded this living fruit in his children, for they are in perfect love with one another. Not one impurity of the material impurities blemished their passion. Apathy didn't affect their relationships despite living far apart from one another, as is happening with many families. The reason for this beautiful depiction of true love and the remarkable bond was that Father, the one who lived clinging to Christ's commandments all his sojourning days on earth.

Also, there was another sign that adorned his sojourning days on earth with the beauty of holiness, for this man established his love upon the Lord's saying, "It is more blessed to give than to receive25." Once he profoundly tasted the joy of almsgiving, he joyfully grasped any opportunity for almsgiving presented to him by grace. Thus, he grew in virtue and became generous with everyone.

The almsgiving, throughout his life, diverted from its traditional concept. He became highly tender and affectionate. Numerous times, his children witnessed him; at that time, he resided next to the Church of Saint Mary at El-Zaytoun in Cairo, calling one of the peddlers whom he perceived weak or poor and inquiring of him about the item that he was selling and its price. If the peddler said, for example, that the price was 20 Piasters[26] per pound, he responded, "My son, the price is low; it should be 25 Piasters per pound." Then he continued saying, "Weigh a couple of pounds." However, when one person in the household objected, as usual, that the price was high and the item was of poor quality, he would tell the peddler with an implicit sign to accept, saying, "It's okay. Accept, and I will restore to you." After the peddler leaves, Mr. Farid hastily gets to the window and throws the extra money to him, saying, "Go in peace, my son, may the Lord bless you."

He believed that with such sacrifices God is well pleased.

- Mr. Farid's life was characterized by unique humility, which was in accordance with the commandments of His master, He who sits at the lowest place, the server of the little ones as well as the great ones, and the last of all. He always preferred others over himself and laid down himself for everybody in a manner that is rare in our present time.

- The prayers, liturgies, and fast consecration were the pillars of that grand edifice. For he always obtained a wonderful, unique grace through heavenly assistance and support. The psalms were his delight, in which he meditated day and night.

A bright end:

When the sojourning days of that pious man drew near, he briefly fell sick. The Lord revealed to him the day of his departure from this world three

---

[25] Acts 20:35
[26] 1 Piaster is equivalent to 1 cent.

days prior …… Similar to the great saints. So, he brought his wife and all his children around him, held his wife's hand, kissed it, and said, "Forgive me; you are more righteous than I." He began to urge his children to follow the great commandment we acquired from the beginning, the new commandment, which is love that never fails, and the adherence to God until the last breath. Everyone marveled because of that strange behavior, and they wept, saying to him, "You are fine and in good health." He responded to them, "Tomorrow I will partake in the Eucharist, and the following day, Christ will visit me."

And so, it was …... The priest brought him the Eucharist the next day, and the following day, that pious man ascended to the high heavenly places while his righteous works followed him as he prayed and said, "Holy God."

Everyone testified that they never heard him utter one idle word; hence, he was worthy to echo the praise of the Seraphim at the last breath. He uttered it as a new hymn along with the myriads of the redeemed saints before the throne of Christ. The word "Holy" was the last word spoken by that blessed tongue.

- He asked of his daughter (living in Alexandria) as she was beside his bed, saying, "Tell Abouna Tadros and Abouna Saleeb to pray for me so that the Lord may repose my soul in the paradise of Joy."

- Surprisingly, upon his departure, Abouna Tadros and Abouna Saleeb went to Alexandria to attend the funeral without prior knowledge of his request. But it was the economy of Christ who willed to grant that pious man his last word. And to testify that the man had found favor with God, not a word of his words failed.

5

Ascended into Heaven

Sister Layla was a young gal in her prime. Undistinguished, according to the outward appearance, by any feature that made her protrude from the others. On the contrary, she was ordinary in everything. She was not a Sunday school servant; she had no prominent role or a renowned name[27]. Rather, she was an ordinary gal similar to all the youth of the Church at Cairo.

She married a relative in Alexandria …. She resided next to our Church[28]. She was regularly attending the liturgies and the vespers; however, she had little contact with the people. Occasionally, she confessed to God before me during the vespers.

I was envying, due to the lack of a better word, that sister for her pure heart and the transparency of her soul. How was it possible for her, despite becoming a mother of two children, to maintain such a pure heart and such a soul that didn't get blemished by the world?

She was, in her marital, an epitome of loyalty and endearment. She literally followed the Lord's commandment, "Do not let the sun go down on your wrath." To the point that not one day passed by while she was in ruction with her husband. Also, when a misunderstanding occurred, she was quick to forgive, absolve, and apologize. Hence, her heart remained clean and pure. Did the Lord not say, "Blessed are the pure in heart?" The son's attachment:

---

[27] In the ecclesiastical milieu.
[28] The Church of Saint George at Sporting, Alexandria.

Her older daughter was four years old, and her younger son was a son of two years. He was attached to her in an unparalleled way. That situation was the talk of those around her. The child couldn't depart from her for a single moment …. She was not able to use the lavatory without him being present. The family voiced their concern about that situation. But as for her, she was constantly calm, full of peace, and unbothered by anything.

Unexpected departure:

Her husband returned from work, as usual, in the afternoon. He found everything beautiful and clean as always ….She cooked him food and prepared the table. Everything was perfect. They ate their dinner, and the husband rested a little, then got up and got ready to return to work for an evening shift. However, she told him, "Don't leave for work today." He was amazed and said, "How come?She answered, "I need you." He responded, "What is it that you want? Don't you know I have work and can't be late?" But when she stressed the request, and he insisted more on the inquiry, she said to him, "I will die today." His mind and thoughts were paralyzed as he stood in front of her in utter astonishment, "What is this talk? You are fully healthy and in the prime of your youth. This is evidenced by the great effort you made today." She calmly said, "Please …. This is what will happen today."

As soon as she uttered those words, she sat down on a chair next to her, turned pale, and within moments she lost conscience. The husband was in shock from all that was happening, almost not believing that he was in a state of awakening. The Children were standing around him in a dramatically tragic scene. He began to slap her cheeks to revive her out of unconsciousness. Behold, she opened her eyes, vomited, started breathing, and regained her conscience. Her husband, who almost flew out of joy, said to her, "Thanks be to God, for you are okay; I almost went crazy moments ago …." She interrupted him, saying, "Listen, I died and went to Paradise, and I met many of the departed. I spoke with my father (He departed to heaven before her several years prior), and he told me, 'My daughter, you are still young, and your children are young …. Go back.' However, I know that I will also die. Heaven is beautiful …. Please, hold unto God, keep His commandments, and raise the children in the fear of the Lord."

Upon uttering those words, she fell asleep in the Lord. The husband did all that could be done by the power of men, but the order was decreed from the Lord.

The Lord preserves the simple[29]:

Everyone was, after several hours, at the house. And besides all those tragic events, an issue presented itself sharply and harshly—the problem of the child who was firmly attached to his mother. The majority of those who were present believed that the child wouldn't survive after the death of his mother and that he would die of sadness. He who did not tolerate her absence for several moments, how can he accept her absence forever?

But God, who works to glorify that pious sister, allowed her while she is in heaven to have the ability to serve her children and pray for them, bestowed that little child with peace and tranquility so that he didn't ask about his mother nor cry for her. Those events embarked, in the mind, the account of one of the Catechumen martyrs. She gave birth to her child while in prison, awaiting martyrdom. The guards detained her infant and deprived him of food for an entire day. Then they brought him before her crying to dissuade her from her faith and influence her affection as a mother. But she was praying fervently and with great longing. Hence, grace was satiating the infant so that he wouldn't cry.

That miraculous Divine work was repeated, in a different manner, in the life of that family. Months after the departure of the mother, and as they were showing some family photographs to the child, he recognized all his relatives and called out their names. But when asked about his mother's picture, he didn't recognize her. He stayed quiet and didn't answer. He lived a normal childhood life, and the Lord poured into his heart and the hearts of the rest of the family extraordinary condolences. The account of that pious woman was a cause for the repentance and console of many.

---

[29] Psalm 116:6

6

After Five Days

Abouna Matta[30] used to visit Mr. Michelle[31] in the house where he resided, along with his relatives. He was a man advanced in the days, never married, and was an employee of one of the government agencies before his retirement several years ago. He devoted his life to others through service, dedication, and self-denial. Mr. Michelle was, for many years, attending the liturgies at St. Mark's Cathedral. So, his presence became unique amongst the people due to his unceasing attendance, except during compelling circumstances.

Abouna Matta used to be pleasant with the man during his visits; hence, they discussed God's great things and contemplated the living and life-giving word. In the last year of Mr. Michelle's life, sickness affected his mobility. Yet, his heart's desire was to attend the Divine Liturgy every day. However, the man accepted sickness with thanksgiving and utmost humility. Abouna Matta was consoling him by the words of grace and by the coming of Christ to him through the Sacrament of the Eucharist once every week. The time of communion was set for Monday and was to be brought by Abouna Matta. After the man partook of the Eucharist with extreme dignity, worship, and prostration, the two of them would sit down for a light breakfast accompanied by words of condolence and edification.

---

[30] Arabic name for Matthew.
[31] Arabic name for Michael.

During his last months, Mr. Michelle requested to receive the Eucharist twice weekly, apologizing to Abouna Matta that it would be exhausting and stressful. But love doesn't get weary for Abouna Matta; he joyfully went to him carrying the Lord's body, the bread of eternal life, and His blood.

One time, after the man partook in the Eucharist and thanked the richness of Christ's grace and his wondrous tender humility, the man's eyes sparkled with a spiritual glow and said to Abouna Matta, "You suffered a lot for my sake, Christ shall reward you, on my behalf, with good heavenly wage. Do not fret yourself on my behalf anymore. The ship is nearly docked, and the alienation is nearing the end. Only five days left." Abouna Matta was very surprised by that talk, almost not believing it, and said to the man, "How can you say this, Mr. Michelle?" The man responded, "Monday, Tuesday, Wednesday, Thursday, and Friday, I will be released for the confinement of the flesh."

Abouna Matta sat down, according to their custom, blessed the food for breakfast, and they ate with thanksgiving. One of the deacons came along this time with Abouna Matta. He was astonished by the Mr. Michelle's words. Then, they talked about the things pertaining to the Kingdom of God, the promises of Christ, and the portion of the righteous in perpetual joy. Afterward, they bid the man a Christian farewell, and Abouna Matta said, "I will come back to visit you after tomorrow." The man humbly insisted, "Don't fret yourself, and don't waste your time."

On Friday, according to the time God had previously revealed to that pious man, his soul departed like Simeon the Elder. When Abouna Matta visited him after the liturgy, he found he had passed away hours ago. Abouna realized it was not strange for the Lord to have righteous witnesses who lived as such in the world, but they were not from this world.

7

Your Prayer Is Heard

I went out for visitation a long time ago, almost 14 years. I took out of my pocket a small diary to retrieve some addresses and street names within the parameters of my assigned visitation area. During that time, the names of its streets were similar in pronunciation and writing. For example: Heliopolis Street, Hemopolis Street, Memphis, Tanis, Manis …. Etc. I read one of the addresses from the diary and committed it to my memory … The building number, the street name, and the apartment number.

I reached the street, located the building number I was seeking, and went up the stairs to the third floor, where the apartment was. However, I had never visited that building prior, so maybe I had the wrong address. I took out my diary to confirm …. I realized that I had come to the wrong street, but I already knocked on the door. I was too embarrassed to leave before the door was opened. After a moment, the door was opened, and I was faced with a man in his forties with messy hair. He immediately said to me, "Yes????!!!!" At that moment, as soon as the door was opened, I glimpsed a picture hanging on the wall. A religious picture of a Christian Calendar…. So, I said within, "Fine, even if I came to the wrong address, there is nothing wrong with the visitation. For this is a Christian home."

- I asked the man, "Are you Christians?"

- He answered, "Yes. How did you get our address? Who gave it to you?"

- I said, "Since you are Christians, I visit you."

- He responded as he seemed troubled for a reason I didn't know, "Please come in."

As soon as I entered and the man closed the door behind me, he repeated his question with great confusion and eagerness.

- "Please tell me who gave you my address."

- I responded while being astonished, "Can I sit down?"

- "Please do."

The man kept standing before me, so I told him with extreme calmness,

- "I wish that you relax first, then I will tell you."

The man sat next to me while the signs of surprise were still apparent on his face. Then, after a moment of silence, I gestured to him, saying,

- "Why are you troubled as such? Have you not seen a priest before? I will not tell you how I came to you unless you tell me first why you are acting this way.

- The man said as a strange emotion possessed him, "My situation is very astonishing …. I can hardly believe what I see with my eyes and what I am experiencing these days. I, as you can tell, live by myself in this apartment. I have been an expat here in Alexandria for more than twenty years. Before coming to Alexandria, I resided in a small city among a Christian family. During those days, I was a religious youth, having a "Living relationship" with Christ and keeping the Sacraments. I completed my studies and was hired as a government employee in Alexandria. My spiritual life began to suffer from apathy, negligence in prayer, wicked friends, carelessness, and the life of sin by all its depictions and methods. Then, I felt lost. In the beginning, my conscience would sometimes revive, and I longed for my life with God and with my Church. But I did not allow those feelings and emotions either the time or the space; hence, they died in their infancy. It has been over twenty years, and I have forgotten everything. Imagine, I did not receive communion all that time. But surprisingly, two weeks ago and without any preapprehensions, my inward parts erupted like a volcano seeking repentance and the return to God. Truthful tears burst out of my eyes. I returned to prayers and searched for my Bible till I found it in a pile of old books. I read it now with an amazing passion. Its words are like sharp arrows penetrating the walls of my heart. The whole world fell out of sight, and I no longer desire anything from it."

I interrupted the man as I was perplexed about his state.

- "But during these recent days, did you not attend a meeting at the Church? Did you not listen to a sermon? Did you not meet with a servant?"

- He responded, "Not at all. And this is what makes me so astonished. My life completely changed; I returned from work, locked myself in my room, and continued with my prayers, shedding my tears and reading my Bible until late in the evening. Then I go to sleep ...."

- I asked him, "How about the friends?!"

- He answered, "They were so surprised and perplexed about my behavior. They are trying every day so that I return to my old ways. Some think that I am sick and have fallen into depression, while some marveled at the change in my conduct, my speech, and my habits. But anyway, I have asceticised friends and all people. Now, my delight is in the acts of repentance within my room. However, I was worried that these feelings were temporary and fleeting or not from God. But, only yesterday, as I was praying and weeping before God, I entreated Him with tears, saying, 'Give me, O Lord, a sign by which I know that You have accepted me despite my many sins and inequities.' I dared to ask as such and said in my prayer; this is the sign .... You send me a priest so that I confess on him...... And to feel that my repentance and pleas have found favor before You."

I was overtaken by trembling upon hearing those words, and I glorified Christ, my God, who works by His Holy Spirit for the repentance of His Children. When the servants are absent, He acts in the hearts and brings back for Himself the lost sheep and finds the lost coin[32]. So I said to the man whose eyes filled with tears,

---

[32] Luke 15

- "Then the Lord gave you the desires of your heart[33]."

- He said, "Yes, my Father. But please tell me how you got here."

- I took out my little diary ... Pointed at the address recorded in it...... The building number and the apartment number were identical to his, but the street name was different. I told him, "God does wonderful things with us, I misread the address and I came to you ordered by the Lord."

We prayed fervently and thanked] Christ, the tender, the good Shepherd, and we offered our heartfelt prostration to He who accepts the sinners and the lover of mankind. Then, that brother offered his confession to be recorded in heaven as a seal for a truthful repentance accepted before God.

I read him the absolution, and I left glorifying God. After that, we had frequent meetings, and he began to attend the Church with longing and thirst for righteousness. Grace satiated him according to the Lord's promise: "Blessed are those who hunger and thirst for righteousness, for they shall be filled."[34] The Grace had restored him the years that the swarming locust had eaten.[35]

And the Lord sealed the sincerity of his repentance .... And he completed his days pleasing before God, supported by the power of His Holy Spirit.

---

[33] Psalm 37:4
[34] Matthew 5:6
[35] Joel 2:25

8

The Service of the Angels

The tram stopped near the Church that Mr. Farid loved and lived within her walls as a "Living Pillar." He had just left the Church about one hour ago after partaking in the Mysteries as his daily custom. The people gathered in crowdedness around the tram, and all of them were asking and wondering about what had happened.

The man bowed his head and submitted his spirit peacefully in the blink of an eye as he was seated on the tram. Everyone around him figured that he was asleep. But when they attempted to wake him up, they realized that he was gone to the eternal world, as such, in serenity and an angelic peace. Those who celebrated the liturgy with him were astonished, for the man, shortly prior, was very active, and nothing abnormal was apparent to him. However, did the Book not say, "For what is your life? It is even a vapor that appears for a little time and then vanishes away[36]."

The loved ones and the relatives assembled at the house of Mr. Farid …... Numerous memories and luminous depictions began to come to the minds of those who were present. He was a beautiful icon of serenity and Christian humility; he did not cry out, and no one heard his voice in the streets like his master. A pleasant smile expressing peace of heart never departed from him, even during the most severe hardships.

Then, the relatives recalled that fantastic act of Mr. Farid when his sister departed; he was entitled to an inheritance so great. Yet, despite the simplicity of his financial situation and his need for a part of such inheritance, the man

---

[36] James 4:14

insisted, despite the opposition of all who were around his scope, not to be the heir of earthly things, waiving everything, voluntarily, to others. The depictions and the incidents presented themselves upon the assembled, for the man's life and actions uttered all that is spiritual. Mr. Farid was pleasant and sweet to everyone. He was about living the "Inner Life" and the "High Religiosity."

He, since his early youth, was enjoying a "Living Fellowship" with Christ. He was waking up very early daily at four o'clock in the morning and began his concealed esoteric activity of prayers, praises, psalms, readings, and intonation till seven o'clock in the morning with great joy and goodwill. That was the spiritual start for every day, the preparation for facing Satan's warfare, the foundation for Christian conduct, and the strength to follow the commandments. There was nothing that could hinder or dissuade him from his intention. As the years passed, the roots of vigil and prayer stretched deep into his life.

His life, which was apparent before men, was the fruition of a deep fellowship with God. Who might have established for him that canon for prayer except the things that he tasted through his cohabitation with Christ? His household testified that nothing prevented him from his early rise except sickness. He has been doing that for more than forty years. Thus, the fountain of the Spirit in him has regenerated. And the prayer, within him, became the primary of instincts and became, for him, as essential as breathing.

When everyone knew about that Spiritual mystery economy, they realized that the Spiritual life (The Kingdom of God) is, as the Lord said, a treasure hidden in a field and also truly was like a pearl of great price that was once found by a merchant, he went and sold all that he had and bought it[37].

How much do we need the life of prayer, by which we can truly offer our lives as the fragrance of Christ, treasures for the world, and salt for the earth?

---

[37] Matthew 13.

9

Poor, Yet Making Many Rich

Her husband died....He was a poor handyman.......He left behind two kids....They were living in one of the slums and residing in a tiny room[38]. There was no support for that widow, either from money or men. She refused to acquire anything except Christ, whom she petitioned according to His promise of being a husband of the widow and a father of the fatherless[39]. Her certainty was firm in God's care and protection.

Her faith in the presence of God in her life was putting me in tremendous shame. I wished, wholeheartedly, to display a photo of that poor widow before those who complain, dissatisfied as they are unthankful and not satisfied with what they possess despite being plentiful. She would, with extreme difficulty due to my persistence, accept some help. Finally, I suggested that she labor, by her hands, as long as she could do so ...... However, in actuality, she had no ability to work because of her weakness and her incommodious circumstances .... However, I encouraged her to work so that it could be an excuse for help without her rejection or refraining from receiving assistance. Thus, she was working in housekeeping to the best of her ability. We tried to offer her money, but she didn't accept any, except for the bare sufficiency.

The behavior of that poor widow was rebuking me: her contentment, her spiritual joy, her perpetual prayers, her praises while working with her hands, and her profound thanksgiving to God for the least possible portion of the things that pertain to this life.

---

[38] The entire living area is one room.
[39] Psalm 68:5

Truly, Christ was filling her life with joy and gladness.

Her whole livelihood:

One of the strange things that I discovered, by coincidence, was that she was saving some of the few piasters[40] that were reaching her hands …. I found her one day at Saint Mar Mina's monastery. There were no visitation trips on that day, nor were there any transportation cars. I asked her. "How did you arrive here?" She answered, "By train, then walking on foot[41].

And I learned that she baked bread with the few piasters that she saved and carried it on top of her head to the monastery. I knew she was attached to Saint Mar Mina, but could it have been to that limit? She spent the rest of the day washing, cleaning, and wiping the floors of the monastery with tremendous joy and overwhelming happiness. She was giving, truly, just as the Lord said, "But she out of her poverty put in all that she had, her whole livelihood[42]

Like the days of Elisha:

Her younger son, six years of age, returned from school and requested something to eat. The mother said, "We have nothing, but go and buy yourself one piaster worth of "Fool Medames[43] .That Piaster was all she possessed that day.The kid returned with a bowl of Fool Medames, seasoned it with some salt, and then asked for oil.The lady didn't have even a jar of oil, for she was done washing the four glass jars she owned and placed them upside down under a table behind a curtain customized from old cloth[44].She apologized to her son for the lack of oil and assured him that soon God would send her money to buy the subsidized provisions[45].

The kid screamed in disbelief and protest, an immature boy, insisting that there must be oil.She kept, with utmost calmness and a broken heart, soothing him, calming his anger, and urging him to give thanks to God, who takes care of them.She signed, on his behalf, the Cross over the bowl of the "Fool

---

[40] Currency equivalent to USA cents
[41] Several miles of walking.
[42] Mark 12:42-44
[43] Traditional Egyptian breakfast similar to the Mexican black beans.
[44] To keep them dry and ready for the new supply of oil.
[45] The Egyptian government subsidizes the essential food items such as rice, pasta, sugar, oil, tea… Etc.

El-Medames." And said to him, "Eat my son." But the kid, with persistence and stubbornness, said to his mother, "You are hiding the oil from me, and I must find it."

The kid extended his hand behind the curtain underneath the table where the jars were. And behold, he brought his hand out, holding a jar full to its brim. He increased in screaming, insisting that she hid the oil from him.

But the woman, by her spiritual instinct, immediately realized that the Lord was doing great things for her …. Hence, she responded to her child wisely, saying, "Forgive me, my son, I forgot about it." The kid added the oil. But when he was about to eat, she said, "We ought to give thanks to God." So, he prayed and ate.

The woman came to me, leaping and praising God. She found the four jars full of oil. So, she sent two jars to Saint Mina's monastery, she brought one to Saint Mark's Cathedral, and she kept one jar.

She kept that secret in her heart and didn't tell anyone of the people because she felt that God's dealings with her and His care were very private matters. And she ought not to either broadcast them or talk a lot about them.

The woman believed that God replaced her husband and fulfilled His promise to her as the husband of the widow and a father to the fatherless. She and her children were similar to the saints in self-denial, even when the Lord did extraordinary miracles for them. However, they maintained their humility as a shield against the snares of the adversary. And as such, the Lord did great things with that widow till she raised her children in the fear of the lord and according to His goodwill.

10

The Blessing of the Lord Makes One Rich and Adds No Sorrow with It

It is a known fact, to many people, that an abundance of money is not without troubles and hardships and that the plaques of the rich person are many: from temptations to pride, to the dependence on money, and then to the love of money which is the root of evil.

But lest anyone think that money, on its own, is evil, the Lord preserved for Himself witnesses for His benevolence from all walks of life. Numerous rich people in every generation glorified God in their lives, as their riches didn't turn them away from the source of true wealth. On the contrary, the talent of wealth became a means of salvation for them. For they traded and gained more precious talents, which immortalized their remembrance with a sweet fragrance from all the generations of the Church.

A living example that lived in the conscience of many people in our generation, whom we have seen with our eyes, was a pious and righteous man. He resided in a typical poor neighborhood in Alexandria. El-Megadess[46] "Abo – Boshra[47]" began his adulthood very poor; he lived in a simple room

---
[46] The title bestowed upon who pilgrimage to Jerusalem.
[47] The "Father of Boshra." It is customary in Egypt especially within the milieu of peddlers and merchants to call the person by the name of his first-born son. Also, they prefer to be called in such manner because they are proud of the son who will inherit their name. Thus, keeping their name and commemoration alive.

resembling huts more than apartment rooms. He, along with his children and wife, were sleeping under that shoddy ceiling that was not protecting them at all from Alexandria's heavy rain. Despite the scarce resources feasible to that poor man, he was fixing the roof with all of his might, but it didn't pardon his little ones from the raindrops that were sneaking in and falling on them during the night of severe winter. To increase the pain of the cold along with the lack of covers and the weakness of the body.

The man was, during the days of his youth, a peddler for seeds. He rented a small cart to carry lentils, rice, fava beans, etc. He was roaming the streets and the allies of Khieet El Enab and Ghorbal[48] .with his small cart, which he was pulling by hand, which took place during the thirties decade. At the end of the day, the man wins a few piasters by this simple trade of his.

The great contentedness:

However, that simple man proved by his poor life and his very modest capabilities ……… One of the most perilous facts in life is that joy, contentment, and inner peace are not derived from material things at all. Abo–Boshra lived a life filled with joy and contentment, and he was happy with that simple life. He was emanating joy into all who were within his scope. He was very thankful to God, always praying most of his day, being saintly in his simple dealings with the women who bought from him, and diligently attending the liturgies with his wife and children.

Almsgiving out of livelihood:

The man's greatest virtue was his love for the poor and his passion for almsgiving. No one would have imagined that a poor man like him could give anything. As man, by nature, offers only out of surplus and excess. However, the Grace once resided in man; its generosity overflows out of poverty, fountains of riches, and satiety. The humble heart of Abo-Boshra was a comfortable tabernacle in which the Grace had found its rest. He was poor in appearance but very rich within, by the Grace. He was a depiction of the verse, "Poor, yet making many rich."

---

[48] The Egyptian government subsidizes the essential food items such as rice, pasta, sugar, oil, tea… Etc. To keep them dry and ready for the new supply of oil.

The man was keen to give tithes from the few piasters he earned throughout his working day. He gave it to widows and poor people who were more needy than him. He was doing such a task with great joy, yet in secrecy so that he wouldn't lose his reward.

He exalts the lowly:

The Lord willed to exalt His humble servant; he manifested him before many souls as a very honorable icon and placed him on a lampstand[49]. So that those who enter may see the light.

The Grace supported his simple trade, and it was growing at an astounding rate. Thus, he rented a small shop at first. Then, the Grace increased its blessings with generosity and abundance, yet the man remained faithful to his life and principles. He was faithful before his God as his love for the poor increased and his passion for serving them increased.

Give to him who asks you:

All the neighborhood's people testified that the man followed this aforementioned[50] saying of the Lord Jesus to the fullest. No one had entered his shop seeking anything, and he sent him away disappointed. The neighborhood was poor, and the requests of the poor people were endless all day. Yet, the man's heart was wide open to all people. He did not inquire, from anyone asking for help, about his name, religion, or the measure of help needed. On the contrary, he never denied anyone's request nor cut short the hope of any person. All day, the poor kids didn't cease asking, "Give me an onion, Mr. Abo-Boshra," "Give me rice, Mr. Abo-Boshra." He never sent anyone empty-handed. He blessed everyone with a generous smile and gave without measure.

The more the man gave, the more Grace rained upon him until he became rich and a prominent merchant in the neighborhood. Yet, his simplicity remained, and he increased in the life of thanksgiving and almsgiving.

With Abouna Bishoy:

---

[49] Figuratively.
[50] Give to him who asks you.

The man frequented St. Mark Cathedral. Loved her from all his heart, and he loved Saint Mark the Evangelist with a Spiritual passion. He was accustomed to entering into the Church with dignity and righteousness.

Numerous times it happened that when we[51] were present at the Patriarchate or St. Mark Cathedral, we met with El-Megadess Abo-Boshra. He greeted us with great joy and great spiritual affection.

He said to Abouna Bishoy, in my presence, and while his tears were filling up his eyes, "O' Abouna Bishoy, you know me very well. I am poor and simple. Before that, I lived happily while profiting from five or six piasters. I was able to manage them and easily fall asleep. But now, the responsibility is huge, and I can't manage it. I am ignorant and can't deal wisely with all this money. Why did God give me all this? I can't render Him an answer for all this. Please, Abouna, pray for me." The man was crying like someone carrying a burden of many sins. My heart was breaking at the sight of that pious man I knew was offering to the Lord liberally and with generosity rarely found in that generation.

The man, upon finishing his talk, would empty his money bag in the hands of Abouna Bishoy. I was asking him, with persistence, to pray for him so that Christ may forgive his lack of almsgiving.

As he did so, the Lord was bestowing him with astounding blessings in everything he set his hand to.

Another incident with Abouna Bishoy:

It happened one time when Abouna Bishoy went to buy Fava beans for the Lord's brothers from him[52]. It was during the days of the lent. He noticed, during the short time he spent at the store, more than fifteen poor individuals came asking for alms. The man didn't send any of them empty-handed, nor did he inquire about his name. That intrigued Abouna Bishoy's curiosity, so he asked him, "Do you, Mr. Abo-Boshra, give to anyone who asks or just to the one in need." He replied to him with confidence and joy, "No, only those are in need." Abouna was astonished and asked once more, "How did you know that they are in need? Do you know them personally?" He responded, "No. But I know one thing: that is our Lord Jesus Christ. Whom I entreat, every

---

[51] Abouna Bishoy Kamel, Abouna Tadros Yakoub Malaty, and Abouna Loka Sidaros.
[52] A pleasant title for the destitute.

morning, to bless my day and send me only His brothers who are in need, and keep away from me the deceivers. And since He is the One responsible for these people, they all must be in need, and I do not need to ask them. Because the Lord Jesus is the one who sent them."

Abouna left the man's shop, glorifying God, who left a remnant for Himself.

In times of crisis:

Towards the end of the '60s, there were particular shortages in food supplies, especially during the days of fasting. The prices of some legumes increased, while some disappeared from the markets. The rich could barely afford beans and lentils at the expensive market prices of those days.

It was during the days of the Great Lent when El-Megadess Abo-Boshra met with us at St. Mark Cathedral, asking, "Do you have any beans and lentils." And before we responded, he said, "Christ shall help me, and I will send to my poor brethren something for the lent." In the evening, a truck arrived at the Church with over forty sacks of beans and lentils. And so, he did as such with many Churches.

He was, by his humble behavior, encouraging many to strive in the path of almsgiving. He was an example for self-denial, for he didn't seek compliments from anyone, nor desired honor for a task he accomplished, nor to record his name on a receipt or in the book of donations, or to be embroidered on the altar's veil or engraved on the Church pews. He behaved in a spiritual manner and fulfilled his Master's commandments in order to receive a full reward in the kingdom of the righteous.

After he completed his days in satisfaction, he was satiated by the Liturgies, with offerings and sacrifices accepted by God as a sweet aroma. And after he raised his sons in the fear of the Lord, he joined the ranks of the pious so that he might shine in heaven by the works of mercy and the reward of the righteous.

11

Fruit According to Its Kind

By the fruit, the tree is known. "You will know them by their fruits. Do men gather grapes from thorn bushes or figs from thistles? Even so, every good tree bears good fruit, but a bad tree bears bad fruit[53]"

Heaven and earth will pass away, but not a single letter of this talk will fall. We practically realize this fact every day of our lives and the lives of our children and families.

He frequented the Church during the summer days in piety and utmost devotion. He continually partakes in the mysteries. I felt extreme embarrassment before that man, his being advanced in age, while he confesses tearfully. I become fainthearted.

The man was a renowned physician in one of Upper Egypt's cities. The fear of God occupied his heart, and the observance of Christ's commandments overshadowed his actions. Since I only encountered him during the summer, I didn't have a chance to know a lot about him except what he uttered during confession or the short meetings at the Church after the prayers of the Divine Liturgy.

The man had been absent for years, but one summer day, I saw him in front of me at the altar. I was delighted to see him, and I began inquiring about his life and how he was doing. His wife had departed to heaven, and he was living alone. His health had deteriorated, but he was in a state of inner peace of heart that added a touch of grace and an elevation in dignity and majesty to his old age.

---

[53] Matthew 7:16-17

The man asked to talk to me in more detail about an issue he was facing, so we postponed the talk until after the Liturgy. When we concluded the prayer of the Divine Liturgy and the congregation left, we sat in one of the Church corners, and I asked him, "Is it well? What occupies your mind?"

The man said, "I have decided to clear my mind from everything preoccupying me. I want to live liberated from everything these remaining days. I decided to settle my financial obligations, especially towards my children, and not keep them confused about anything or leave anything pending." I responded, "You do well; what is the problem then?" He said, "I have only one son who recently graduated from college, and two married daughters in Alexandria. One is married to a physician, and the other is married to an engineer. And I thank my God that both are successful in their lives, comfortable, and not short of or missing anything at all. As for me, the Lord had given me some possessions of this fleeting world. A piece of land (Several archers), and two apartment buildings. I wanted to distribute them amongst my children while I was still alive. When I discussed it with my son, he was overwhelmed, cried profusely, and refused to do such a thing. But I insisted on explaining that this would comfort me and elevate my joy and peace since I no longer needed anything. After a prolonged discussion between him and me, he hesitantly agreed, but under one condition: his portion should not exceed the portion of any of his sisters[54]. I was delighted by his spirit, full of love and asceticism, of all that was earthly at that young age. Then, I came to Alexandria and visited my oldest daughter's home, and I spoke to her regarding the same issue. She adamantly rejected that I do as such, and I spent long hours pleading with her to accept for the sake of my comfort and inner peace.

Finally, she accepted my plea. But when I conveyed her brother's request for equal division among them. She erupted and wept with copious tears, begging me, saying that she didn't need anything and that God's grace was more than sufficient in her house. And that her brother is a young lad, in the prime of his youth, and I ought to give everything to him. And if it was necessary for her to receive something, it should be a little blessing so my soul is at peace." I said, looking at the man in astonishment, "What then?"

The man said that the strangest thing was the stance of the youngest sister. It was a total refusal to accept anything. Rather, she threatened, if he followed through with his plan, to boycott him and not to ever talk to him. I told the man, "It is truly a problem, and it is a quarrel of the strangest type." The man

---

[54] The Egyptian law follows the Islamic Sharia, the male inherits twice the female.

Fruit According to Its Kind

responded, "Please, come with me to the girls and convince them that I don't want them to live in distress, for I trained them to be always in peace with God and peace amongst each other."

I went with the man to witness that wonderful fruit of the faithful spiritual life. The man saw, before he departed that world, with his own eyes the fruit of the spiritual life that he lived and how the sound principles that he planted in his children blossomed, like the paradise of God, in souls that tread, by their feet, greed, and love of oneself, and despised the vanity of the world.

The account of that pious man and his children brought back to my mind the image of the early Church with her rejection of the world and adherence to the Biblical commandments. "Let each of us please his neighbor for his good, leading to edification[55]" "In honor giving preference to one another[56]" "It is more blessed to give than to receive."

I was greatly distressed by the circumstances that we encounter every day and the awful problems of greed, the love of the most significant portion, love of oneself, enmities, and lawsuits over inheritance. Even hatred and evil ...... Etc. I wished that I had witnessed, once more, during my life another similar account. But can such a fruit blossom out of nothing? NO. Every tree bears fruit according to its kind, as the Lord said.

---

[55] Romans 15:2
[56] Romans 12:10. Acts 20:35

12

The Deacon Youssef Habeeb

A rare example of consecration with a pure intention for the sake of pleasing and loving Jesus Christ only. Without a desire for a gain on earth and without expectation of a reward from people, whatever they may be. The approach was a complete and adamant refusal of earthly reward, whether it was praise from people, an elevated position, a renowned name, a specific style of presentation, or wearing special garments, or occupying a rank, or acquiring money or authority, and so on and so forth.

That was how the truly ascetic deacon "Youssef Habeeb" lived till the last day of his sojourn on earth. The city of Alexandria knew him, in the prime of his youth, as a servant and a deacon at the Church of the Virgin Mary – Muharram Bey.

He was, according to age, older than the generation of servants whom Father Bishoy Kamal entrusted to serve at the Church of the Virgin Mary –

Muharram Bey. But his spirit was young and was close to those youth who were full of spiritual zeal. Thus, he was attached to them in all aspects of the service.

The beginning of Consecration:

When the owner of the vineyard called His "Faithful chosen one" Abouna Bishoy Kamel and appointed him a shepherd and a priest for the flock around early December of the year 1959, El-Megadess Youssef was employed as the head of the "Bureau of Traffic" in Alexandria. The image of Abouna Bishoy Kamel's ordination in front of him was a turning point in his life. He was inflamed with a holy zeal and said to himself, "The young lads accept consecration for the love of Christ, and they sacrifice their youth joyfully for the One who died for their sake. And you are lazy and negligent!!"

After the Liturgy prayer and completion of the ordination, Youssef went to his work, and on that same day, he resigned. He consecrated himself, his time, and his effort for a better job.

His Life of Consecration:

As soon as Abouna Bishoy returned from the Syrian Monastery upon completing the forty days required of the priest after his ordination, he found El-Megadess Youssef ready for service, day and night, at the new Church—the Church of Saint George at Sporting.

He took it upon himself, without assignment from anyone, to support Abouna Bishoy at the beginning of his service. The new Church had no deacons, or a chanter, or servants. The Church was at the initial stage of all things. Thus, El-Megadess Youssef became her chanter, caring for the children and the lads who started to frequent the Church. He began to care and water those new plants.

He was an ecclesiastical man of a rare type, memorizing all of the Church hymns with perfection and reciting them in the spirit of prayer with a very affectionate tune. As such, El-Megadess Youssef remained a tutor for the children, helping them absorb the spirit of the Fathers and raising them on the love of the Church, the mysteries, and the hymns. As the Church established for herself a chorus of deacons, acquired a chanter, and her affairs were stabilized. He withdrew with an astounding humility and self-denial, and he aimed, with all his might and effort, towards a new field of "Heritage Revival."

Youssef Habeeb ...... And the Saints' Biographies:

During that time, El-Megadess Youssef was fond of the Saints' biographies. Especially those whose fragrant biographies weren't published. Thus, he began visiting the monasteries, searching for their treasures for all that were hidden within. He brought out into the light tens of saints' biographies and rare accounts that encouraged many generations for repentance and life with God. He purchased himself a monthly pass for the train. He traveled twice a week to Cairo .... Searching the libraries, especially the Coptic Museum and the Patriarchate library .... Translating the biographies and the sayings of the saintly Fathers, then publishing them in small books that were useful for ministry and necessary for edification.

The man was, by his extreme asceticism, spending all his pension on those matters joyfully .... He didn't save anything for himself, and the many books he published didn't bring him any money. On the contrary, he lived poor and did not owe anything at all. Ascetic and hermit in his appearance, eating, drinking, and apparel till the day of his departure.

The fleeing:

Books multiplied and spread throughout the ministry, becoming holy first fruits for a blessed work. The matter reached the hearing of the departed Pope Kirollos the Sixth as we visited him in Cairo. So, he said to our father (Abouna) Bishoy, "My son, bring to us this Youssef Habeeb, for he is useful to us. He can be with us here."

When Abouna Bishoy returned to Alexandria, with all wisdom and calmness, he said to El-Megadess Youssef, "His Holiness Pope Kirollos wished to meet with you." The man marveled and said, "What does he want of me?" Abouna responded, "Maybe he will allow you a bigger opportunity to research and study at the Patriarchate library." And Abouna assured him that there was nothing to it. Thus, we agreed he would be with us on our next visit to the Patriarchate.

And so it was: We traveled to Cairo as a group of priests from Alexandria to meet with the Pope. Youssef Habeeb came with us. We entered the Pope, only the priests at first, and Youssef Habeeb waited outside.

After the meeting, Abouna Bishoy and I met privately with the Pope. The Pope inquired about Youssef Habeeb; we said, "He is waiting outside." The

Pope said, "Let him in." We went outside, and behold, we didn't see anyone. We asked those who were present, and they informed us that he left the patriarchate once the fathers entered the meeting. We looked for him inside the Church and in the library but couldn't locate him.

We returned to the Pope, and Abouna Bishoy said, "He fled Your Holiness." The Pope responded, "He who flees from dignity knowingly, it will follow him." Hence, we returned to Alexandria. When we met with El-Megadess Youssef, we asked him …He replied, "I thought to myself, what the Pope would need from a poor fellow as myself? So, I ran out of the Patriarchate, and the Lord saved me."

Thus, Deacon Youssef Habeeb was humble and didn't desire any sort of dignity. He always said that it is suitable for a person to be little.

The Church Saint Takla Haymanout:

The Lord permitted us to build a new location towards the end of the '60s. The start was at the Church of Saint Haymanout at Al-Ibrahimeyah in Alexandria.

El-Megadess Youssef felt, once more, the responsibility resting on his shoulder. So, without any hesitation, he gave himself up for the service and all the liturgies and vespers, assuming the role of the Chanter and the Deacon with a spirit of patience, sacrifice, and self-denial, even though the Lord had adorned his life with scarce talents.

It happened one time while we were raising the Matins' incense; during the early stages of the Church, the reading books weren't fully available. We were reading chapters from the Holy Bible, and when it was time to read the Matins Gospel, he couldn't locate a copy of the Scripture. (The Arabic version) So, with the utmost simplicity, he held the Coptic Katamaros, retrieved the day's chapter, and read the congregation the Gospel as he instantly translated from Coptic to Arabic.

And so was he, El-Megadess Youssef, an expert in the Coptic language who spoke it fluently (Bohairic and Sahidic). He translated many manuscripts and brought out of their treasures things new and old.

A wish granted:

El-Megadess Youssef lived alone and cared for himself with great humility. He was truly humble in everything, including his eating and his apparel.

He was living on subsistence and was always saying, "My wish of Christ is that I will be able to keep walking on my feet till my death. I don't want to be bedridden, be a burden on someone, or have someone assist me. Just walking on my feet is a great blessing." The Lord granted his faithful servant that wish, for he didn't get sick or need people's help. The Lord brought him to Himself and peacefully reposed him from all the troubles of the world.

His love and care of the Youth:

He once told me, "When a sinful youth comes to you, know full well that he is sent to you from the Lord. As if he is carrying carte blanche from Jesus Christ Himself, telling you, 'Please care for him for the sake of my wounds and my shed blood, and I shall reward you for your kindness.' You must accept him with tenderness and love and care for him tremendously."

The Angel of the Altar:

He told me some other time, "You must befriend the Angel of the Altar and let him be reconciled with you, especially during your procession around the altar. If he is satisfied with you, the Angel will accompany you as you penetrate the rows of your congregation and hold your hand while you wander with the incense. Thus, you will be revered by all people, and your word will be heard and preserved in the hearts. He will accompany your steps in every good deed, heal all diseases of your body, and strengthen you during prayers. But if the priest is not reconciled, the Angel of the altar departs him. Hence, he loses his reverence, becomes powerless, and is in a state of abandonment.

I was greatly astonished by that talk and asked if he quoted one of the saintly Fathers. He didn't reply but rather said, "Isn't the Angel of the altar you serve the one who raises the prayers and the sacrifice of praise to the heavens!?"

Wise in his silence:

The approach of El-Megadess Youssef concerning public issues and ecclesiastical problems was an approach that genuinely expressed genuine humility that occupied the man's heart and soul. He considered himself unworthy to delve into the matters of great people…. And as such, he used to say to those who contacted him.

No one of those who knew El-Megadess Youssef recalled that he was involved, even once, in a discussion or a debate concerning an issue or a person from the Church leaders and Fathers. He always kept silent. He once told me at a time when there was lots of talk, controversy, and prejudice. He said, "Are you aware of the fundamental reason for the silence of Saint Arsanious the wise? I replied to him, "What was it?" He said, "During that time, powerful waves of controversy swept the Church concerning Origen. Some supported and defended him with enthusiasm and strength; others opposed him and resisted his ideology, considering him excommunicated from the Church's fellowship. Saint Arsanious didn't wish to get involved with that vortex of useless controversy. He didn't receive anyone or talk to anyone. He maintained silence. He transformed silence into prayer and fellowship with God. He loved all people by staying away from people."

When he said that to me, I found out that he published a book about Saint Arsanious, he was attached to Saint Arsanious and emulated his spiritual discipline in transcending circumstances and having love for all people without arguments and faction.

13

George from Rome

She was one of the widows whom the Church fully supported after her husband departed, leaving behind seven children. She was visually impaired, fragile, and illiterate. However .... She was constantly seeking and praying, crying a lot, and holding fast throughout her life, after the departure of her husband, to the Lord's promise that states, "He is the husband of the widow and a father of the fatherless." She strived tremendously to educate her children, and the Lord was holding her hands in miraculous ways to the point that she once came to the Church inquiring about a person who extended her extraordinary help, wanting and insisting on meeting him. She asked the deacon, "Tell me, where is George?" He answered her casually, "George, who?" She replied firmly, "George, who is from Rome." So, he asked her once more, "Where does he reside?" She said to him, "He resides here at the Church." It coincided, at that time, that I was entering the Church, so the deacon told her, "I don't know anything. Abouna arrived, and you can ask him about it."

I asked her, "Is all well?" She started telling me something stranger than fiction, "My daughter's (So and So) grades for the elementary level this year were abysmal. She didn't get accepted into public High Schools. And I am tired of roaming, with her, between the schools. Finally, I went to a private high school yesterday and met with the principal and teachers. They insisted that I pay a first installment of eighteen Pounds[57]. I only had eight pounds, which I received from the Church. I begged them and cried to accept her file and the eight pounds. But they refused. I left the school as tears ran down my

---

[57] Equivalent to 18 USD. Based on a 1:1 ratio

cheeks, lifted my eyes towards heaven, and said, 'O Lord, you are a father of the fatherless, a defender of widows.' And I have no ability. After several steps, I heard, behind me, a voice calling me by name. I became afraid because I was carrying the bag of money. I hid it out of fear that it would get stolen by anyone. I didn't turn around because of fear, but the voice that was calling me drew closer to me. When I turned to it, I saw a man whose face was very luminous, and his appearance was magnificent. He said to me first, 'Wipe away your tears.' Then he said, 'What do you want?' I said, 'I want my daughter to get accepted into High School.' He said, 'Come with me.'"

He made her ride a huge car and drove her to the "Education District." Which was, according to her description, a huge house with many employees. He accompanied her as she met with the district administrator ...... He handed him the girl's file .... Then they left together, and without inquiring about her address, he drove her close to her house. He informed her, "After three days, you will receive, by mail, a yellow card. Which is your daughter's acceptance letter into public High School."

She wished him a long life and insisted that he enter her house so that she could offer him hospitality. He thanked her. She inquired about his name. He responded, "George from Rome." And about his residence, he answered, "I am always present in the Church of Mari Gerges at Sporting."

And it happened precisely as he informed her. Her daughter got accepted into High School, and she noticed that the school principal was very enthusiastic about her daughter as if previously advised to do so.

After that poor lady told me her story, as I couldn't believe what I was hearing, she said, "Do me a favor, Abouna, and let me meet this man. I want to kiss his hand and thank him." I said to her, "Describe his looks to me one more time." She responded, "My eyes are weak, but he is white with blue eyes and resembles the sons of Kings."

I told her, "He is always, during every liturgy and very vesper, present in the Church. If you enter the Church during prayer time, you will see him. But take heed not to stare at people. He is always at the last pew of the Church guarding his children."

I was certain that the author of that task was the great Saint George the Roman and that he appeared to that poor widow who had no helper in this world. I glorified God, who is accompanied by His power and sends his saints to help those who seek His Face and call upon His name.

"We recognize a tree by its fruit… we ought to be able to recognize a Christian by his action. Being a Christian is more than making sound professions of faith; it should reveal itself in practical and visible ways."

– St. Ignatius of Antioch, Epistle to the Ephesians

14

Let Me Die the Death of the Righteous

One of the strangest accounts I heard of concerning the departure of contemporary righteous was the account of the departure of the pious man Mr. Bishara El-Kasisees. (The brother of the blessed Pope Macarius III, and father of His Eminence Abba Athanasius, Metropolitan of Beni Suef, and the departed Hegumen Mikhail Bishara, the priest of Saint George Church in Mahalla al-Kubra)

I heard the account from Abouna Mikhail Bishara in the presence of some of his relatives. They all were "Eyewitnesses" to the final moments of the departure of that pious man.

During his life, the man was recognized by all people as a righteous and saintly person who feared God and loved him with all his heart. He was blessed by the Lord in his household and his children. He was revered by those of the insiders[58], and had a good report amongst the outsiders[59] as well.

He was famous for his love for everyone and his hospitality to strangers and passers-by. It was said that one day, while he was sitting at the entrance door of his house, a group of youths passed by him. Hence, he invited them, saying, "Please come in." It was his custom to welcome everyone and offer his table[60] to anyone who asks …. When the youth accepted the invitation and sat

---
[58] The Believers. (Christians)
[59] The Non-believers. (Muslims)
[60] Food.

at the table, he immediately rose like Abraham the Patriarch and asked his wife to provide food to his guests, even though he didn't know them personally. She apologized, saying that she didn't have enough bread sufficient for them and that she was about to bake bread that day. And there was nothing in the breadbasket except some small fragments. He told her, "Offer what you have, and God will bless."

The youth, on the outside, heard what transpired between the man and his wife. They seized the opportunity to embarrass him. They decided to eat all the bread he offered and then ask for more.

The man came out to them carrying the fragments of bread and some pieces of cheese. He placed it before them, blessed it as usual by signing the food with the sign of the Cross, and invited them to eat. They began eating hungrily and voraciously so they might devour the entire food. But ironically, the food was not used …. Until they were completely exhausted and sick from excessive eating. At that moment, they said, "Mr. Bishara, reveal to us the spell that you recited over the food so that it doesn't get used up."

As such, the Lord's hand was with the man, and His blessing was descended upon him.

At the time of his departure, he was residing with Abouna Mikhail. The man appeared and acted very naturally, but at midnight, he awoke and asked the people present to wake up Abouna Mikhail because he was going to be with the Lord. All were surprised and took heed not to disturb Abouna, especially since the man appeared before them to be in good health. But due to his persistence, they woke up Abouna from his sleep. When Abouna woke up troubled, he perceived the man in a normal state as he was coming out of the bathroom and walking on his feet. He inquired about his state ….To which he assured him that he was okay. Then the man approached his bed, went up to it on his own, and began to advise Abouna Mikhail with Spiritual commandments concerning the Service, the Praises of the Church, the congregation, the love, and concerning his brethren. Biblical Christian Commandments. Then he asked Abouna to pray him the absolution. Abouna got worried and was exceedingly troubled, but he was forced to do so as per the request of that dignified elder. And while he was reciting the absolution, Abouna got confused and stuttered in speech. The dignified man opened his eyes and said, "Recite the absolution properly."

As Abouna was reading the absolution, the man shut his eyes ……The women who were present began to hue and cry ….So, he opened his eyes for the second time and said. "Why such disturbance and screaming? It is better to pray." Then he began to personally distribute Psalms to each of them.

Then he asked Abouna to continue reading the absolution ... When Abouna concluded reciting the absolution, the pious man submitted his spirit in the Lord's hand in peace and by the comfort of the saints.

That spiritual view was witnessed by more than ten individuals who were present and assembled around his bed, which the angels deemed with great honor. When he submitted his spirit, the women began to weep, but Abouna Mikhail firmly prohibited them and asked them to continue with their prayers and psalms that were initiated for them by Mr. Bishara.

15

Jesus Helps the Tempted

There are chosen ones for the Lord in every generation, whom He has endowed with talents and gifts, as He liberally bestowed them all with wisdom and prudence. The Lord bestowed Sister Fawzia Ishaq with unparalleled purity of heart and transparency, which revealed terrific things for her. She was accustomed to seeing God's visions and acknowledging, by spiritual insights, great things before their occurrences. She, for example, at the dawn of Tuesday the 9th of the year 1971, woke her husband up while she was highly affected and said, "Huge loss, Onsie[61], Pope Kirollos went to Heaven." He asked her, "How did you know this?" She replied, "My departed sister 'Julia' (She was her older sister. She went to heaven after a pious and holy life) came to me saying, 'We sent a

---

[61] Her husband's name.

special great procession from above to bring along, with us, Pope Kirollos so that he stays in the same place with us.'"

That transpired at the dawn of Tuesday, and Pope Kirollos went to heaven several hours after that vision. At that time, she was living in the city of Luxor. , separated by hundreds of miles from the Patriarchal Seat in Cairo.

Great Revelation:

And so it happened at the time of her father's departure at Alexandria, as she was still residing at Luxor .... She woke up in the middle of the night and said to her husband, "My father, O Onsie, departed now and is relieved from all his sufferings. I saw him now and the Angels ascending him into heaven."

They received the announcement of death the following day, and when they traveled to Alexandria, they found out that the hour of his death was precisely the hour she saw him in the vision going up toward heaven.

Procession of the Angels:

She, while being a wife and a mother of children, was distinguished by serenity of soul and purity of heart. Uncaring for the vanities of this world and its false frills, but living a simple life in its appearance and significance. Until the Lord permitted her to be tempted with sickness; hence, she had cancer. In the last two years, before her departure to heaven, she suffered pain beyond human's ability to endure. But her account with the Lord exceeded the sufferings by an immeasurable balance. Thus, she depicted the saying of the Apostle, "For our light affliction, which is but for a moment, is working for us a far more exceeding and eternal weight of glory."

Agreement on the time of Departure:

But what is stranger than fiction was how the Lord determined for her the time of her departure from this world. One day, she was burdened by pain beyond measure, and that was on January 4th of the year 1984. In the early morning, she signaled her husband and said, "Come here, Onsie, I have some words to say to you, but don't be sad; last night I was with Christ, and He said to me, 'You are done, you endured all your sufferings, and your crown is prepared for you as well. If you prefer to come to Me, I am ready.' But I

Jesus Helps the Tempted

replied to Him …. 'Sorry, O Jesus, it is true that my sufferings now are beyond my ability to endure and are extremely severe if it was not for You helping me. But You know how much I love my children and how much I am willing to endure for their sake. And I hope they celebrate the Nativity Feast and the Theophany Feast as well. And afterward, they enjoy, along with their friends from the Church, the mid-year vacation. Therefore, I would love to come to You on the last day of the vacation, which means Friday, the 27th of January, so that the kids return to their colleges the following day. Jesus agreed with my request and promised me to fulfill it. Hence, on Friday, the last day of my mid-year vacation, I will go to heaven. Do you agree, or are you upset, Onsie?"

The man controlled himself and, with effort, replied to her, "Is that possible, Fawzia? The thing that Jesus agreed to, I object to and oppose. His will shall be done."

The Lord truly fulfilled His promise and peacefully released her from the confinement of the flesh on Friday the 27th, the day and hour that she agreed upon with her beloved one.

O the wonder, is it to this degree of revelation, affection, and agreement? How excellent is Your name, O Lord, how excellent is Your love, and how excellent is Your glory that You reserved for Your saints?

The Lord was comforting the saints by revealing to them the time of their departure several days prior. But we have never heard of such a situation. Thus, her husband conveyed to us, from his diary, excerpts about the work of grace that supported her faith till the end. Was it possible for dandling to reach that level of love to the point of negotiating an agreement?

Indeed, how wonderful is the life of adherence to Christ? Her husband, the dear Dr. Onsie, shared with us some of what he had documented, including her visions, revelations, deep fervent prayers, and precious commandments helpful for every soul.

She, may the Lord repose her soul; during the night and while she was in a trance between sleep and wakefulness, she did not delve into deep sleep due to her continuous severe pain; however, due to the efect of pain relievers and hypnotics falls into a light coma, was uttering simple, clear, and profound words depicting her feelings and manifesting them in the form of contemplations and sometimes as tips and advice.Her words also were a revelation of her heavenly spiritual visions as she was under the pressure of her severe, harsh pain.

There were certain visions that declared and confirmed that she had meetings with the beloved of our souls, the Lord Jesus.He who, by his humble love, appeared to her numerous times, declaring His person to her, spreading His light and beauty around her, and engaging in a conversation with her, through which He provided her with hope, support, and comfort. Thus alleviating her suffering, so that not only does it become bearable for her, but she gets to endure it. Rather, be thankful for it and be joyful as well.

Now, her husband lists, for us, some of what he recorded of her during the final months of her sickness and during the times of her suffering. He says,

My beloved wife, May the Lord repose her soul, was uttering these sayings with clarity and simplicity. She didn't intend to direct them to any one of us. But she was uttering them off-hand, expressing her feelings and the reservoirs of her sentiment. Despite their simplicity, they were logical sayings, vivid, and carried a deep, profound ideology. I felt, upon hearing her during the night, that they were derived out of a heart filled with serenity and immersed in perfect peace. And I felt as if there was a Holy and Meek Spirit inside her teaching her these expressions so that her sayings come out demur, firm, and not shaky at all. Truly, they are the words of the Spirit who spoke in a heart destroyed by the cruelty of pain but was filled by the person of the Lord and His Spirit who brought along assistance, joy, and peace. During one of the nights, I heard her say,

"O Jesus Christ, You are our only satiation. We will never achieve satiety by our flesh, no matter how much we eat, get dressed, or receive .... As of now, my body perishes day after day. Even the tiny morsel gets stuck in my throat. But I thank You because You are my satiety, and I, in my severe pain, preserve You close to me. A long time ago, when I was well, I couldn't acknowledge You. That is why I'm patient, thankful, and joyful. If only people learn to make a place for You in their lives ... Satan is deceiving them so that they fill their hearts with earthly matters till there will be no room for You. I implore You, my Lord, to make everyone rejoice in You, help them establish a place for You in their hearts and thoughts, and rejoice by the true joy. The joy that the mightiest sufferings can't eradicate. Here I am, amid my inexpressible sufferings, You bestowed me with grace .... Amid my sufferings, I realize Your great gifts for me which I am unworthy to receive. Hence, I rejoice, be patient, and say, 'Just I received from You the sweet things, I ought to thankfully accept from Your hands the bitter things. Even these bitter things themselves are a great gift because I realize they are a tiny piece of the Cross that allows me to be a partaker with You in its suffering.'

When I perceive that my beloved believers strive to be satiated by earthly things, I get upset. Just as in window shopping, they believe that it brings them happiness. Let them realize, O my Lord, that their living fountain is You, the lover of mankind and the rich God who delights in perpetually granting us gifts. And when You perceive us delighted by Your love and Your person, You also be delighted and give us abundantly. Your fellowship, O Lord, is the utmost true success. You were with Joseph. Thus, the Book states that he was successful in all things."

"O my Lord, let my children live for You and in You so that they live the true joyful life in Jesus, in chastity, in honesty, in humility, in meekness, and conviction. For the sake of my sufferings, keep their lives in Your benevolence, and that they love one another and love all people, even the not-so-good ones. They offer them love for the sake of the Lord, and pray for them for the sake of Your Cross that redeemed everyone."

"I thank You, my Lord Jesus because my tribulation revealed to me Your beauty, which is fairer than the sons of me. I have seen plenty, and You have given me plenty …. I was happy copiously, but all that happiness is finite and perishes quickly. Yet, my rejoicing in You is in perpetual increase and remains forever. If it were not for this joy, I wouldn't be able to endure one single moment of the severe suffering that I am experiencing every moment of these lengthy months …. I am delighted in You and by the garment of glory that You prepared for me, which You informed me I would wear after a while."

"I, my children, want you always to rejoice. For life with Jesus is the life of perpetual joy. After I depart from you, rejoice. Because I will be putting on the garment of glory and light after putting off the garment of pain and sorrow …… Would you hate for your mother to go to heaven? There, her spirit will be with you way more than here, and she will have a message for you greater than here. I, on the day my mother departed from this world, kneeled next to her bed and prayed for her sake and also for my sake so that the Lord grants me faith and strength. The temptation passed by peacefully, and God helped me to always feel her presence with me and mine with her …. I want you to be as such and never be sad so that I won't be sad while I am at my heavenly joy. I am certain that God will be with you more and more after I go to Him.… He will be glorified with you more, and you will succeed in all things …. Provided that you serve Him and His Church, your true mother who gave birth to you by her baptism. Live the life of purity so that the Holy Spirit dwells and stays in you. Do not care for the world, and always do the right thing. If people were satisfied, fine. And they were not, that is okay. I learned a lot from my tribulation ….Long time ago, I cared about peoples' opinions, and I was concerned about the outer appearance. But after the many lessons the Lord taught me, I realized that all those better than me had returned to dust. I realized that this is a deception that we ought to avoid. Since then, I have cherished perfect simplicity and natural things that are void of everything, to the point that many people have criticized and insulted me because of my outer appearance and other things. But I didn't care for anything since I wanted Christ, who was meek and commanded meekness in everything. Not just in clothing but in everything. In eating as well, we ought to be simple. All is vanity, my children; all is for corruption and stench. You ought to care only for your spirits because they are everlasting. The flesh, if given more than what is sufficient, will cause our perdition and the loss of our salvation. Seek success in your earthly life so that with it, you can serve the Lord and glorify him. But do not trust that your success is worth anything. If it is not accompanied by spiritual success, then it is useless. What is important is the success of your spirits before all things. But the secular success will perish and renders nothing at all."

Then she groans from severe pain and says, "Oh, Oh, the pain is extreme, but it is sufficient, O Jesus, that I am seeing You, and You are with me. This comforts me, lets me rejoice, and allows me to bear all things."

On another night, after she groaned because of the severe pain, she fell asleep upon receiving a shot of Morphine. Then she wakes me up saying, "Oh, how beautiful is it what I am seeing." I asked her, "What are you seeing?" She tells me, "I see Jesus. He is so beautiful; I can't describe Him." I tell her, "Of course, isn't He not fairer than the sons of men?" She responds, "True. True." I asked her, "Did he say anything to you?" She replies, "Yes. He asked me, 'Would you like to come to Me now?I told Him, 'Yes, I am anxious. But not now. Let me talk to my children and advise them a bit more about living for You. And this will be it, and I shall come to you." Then she groans and says, "Oh. Oh, the pain is strong. But I thank You, Jesus because You are holding me. I never deserve Your gifts. Even the shot of the pain reliever, which not every suffering person can acquire, I don't deserve it …… I thank You, O Lord, a thousand times. I am so delighted with You and have no void in anything. I wish all people would be satiated by Christ's satiety, the true bread of life. I hope all my loved ones strive to get satiated by Him only. They shall never hunger or be in need of anything, nor will they be afraid of anything. I command you again, my

Jesus Helps the Tempted

children, to always live rejoicing by Jesus. Rejoice for me when I am in heaven with Him until we all are together there with Him."

She, May the Lord repose her soul, was talking to each one of her children separately. Conveying to him the exact expressions and ideologies, but perhaps on a more extensive and deeper scale than what she was uttering during her sleep. It was imperative to her to establish these ideologies in their hearts so that they remain anchored in them all their lives.

During another night, upon administering the shots of anesthetics and hypnotics, and while she was not fully asleep and not fully awake, she said, "Today, I am rejoicing in Him and by the grace that I am immersed in. Today is the day that I experienced the most severe pain, and as you know, Onsie is also the day in which I received the most shots of pain relievers. But also today is the most day Christ encamped me, and made me rejoice by Him to ease my suffering …. I rejoice in Him …. What good did I do to deserve that He lets me see, with my own eyes, all this goodness while I am still alive? I don't know how to thank Him. No matter the magnitude of the Thanksgiving, it is not enough. Today, there is more pain, but there is also more love. Therefore, I rejoice in my suffering …. He is supporting me, and I feel His two hands. These are mercies above understanding …. Thanks be to God truly."

It seems that Christ, glory be to Him, didn't leave her either by night or by day – Rather, I became confident that He was taking her for periods outside her body and out of this world to grant her periods of rest, happiness, and consolation. Similar to how He took the Apostle of endeavor Paul the Apostle to the third heaven after he was stoned at the city of Lystra and was almost dead, He took him to strengthen him, comfort him, and support him. But how I became sure of this …. It is based on the following incident:

On the morning of one of the days, we found our departed beloved in a strange state. She was neither awake nor asleep, and as we were thinking about the situation, we were perplexed. We were visited by Sister Dr. Mofeeda Moawaad. She is a faithful friend who frequented her three times weekly and spent some time with her as she was very comfortable with her during the time of her happiness and her sorrow. When she examined her, she was very perplexed as well. The situation was not a coma in its known form and was not a state of death nor a state of living. Meanwhile, she continued to administer all methods and diagnostics so that she would be alert, and after thirty minutes, suddenly, she opened her eyes. Immediately, Dr. Mofeeda asked her, "What is the matter, Fawzia? Where were you? And what happened with you?" She answered her, saying, "You now cut short for me my happiest moments, Dr. Mofeeda." But she didn't elaborate more than that. However, the following night, I was awakened by her voice. She was half asleep but spoke with an audible clear voice, saying, "The previous day was extraordinary. It began with amazing comfort and without any pain at all. This was the first time I lived several hours pain-free for many prolonged months. I felt perfect happiness, unlike any other happiness I experienced before. The happiness of a new type is indescribable. And more than this, I saw Jesus early morning, and He said to me, 'You are of My daughters whom I love … And those whom I love, I make their Crown bigger and larger … And also, he who truly love Me, bear with Me, and accept from Me everything.' I felt like I was getting lighter and lighter till I left the world in actuality and crossed over for moments, which I couldn't tell how long they were or ever describe. I felt the pain and suffering of my entire life; I was totally put off, so I got prepared to put on the heavenly white garment. I was in extreme joy afterward when Dr. Mofeeda came in, and I said to you, 'You cut short for me my happiest moments.' And Dr. Mofeeda thought I was in a Coma. No. I was crossing over the life and the world. As Jesus revealed to me, the sweetness of the crossing over is so that I will be calm during the hour of my departure, which is very near."

Afterward, she repeated the same account, and she said to me while she was awake during the day, "I truly give thanks to God because the only thing I feared was the moments of death. But seeing the love of Christ, O Onsie relieved me from my body, crossed me over the world and life, and taught me that the hour of departure is an hour of joy and dash to Christ. Now, I am not afraid at all because I realized how sweet and beautiful it is."

She always talks with Jesus while observing His beauty and light. One night, while she was talking with Him during her sleep and as I was listening to her, I said to her, "I want you, Fawzia, when you are with Jesus, to remember us always. So that he helps us, strengthens us, and has mercy upon us." She replied, saying, "Of course I will remember you." I said, "Is that a promise?" She answers, "It is a promise, Onsie. Do I have any task other than this? It will always be as such when I am with Him there." Then I tell her, "But you will be overwhelmed by Him and His Grace." She replies, "Part of my task with Him is to remember you one by one."

She was, during numerous nights, uttering many contemplations and profound testimonies concerning life with Christ and the beauty and sweetness of His fellowship. And about the work of His Grace with us and within us, as

Jesus Helps the Tempted

well as the necessity for our adherence to Him and tasting His benevolence. And other things that there is not enough space to list.

She declared, in her talks, different visions of the heavenly views and the appearance of the saints and so on and so forth.

One night, around two after midnight, she woke me up saying, "Onsie, don't be afraid of anything …. All these whom you see are outside the bedroom." I ask her, "Who are they? She says, "These might be a group whose appearance is terrifying, whose color is black, and who are very tall. I see them gathered to enter unto us. But no one can enter unto us as long as this beautiful lady stands at the door. She assured me that she would be standing all the time so no one from this group would be able to enter. Do you see her, Onsie? How beautiful is she? She is wearing a light, heavenly dress, and her face is luminous. She is resting her hand at the door, blocking them. I thank You, O Lord, because You truly protect us."

Of course, who could that luminous lady be other than our mother and the lady of us all the lady Virgin Mary? Now I understood the meaning behind the Agpya prayer, "And when my soul departs my body attend to me, and defeat the conspiracy of the enemies, and shut the gates of Hades, lest they might swallow my soul, O you, blameless bride of the true Bridegroom."

It was truly a fundamental matter that allowed us to know and understand. This is truly one of the tasks performed on our behalf by the ultimate intercessor. Rather, it is the greatest and last task in our lives.

One night, she asked me, "Do you see, Onsie, that great light that filled the room? That is very strange. I always tell you that my eyes can't tolerate electric light, even if it is weak. How come I can look at this light, be happy with it, and have my eyes relaxed? Truly, the light is strong but comfortable and very relaxing."

Truly, our beloved, it is the light of our Christ the beloved. He is the "Sun of Righteous" and the "Light of the World." She was always balancing between her vicious sufferings and what was revealed to her by Jesus, her loved One, and says to us, "Why do you suffer? Why do you shed your tears and make me upset? If I am happy for my suffering, that is because I see Christ and all His Glories. Why do you get upset?"

One time, she was in severe pain, to the point that her face turned red because of the magnitude of the pain. The bed shook with her intense shivers of pain. At that hour, our holy father Kirollos Dawood, the priest of our Church at Mostafa Kamel (The Church of Archangel Michael), was present with us. When his reverence saw her, he was very hurt and prayed with his tears. Truly, it was a powerful, fervent prayer from the bottom of his heart. After his reverence left, she asked me, "Do you realize now that behind every pain, a great blessing greater than it? If I didn't suffer with this pain in the presence of our father Kirollos, we would have lost the blessing of this blessed prayer that we received."

As such, she was by the Spirit analyzed all matters throughout her suffering with her cruel and terrible illness.

These are examples of the overwhelming consolation that this righteous soul encountered through her physical sufferings. She is, in fact, a unique example of God's dealings and unsearchable benevolence. That soul had become a source of blessing and consolation for many of her loved ones and acquaintances. The account of her endeavor and endurance has become a preaching for bearing the Cross and offering thanksgiving with joy. Also, God's consolation and His genuine promises to her became an edification of faith and confirmation of hope.

May her life be a consolation to all those who suffer, a hope for a better life, a crown that does not fade, and an inheritance preserved for us in heaven.

PART 2

16

Illuminated the Insight

One of the souls accepted the faith and entered the fold of Christ, the good shepherd, as she was advanced in age. Some individuals were indeed chosen before being formed in the womb. Their selection manifests vividly as the mid-day sun; we witnessed that with our eyes. Thus, we obtained consolation through grace and hope.

The Church of Christ will continue to bear sons to Christ until the end of times because the Holy Spirit enriches her, being present within her in perpetual dwelling. Also, the Church neither gets old nor suffers infertility. Rather, she is fertile and bears children. This undermentioned is a sample of whom the Grace placed in our way for consolation and encouragement. We saw that it was fitting for many souls to be comforted by the consolation that we obtained from God.

One of those souls was a lady who accepted the faith in her late forties while being a mother to several boys and girls. When her heart was opened for the Lord, it was open without objection or hindrance. Thus ... She loved the Lord with a supreme, overwhelming love. And she enjoyed the Cross of Christ and his precious blood to the fullest extent.

She, upon receiving the grace of Baptism, persevered in prayer, in attending the Liturgies, and partaking in the Eucharist with an inexpressible passion, hunger, and thirst.

In April of 1979, I was baptizing a group of Americans at the Church of Saint Mark the Evangelist in Los Angeles. During their procession around the Church after the Liturgy while wearing white garments and holding lit candles, that lady was ululating with a loud voice. Joy and happiness, along with copious tears, were running down her eyes as she said, "I am the only one who feels what they are feeling and values the Grace that they received .... For you[62] were baptized at birth and grew up in the Grace, but as for me .... I was deprived of it for a long time. So, when God permitted me to taste His benevolence, I have come to appreciate Christ's generosity and His abundant Grace upon me." She told me, "If it is permissible for envy to exist in the Christian life, then I envy those who were born in the Grace, raised in it, and enjoyed it forever." I would then respond to her, "The Grace cannot be measured, for God does not give the Spirit by measure. What a person obtains in a moment may not be matched to what another person obtains in years and years. So, the last will be first, and the first last. For many are called, but few chosen."

That lady, by humility of heart and humble faith, was rejoicing by the word with a wonderful spiritual joy. She comprehended it with a spiritual stature that surpassed many of those who had been in the Church for a long time. However, there was one obstacle that hindered the spiritual growth of that lady. She was illiterate and unable to read or write. She was suffering because she desired to provide herself with the fountains of life so that she may increase in knowledge .... She desired to read the Bible and pray the Psalms. The only source for her learning was "Hearing." She was hearing the words of the sermons, hearing the hymns, and hearing the Gospel. But she was not able to learn on her own. Books, to her, were sealed. And it happened as the days passed by and as she was frequenting the Church that her desire for knowledge increased as well as her longing for reading the word of God.

One day, as the deacon was distributing the Psalms to the congregation at the beginning of the Liturgy, he passed by her and assigned her a Psalm. She shook her head but was not holding an Agpya book in her hands. She was deeply affected. After the Divine Liturgy, she returned to her home, entered her room, and, with astounding confidence, confronted the Lord about how it was feasible for all people to enjoy His fellowship and pray to him. At the same time, she was deprived of that grace. She implored Him, saying, "You have to give me this Grace so I can read." She was crying bitterly with a broken heart. And behold .... She opened the Agpya that was in her hands, and the Lord illuminated her mind. She immediately began reading without the help of a teacher, while she couldn't recognize the letter "A" from the letter "Z." She came to me in a state of joy and praise .... Leaping .... And how surprised I

---

[62] Those who are Christians by birth.

became as she began to read the Psalms, before me, fluently without errors … I glorified Him who said, He is faithful in His promises, "None of them shall teach his neighbor, and none his brother, saying, 'Know the Lord, 'for all shall know Me, from the least of them to the greatest of them.'"[63] And also, "And they shall all be taught by God[64]".

---

[63] Hebrews 8:11
[64] John 6:45

17

Chosen Vessel

What the Lord had said to Ananias regarding Apostle Paul that he was a chosen vessel, is truly marvelous! For the Lord has chosen vessels at all times and all places. Those vessels may be living far from their appointed path or lost in the mazes of the world. Not knowing their calling nor realizing they are chosen until the fullness of time arrives. Only then would they recognize their calling and walk the road of salvation. Devoting themselves to the One whom they were called by.

One of those chosen spirits, an American youth from San Francisco, whom I met in 1979 through a beloved member of the Church who informed me saying; "This young man has an amazing story concerning his faith in Christ; I wish you would hear it; I brought him so that he may increase in knowledge and faith, and to accept the Holy Baptism." I sat down with this youth; he was young and very tall, with pleasant features. He started telling me his exciting story; he was Jewish from a religious family, very conservative, despite living in an area infested with temptations and sins. He studiously went to the synagogue every Saturday, keeping the commandments and the Mosaic Law as much as possible. He worked for a wealthy lady, administering her business and colossal wealth. He was honest in his work, giving it all his efforts and beyond.

The lady was in her forties, enjoying an uninhibited luxury life, living in debauchery according to the rich's environment and traditions. The youth was twenty-eight years of age. The more he was loyal, dedicated to his work, and honest in keeping all her money, the more she appreciated and lavished him. He was happy with his work, and her appreciation boasted his honesty and loyalty. Then the unthinkable happened: she got attached and fell in love with him. She offered herself.... however, he never thought of such a thing; what she was asking evoked revulsion in him. So, he seized every opportunity to avoid her by increasing his workload and reducing their chances of meeting. She was insulted by how he, who was just an employee, could dare to refuse her. She became more persistent, and he became more adamant in his refusal. Her dignity was shattered, so she initiated a chain of inconveniences. The youth placidly tolerated her.

One day, she boldly threatened him that if he did not comply with her desires, she would retaliate. Several days passed, and without warning, he was arrested and imprisoned. The lady and her lawyer accused him of money dissipation due to severe negligence. They were false accusations, but she had power and money.

In prison, the young man was under tremendous stress and feeling oppressed. He waited a couple of days till the investigation was completed. He had no outlet nor refuge.

And so, it happened that an Anglican priest visited the prison, chatted with him, and left him a Bible. But being Jewish, he did not believe in the Bible, did not know it, nor did he ever read it. Additionally, he was proud of his Jewish heritage. So, he put the Bible aside. Time in prison moves slowly, and boredom is a killer. He stretched his arm and held the Bible, thinking there was no harm in reading to pass the time.

He started reading ... First, it was the miracle of feeding the multitudes, then the struggle of the disciples in the sinking ship, then Jesus walking on the water and ceasing the wind with astonishing authority. The young man was cut in the heart like never before; he started praying an unusual prayer; he told the Lord, "Are these words true? Is it your great ability, your authority over nature, and your power that prevented the danger from your disciples? If you lift the oppression off me today, I will be your servant all the days".

An hour later, he was taken to the attorney general, who thoroughly interrogated him. To which the young man answered him with complete honesty. Immediately, he was released without bond. He did not believe it; his heart was flooded with the faith of Christ. Joy overwhelmed him from within. He prostrated, thanking Christ, the mighty God. He went home and met the beloved brother, who resided next to him, requesting to meet with a priest so he could receive Baptism. When they got the chance, they met with me. The young man read the Bible a lot and was taught about the Orthodox faith and the history of our church.

I was joyful by that pure young man; I kept him with me for days, teaching him the Old Testament, which he knew. But now, once he learned it in the light of Christ, he leaped with joy. He received the grace of the Comforter, accepting the Holy Baptism, born again from above. He became a new creation in Christ Jesus, for the old things have passed away.

18

The Word of God Is Living and Powerful

Abouna Bishoy Kamel talked to me about several "Accounts of Faith." He said, "At the beginning of the Seventies, one of the beloveds approached me; he was a civil employee for the army, along with a youth in his twenties who was an army volunteer. He introduced me to him. The lad sat beside me while reciting one of the astonishing accounts of God's dealings with mankind.

He said, "We live in an underprivileged neighborhood in Alexandria …. We have no Christian neighbors. I never dealt with any Christian person at all. We are a poor family, and my father works as a guard at the police precinct. I have seven siblings, and I am their eldest. I was fierce in my behavior and cruel towards my brothers, and I didn't know or show mercy. As such, was the milieu in which I lived ……? Full of shouts, insults, and profanities …. No serenity or peace. Not to mention being occupied with songs and all sorts of defilements.

One day, I was purchasing an item from the deli. The deli man handed it to me, wrapping it in paper. I unfolded the paper and, with curiosity, began to read it. Behold, I was faced with words that were foreign to me. So, I read more closely. The words entered not into my mind but into my heart. I discovered I was facing words from above …. Transcendent Divine Heavenly words."(The paper was from the Gospel according to Saint Matthew, Chapters 5, 6. It was part of Christ's Sermon on the Mount.)

The fantastic thing, to which he had no explanation, was that those words, which he read multiple times, radically changed his morals. Hence, he became meek and peaceful, serving the feeble with all tenderness. His tongue refrained from uttering a single word of profanity. He even confessed that his eyes became chaste; he could no longer look at a girl or a woman with a vain and unholy look. He felt that the words of the Bible can transform astoundingly. Even those close to him noticed that conversion and marveled at his change. In fact, his father thought he was depressed. Hence, he asked, "What is it with you, my son? Is there something wrong with you, or has something bad happened to you? You are not your usual. Rather, I perceive you unusually quiet." He assured him that he was fine.

He became passionate about getting acquainted with the Holy Bible. He wished to read it in its entirety. So, he got close to the person who later became his Godfather. He asked him to lend him the Holy Bible, and he gave it to him. So, he began to vigil all night until dawn, reading without fatigue or satiety …. During his confessions, he said, "The entire Book brings joy, gives satiety, comforts the soul, inspires hope, and leads to salvation. But no matter what I read, I always return to the Sermon on the Mount. It is, for me, my first encounter with my Savior and the first experience. It is like the procession of the primary ray of light that illuminated my entire life. How could I forget any of its words?"

On the day that brethren accepted the Grace of the birth from above and the regeneration by the Holy Spirit through the Holy Baptism at the Church of the Evangelist in the city of Alexandria. On that day, I testify before God, that I saw his face as the face of an Angel. And the moment of his emergence from the womb of the baptismal font, the Grace of God was upon him. He also testified, for that, some of the beloved deacons whom I invited to follow up with him and deliver him the rituals, the practice of the Sacraments, and the Christian life.

Truly, The word of God is living and powerful.

19

They Shall Be Taught by God

Also, Abouna Bishoy informed me, concerning the accounts of the chosen souls – About an account of a lady. Thus, he told me, "I met her at the Church of Saint George the Martyr at Sporting in the early Seventies. She was always standing at the last pews, greeting the priest with caution tinged with fear. I asked her, 'Are you Christian?' She replied, 'No …. But I love Christ so much.' When she met with me later, she revealed her secret to me. She works for one of the wealthy families in Cairo. She met a young Christian man from Alexandria. He teaches and talks to her about Christ despite his simple knowledge. And as much as she was learning, her love increased for the Lord and for His life-giving Cross. I asked her frankly, 'Does he intend to marry you?' She simply answered, 'Yes.' I said to her, "My sister, Christianity is not like this? It is not a bridge to cross to reach another purpose. A man shouldn't convert to Christianity to obtain another goal. The Christian faith didn't spread by marriage. This is not Christianity in any way. Christ is sought for His own sake and loved for the sake of His Cross, and not for any other purpose.' She said, confirming my words: 'I seek Christ for Himself only, and I would like to enjoy His fellowship and live for Him. Regardless of the other issue, whether I am linked to this young man or not …. I have tasted the grace of the faith in Christ, and I will never abandon Him no matter the cost,' I informed her, 'The only condition for receiving the holy Sacrament is that you are not to marry this young man.' She immediately agreed. So, I handed her over to one of the female servants to take care of her, deliver her the faith, and teach her the Gospel, the holy commandments, and how to walk in the Christian conduct and virtues. And so it was when she received the Divine mystery …. And God's grace came upon her …. She said to me on the day of her baptism, 'I almost died in the baptismal font … Because of the sheer joy that overwhelmed me.' She also said, 'It is because of Christ's tenderness and love that He doesn't reveal to the soul all the spiritual goodness and the riches of the glory of His inheritance all at once. Otherwise, no one would have endured. He gives little by little because of the feebleness of our nature and its inability to bear.'"

"And it was an amazing thing …. That this blessed sister became, since the time of the Holy Baptism, as if she were inspired concerning what is fitting and what is not fitting, what is helpful and what is not helpful, what is lawful and what is not lawful. As if she had memorized the texts of the commandments …. Rather, it was as if she had obtained the spirit of the commandments; she recognized what was compatible with the Christian life and what was appropriate for the Spiritual conduct without prior knowledge of what is written. She lived in our home during the period of the Holy Forty Days, in a life of fasting, prayer, and perseverance with a longing for the heavenly things that rejoice the heart. Whenever she read the Holy Bible and contemplated, her tears would flow abundantly as evidence of the spiritual response with God's living word, which is sharper than any two-edged sword."

20

Saint George and the Quick Help

The Church intendant approached me, at that hour I was in the baptismal room officiating the Holy Mystery for one of the infants, saying a lady and her mother were seeking to meet with me. I responded by saying, "As soon as I conclude the Baptism, bring them into me here."

The lady and her mother entered...... Trembling in fear .... With caution, they greeted me. I instantly realized that they were foreigners to the Church, and perhaps they never entered a Church prior. I welcomed them while calming down their anxiety .... I invited them to sit, saying, "How can I serve you? As soon as the young lady relaxed, she seemed about thirty years of age; she began narrating a strange incident ... She said, "We, as you can tell, are not Christians. But we belong to a religiously conservative family and live peacefully with our neighbors. Among them is a Christian family with whom we established bonds of love .... Our neighbor, the Christian lady, brought us here and let us in because we are not accustomed to stepping inside a Church .... Rather, this is the first time we speak to a priest." The young lady continued, "From my early youth, I am attached to Saint Therese. I heard of her at school, and I read her biography. Hence, I loved about her the tenderness of emotions and endurance of illness while offering gratitude for it. I felt that her calm and meek life was the best life. I don't know how she became my friend and why I talked to her. My love for her strengthened my relationship with her. Therefore, I loved all that she loved during her life. And I wished I could live like her. Several years ago, I was introduced to a devout young man from a family known to us. He occupies a respectable position …. He prays the obligatory prayers on their due time and fasts the holy month.[65] And he performs all the duties imposed on us by our faith. He is a bearded man, with good manners, and respected by all people …. I got engaged to him …… Then we were united through marriage …. And one of the memories that I will never forget is that one day before my wedding …. I saw in a night vision Saint Therese handing me a bouquet of roses …. How happy I was with her as I felt an overwhelming sense of joy …. Nothing could have made me happier on my wedding day more than my joy with this gift. As if she was blessing my life. I told her, "This is a beautiful thing …. Saints, while in heaven, feel for those who relate to them on earth." She continued narrating her account, and she elaborated, saying, "My life went on calmly and normally, with nothing disturbing it except a troublesome nightmare that would recur from time to time over a year." I asked her, "What is it?" She responded, "I was seeing as if a strange person, very troublesome, his countenance is disgusting, and appeared vicious without mercy …. He was chasing me, desiring to attack and rape me violently…. I was extremely terrified of him. On the day I dream of this troublesome nightmare, I wake up from my sleep exhausted and distracted, as if I were sick and can hardly be able to regulate my strength. When my husband inquires about my condition, I tell him about the matter. He, one time, comforts me; another time, he mocks me, and another time, we go to one of the Sheikhs and to the people who possess knowledge …. Every one of them renders advice, but the reality of the matter remained as is …… So, my turmoil increased to the point that I feared sleeping to avoid what I suffered during my dreams. Yesterday, I fell asleep around 10:30 PM …. And at midnight, this annoying nightmare recurred …. The scary demon chased me …. O the fear …. He caught up with me, threw me to the ground, and fell on top of me …. I felt, at that moment, thick darkness covering me. Rather, darkness penetrated inside me. I almost died, and I couldn't breathe because of extreme fear, pain, and darkness altogether. However, I, with all that remained within me, of feeble ability and with a faint voice as if from a deep well, kept saying, "O Lord save me …. O Lord rescue me." Immediately …. I heard a loud noise …. Resembling a horse running…. Till it drew close to me as I was laying as such …. I opened my eyes in fear and saw a luminous view …. A man riding a horse, holding a spear in his hand; his face was brightly beautiful, and his entire appearance was splendid. Even

---

[65] The month of Ramadan.

his horse was lightsome .... Then a voice came from the horse rider .... He rebukes the darkness within me, saying, 'Get out of her.' He answered him dryly, 'No.' A harsh argument occurred as I was listening in fear, horror, and extreme panic. When the stubbornness of the ghost, which crouched inside me as darkness, persisted .... The horse rider quickly pierced him with his spear with great force .... The spear came out of my back ... Immediately, and with the speed of lightening darkness fully dissipated from within me; light, peace, and astounding serenity came upon me. I woke up at that moment .... When I opened my eyes, I saw my husband sitting in bed while being in a state of panic and terror. I asked him, 'Why are you sitting as such?' He responded, 'Are you okay?' I said, 'Thanks be to God, I am fine.' I sat up and told him about everything that had happened to me with great affection. He said, 'Be easy on yourself, and let go of this nonsense.' I tried to know what woke him up or what he saw or heard. But he didn't answer me by one word.'"

"In the morning, I woke up happy and joyful. And as I was changing my garments, I found my undergarment smeared with blood." She took out her garments from a hand-held bag .... Behold, there was a circle at the front and the back due to the effect of the piercing of that wonderful knight's spear.

I asked her, astonished, "Do you know the Champion, Saint George?" She answered, "No." I said to her, "Follow me." I took her to where the Saint George's Icon was. When she saw the icon, she screamed, "It is him. It is him."

I talked to her about the life of the "Prince of Martyrs." .... She was paying attention, as her face shone with joy. I said to her, "Even though you don't know Saint George and the fact that you didn't ask or request his help .... But when you asked God, 'O Lord save me .... O Lord, rescue me.' Then God, Glory be to His name, immediately responded. He sent you one of His holy men, who is mighty, quick to help, and a conqueror of demons. Saint George is a courageous Knight. His horse was known for its courage and bravery when he was alive on earth. In heaven, upon his martyrdom for the sake of Christ, his lightsome horse, which you saw, became an expression of the power of God. As for the spear that he is holding in his hand, it is not a physical one. But it is the Holy Cross, the sign that scares the demons and perishes their sting."

Afterward, I taught her how to sign the Holy Cross and be attached to it. That became a marvelous beginning for an astounding life. It was initiated by Saint Therese with a simple friendship and perfected by the courageous Knight, the Prince of Martyrs, with his mighty spear. May his prayer include and guard us and our children ...Amen.

21

Peace, Peace, to Him Who Is Far and to Him Who Is Near

Brother Mazloum was a colleague of ours at the university. That was towards the end of the fifties. We were a harmonious group bonded by Christian love. We had decided, during the first year of college, to establish an ecclesiastical assembly dedicated only to us. We chose the Church of the Lady Virgin of Rod El Farag[66]. We assembled there to pray and study the Holy Bible. Thus, our friendship kept increasing in intimacy and friendliness. That was the primary ecclesiastical assembly for college students, as the concept of assemblies was not yet established.

As such, we were bonded by fellowship at college and brotherly love at the Church. Hence, the love bonds were strengthened day after day ....Years passed quickly, we all graduated, and everyone went on his way according to God's plan for each one.

In 1968, some traveled to America as immigrants, and some traveled to England. While some went on study missions to India and Russia .... The majority were at Cairo, Alexandria, and the capitals of some governorates all the way up to Aswan[67].

After a few years, Brother Mazloum, at that time he was working for the Medical Examiner Department, suffered from an Upper Respiratory Disease. It was misdiagnosed as Tuberculosis, as well as inflammation of the lungs.

---

[66] A district in the Northern Area of Cairo, Egypt.
[67] A city on the Nile River, has been southern Egypt's strategic and commercial getaway since antiquity.

He underwent treatment for a long time until a professor at Al Qasr Al Eyni examined him[68]. And he decided to operate on him. He scheduled for him the day of the surgery; our brother went to Al Qasr Al Eyni and entered the operating room. That day, the operating Surgeon[69] didn't show up for one reason or another. So, one of the assistant surgeons performed the surgery according to his own logic …. He removed a large part of the lungs, causing lots of damage. Brother Mazloum came out of the operating room worse than before.

The professor reexamined him. When he saw him in that condition, he kept cursing, imprecate, and blaming. After several weeks, he decided to perform an operation to eradicate the results of the first surgery and to rectify the case.

Our brother once again entered the operating room. On that day, the professor performed an interesting surgery. He removed two rips from the Thoracic cage to expand lung space. That brother came out of the operating room in the worst condition; the sight of him evoked pity as if he were actually handicapped …. All those circumstances left a deep scar in the souls of his four sisters, for he was the only brother, as well as in the souls of his beloveds and colleagues. All were suffering, but they had no means of helping except prayer, supplication to God, and the intersessions of the Saints.

As the news reached the brethren who were abroad, for they were earnestly following his condition with sorrow, they contacted one another and decided that he should come to England so that he may find much better medical treatment than what he had received in Egypt.

Brother Mazloum didn't have the financial means to travel anywhere; he spent all he had on physicians. However, the brethren abroad perceived him as a beloved brother. So, they took care of the travel expenses and, if necessary, the treatment as well.

And as so it was …. Brother Mazloum went to London …. Those who bid him farewell[70]. At the Cairo International Airport were his four sisters, their spouses, relatives, and friends[71]. It was an emotional day. One of his sisters, who resided at Al Ibrahimeyah in Alexandria, was constantly in contact with us … She was praying a lot with copious tears.

I followed up with her, inquiring about her brother's condition. A week has passed since he left for London. I asked her. She said, "There is no news, letters, or phone calls." Then, another week passed by, yet there was nothing

---

[68] https://en.m.wikipedia.org/wiki/Qasr_El_Eyni_Hospital
[69] The professor who examined brother Mazloum.
[70] That took place in the late sixties. There were no instant communications as nowadays.
[71] There was a high probability not to see him alive again.

new. I asked her, "Do you know the hospital's address to which your brother was admitted?" She said, "No." I asked, "Do you know the address of the person who received him in London?" She answered "No" as well.

A whole month went by since he left. Because we didn't receive any information, her anxiety increased, and she was always coming to meet with me while her eyes didn't cease crying. We officiated Liturgies in his name and pleaded abundantly to the Lord.

Days went by without any news. After two weeks, we were officiating a special Liturgy for him .... After the Divine Liturgy, she held my hand and cried out, "Do something; I can't bear this any longer. My sisters in Cairo are having a nervous breakdown." I couldn't contain my emotions and said to her, "With men, it is impossible, but not with God. Because everything is possible with God."

She immediately went to her home and entered the guests' room. In that room was an Icon of the Lady Virgin carrying the baby Jesus. She began to reproach them harshly, almost close to a quarrel. With all her heart, she talked to them as her tears ran down without ceasing. Then she turned towards the Holy Virgin and cried, "Assure me ... I won't let go of you until you assure me."

She prostrated for a long time, then she got up and sat down on the floor. She retrieved her Holy Bible and said, "Lord, let me hear Your voice ....Reveal to me Your will." Then she opened it randomly. Behold, it was opened at the place where it was written, "I have seen his ways, and will heal him; I will also lead him, and restore comforts to him and to his mourners .... Peace, peace to him who is far off and to him who is near," Says the Lord, "And I will heal him." Isaiah 57: 18, 19

She couldn't believe her eyes .... Was what she was reading real? Her heart leaped from joy, and she was filled with happiness and peace. She prostrated on the floor once more, thanking God. What sort of gratitude ought to be rendered to God to compensate for that Consolation? With all confidence, she rose up and called her sisters on the phone, telling them the good news. They asked her, "Did you receive a letter or anything reassuring? She replied, "No. But rather, I received what is greater than a letter .... Greater beyond measure."

Indeed, the Lord has done great things for us. The following day, she received a letter of assurance, and the good news continued coming afterward. It was only a few months later that Mazloum returned from London in total health. He felt that the Lord's hand was working with him every day. He was supported by the prayers of many people and by the faith of those close to him. Indeed, how great is the goodness of the Lord, and how truthful are His promises?

22

Saint Mark the Evangelist

We were at the Monastery of the martyr Saint Mina the Wonder-worker in March 1967. We were gathered around the departed Pope Kirollos on the 6th. That occurred on one of the Sundays of the Holy Great Lent. The Pope had just concluded the evening prayer. (Sunday vespers is the only "Evening" on which vesper prayers are officiated in addition to Saturday vespers …. Because all hours of Agpya and Psalms are prayed on the rest of fasting days. Then the Divine Liturgy ends at Sunset)

As our father, the Patriarch, was exiting the Church, he was surrounded by some of the brethren. They were inquiring about the help of the Saints and their intersessions. The conversation mentioned Saint Mark, Saint Mari Mina the Wonderworker, and Saint George, as well as the wonders and support the believers receive through their intersessions and their accepted supplications. The Pope said, "It is we who hinder their work by our bad conduct, despite them interceding on our behalf perpetually." I asked him, "How can this be?" So, they turned to me and said, "Pope Kirollos the 5th was spending lots of time in the cell of the Patriarchate in Alexandria. And it was in his day, a gardener charged with the maintenance of Saint Mark Cathedral's Garden. He was a pious man who stayed vigil many nights in continuous prayers. He was watering the trees and the plants late in the evening. He was a man of open eyes, seeing God's visions …. He saw Saint Mark every night, carrying a censor full of incense, roaming the entire area. The man was delighted with what God had bestowed upon him and with that inexpressible blessing. No one knew anything about those matters."

"One of those days, that good man didn't see Saint Mark as per his daily custom. He kept praying and chanting to God, but he didn't see him either the second or the third night. That heavenly vision disappeared before his eyes; hence, he became sad and heartbroken."

"As he was perplexed and wondering what should he do? He went up to the cell of the Patriarch …. Informing him of his situation and asking him what these things meant. The Pope said to him, 'Okay, Monsieur[72] . Pray so our Lord intervenes, and we get to find out why that happened!'

"The Pope investigated the conditions of the Church and her servants and discovered that two priests, servants of St. Mark's Cathedral, had a disagreement for several days, and they were quarreling. The Pope summoned them and reconciled between them. They came down from the Pope's cell in peace. A day later, the Pope summoned the Gardner and asked him, 'Is all well?' The man prostrated at the Pope's feet in gratitude …. And said, 'Praise be to God, Our Lord. Saint Mark resumed what he was doing.'"

Then Pope Kirollos the 6th commented, "You see, my son. We, by our conduct, can prevent good from us."

---

[72] Sir in French. It was Pope Kirollos the 5th to call people with that French title.

23

The Guardian Angel

The Church of the Archangel Michael, at Kafar Al Nahal in Zagazig[73], is located very close to the cemetery. It is a very poor neighborhood, and the majority of the housing adjacent to the Church is occupied by non-Christians. This Church experienced, since her establishment, all sorts of assaults such as burning, demolishing, and so forth. However, she is protected by God's providence.

In 1946, a simple monk was serving the Church .... He relied on God, and he was, within the means of his generation, serving God, visiting some of the families and officiating the "Sunday Liturgy" every week. The Church, during that time, was a small building encompassed by a brick wall. The outer gate of that wall was made of iron bars and was locked from the outside by a lock.

That monk was visiting a family at the sunset of one of the week's days. (It was one of the devout families; the head of the household was well off. And his wife was a pious woman. They had no children for quite a long time. Then God gave them, after many years, a child. He was, for them, the light of life. They were grateful to God for all that He had done)

The monk convened with the man, his wife, and their child, contemplating God's acts and the wonders of His saints. On top of the table in the family room was a small plate containing a few grains of lupine. The child, who was one year old, was crawling around the table and holding on to it so that it assisted him in standing up. In an inadvertency of the adults, he placed his hand on the plate .... Took a grain of lupine .... He put it in his mouth and

---

[73] A city in Egypt.

tried to chew it. It crumbled in his mouth ... He tried to swallow it, but it got into the trachea. Suddenly, they found him falling on the floor, coughing with a severe, continuous cough. He was almost suffocating.

The father and the mother screamed in fear. The monk stood still, perplexed. What should he do? It crossed his mind to run to the Church and bring oil of the "Unction of the sick," or "Lakkan water," so that he may rescue that poor child.

And indeed, he dashed to the Church .... The Church was several minutes away. He reached the Church, but it was locked .... No one was inside .... It seemed that the Church's oblation baker locked her and left for another destination. The monk was bewildered .... He tried to call anyone .... But no one responded. He wanted to take anything from the Church .... Minutes were passing, and the Child was in danger. When he couldn't find anything, he inserted his arm between the iron bars and grabbed a handful of dust. (The Church's dust) .... Then he hastily returned running .... He reached the house .... It became crowded. As the neighbors gathered upon hearing the screams of the child's father and mother .... Rescue methods in those poor neighborhoods and small villages at that time were very scarce. People didn't possess anything except tears.

The child was still alive .... But he was not able to breathe. He was turning blue ... He was suffocating. The monk came in running, almost out of breath. He entered where the child was while holding the dust in his fist. He removed the child's clothes, exposing his chest, and he placed the Church's dust, in the manner of the sign of the Cross, on his chest. And he cried out to the Lord, interceding by the venerable Archangel Michael. The child sneezed repeatedly. Along with the sneezes, the crumbs of the lupine grain came out. Instantly, he began to breathe normally. Those who were present were astonished as they witnessed the act of God. They discussed that miracle, exclaiming, "Even the dust of the Church is blessed, and the Lord does wonders with it."

That was not the only incident .... Repeated remarkable accounts occurred in that Church. It happened that a group of non-believers in the year 1948 attacked the Church, burned some of her pews, and of them began to demolish the Church from the inside. But the Lord of the Church was glorified that day. The person holding the ax fell from the top of the Altar's veil, and his head was spit open. He was removed from the Church with a split-opened head. The others, who were throwing balls of fire at the Church, were horrified. The Church survived by a miracle because Archangel Michael was guarding her.

The Guardian Angel

On that day, the believers recalled what had happened with a little child, the daughter of one of the deacons. Her mother had sent her to inquire about her father's whereabouts, who was, during the sunset of one of the days, with a group of deacons memorizing hymns. The mother sent her six-year-old daughter to look for him as he was late for home. When she approached the Church, she saw Angel Michael appearing as a huge man. Standing in front of the Church's gate, his legs were the same height as the Iron Gate, and his hands were wings encompassing the Church and its domes. The girl got afraid and screamed upon seeing that view. But he leaned towards her, with his fantastic stature, reassuring her, saying, "My beloved, don't be afraid. What do you want?" She replied, "I want my dad." He asked, "Who is your dad?" She answered, "My Dad is (so and so)." He told her, "Yes. He was here with the deacons, and they concluded the hymns lesson and left." She asked, "How about you? What are you doing?" He said, "I am the Church's keeper." The little girl said naively, "What is your name?" He replied, "Michael."

Thus, the venerable Archangel was not only a supporter and a guardian of that Church. According to the Fathers' ideology, he was the guardian of every Church. Therefore, they built a Church in the name of the Archangel, located at the monastery fortress, in all monasteries as proof of the power of his intercession and guardianship.

24

Hail to Mari Mina

Mr. Aziz was a simple man who loved Christ with a pure heart. He was an owner of an auto mechanic shop in Alexandria. Abouna[74] Bishoy Kamel and Abouna Mina Iskander were the only two among Alexandria's priests who owned cars for ministry. Mr. Aziz was exceedingly happy when he serviced their cars, fixing them with all loyalty and prioritizing their service before all other tasks. He didn't accept wages for his services. In vain, the fathers tried to even pay for the parts, but he adamantly refused. The Lord's blessing was with him in his life and his house.

Mr. Aziz attended, to the best of his ability, the liturgies and partaking in the mysteries. By his simplicity, he was a witness to the "Christian Life" in his work milieu and his dealings with people. He was apprenticing certain selected youth, the trade. He was requesting that the fathers introduce him to poor families. So, he mentors one of their youths, and once he has mastered the trade, He becomes beneficial to himself and his family. Truth be told, those youths found Mr. Aziz to be the best father and teacher. For he, as he was teaching them auto mechanics, was delivering, to them, how the "Christian Life" ought to be lived.

(It is not hidden from anyone that the milieu of trade workers and industry have certain conduct, a particular character, and certain foreign secular expressions. Not to mention cheating, lying, deception, insults, etc. Therefore, even the poor Copts refrained from sending their youth to the people of trade.

---

[74] Our father.

Lest they adapt to this unpleasant conduct. But Mr. Aziz and others like him were a perfect refuge for those feeble kids. And a blessing to many families.)

Mr. Aziz was one of the departed Pope Kirolos' beloveds. As soon as the pope arrives in Alexandria, Mr. Aziz takes the initiative to go to him to receive the apostolic blessing and service the old car that the Pope utilized in his transportation. That car was left behind by the departed Pope Yousab the 2nd, which Pope Kirolos didn't wish to replace despite its numerous problems and issues. When the monastery of Saint Mina acquired some equipment, such as a tractor and a truck for water transportation, Mr. Aziz frequented the monastery to receive Mari Mina's blessing and to extend a helping hand with great joy[75]. Mr. Aziz was linked, by heart, to the great martyr Saint Mina, the Wonderworker, along with his love for all the saints, whom he didn't cease mentioning their names and talking to all day while accomplishing his work. Thus, if you had encountered him at any given hour of the day, regardless of the busyness and the magnitude of work required of him, you wouldn't see him but jovially smiling and being in profound peace with God.

Therefore, Mr. Aziz's language was void of the laborers' vocabulary. Not a corrupt word proceeded out of his mouth. He and many other laborers in Alexandria addressed their subordinates and communicated with them by saying, "My son; my beloved; Please; Thank you; Do me a favor; Please help me with …." And all the rest of these words of communications that manifest the "Christian Life." And proof that regardless of the person's trade, it doesn't hinder him from living as a Christian. This refutes those who seek excuses for themselves, claiming "Sins of the trade." Meaning that any trade imposes on them a type of conduct against their will …. However, this is not true.

It was astonishing that the youth who apprenticed with Mr. Aziz and those similar to him acquired the same characteristics and language when they established their own private businesses.

Even though Christian life is obtained through education, it is far more obtained by receiving it from generation to generation, learning how to behave and please God.

The Temptation:

---

[75] Servicing the equipment.

Life is not void of temptations. Yet man is born to trouble as the sparks fly upward. As it is written in the Book of Job[76].

Temptations are common in the life of mankind. But for God's children, the temptations convert into reinforcing of faith, patience, and hope. When patience has, in their lives, its perfect work, they become perfect and lacking nothing according to the saying of the apostle[77].

Thus, the temptation began knocking on Mr. Aziz's door. His eldest son had a mental illness. He[78] almost lost his mind, for his son was in the prime of his life and about to begin college. He was a meek, devout youth who adopted Christian behavior and conduct, was pleasant in his dealings, and extremely polite.

Mr. Aziz had no refuge but God, seeking Him wholeheartedly with prayer and supplication. He had no support but the saints, seeking their help. He was praying during work, and many times, his tears ran down from his eyes without anyone noticing. During the time of the temptation, he was bitter in his soul, but he was a man of prayer and reliance on God.

A visit to the Monasteries of Saint Macarius and Saint Bishoy:

One day, I passed by Mr. Aziz to check on him and inquire about his son. He informed me that the situation was not good and was getting worse. But he said, "I have hope in Christ, and I am holding fast to His saints." And he implored me to accompany, next morning, him and his son to the Monastery of Saint Bishoy. Because he heard of Anba Bemwa, the monk, and he trusted that the Lord would heal his son through his prayer. Also, he desires to obtain the blessing of the Monastery of Saint Macarius, the three Macarai, and the forty-nine elders and martyrs of Skete. I couldn't deny him his request. He was a man of many favors, and I was overwhelmed by his love for us and the Church. So, we agreed on the time of our meeting.

We got up early in the morning and rode the Mercedes car that he owned: he, his son, myself, my wife, and Arsani, my son. And we departed Alexandria. In the car, we recited the Prime Psalms and then began talking about God's

---

[76] Job 5:7
[77] James 1:3
[78] Mr. Aziz

acts and the wonders of His saints. The ambiance of prayer and the pleasant talk made us forget about the issue of sickness and mental illness.

As we approached Kilometer 30 of the Alexandria—Cairo route, the exit route to Saint Mina's Monastery, I said, "Let us exit and go to Mari Mina the Wonderworker." The man responded, "Please don't say that. I purposed in my heart to go to the monastery of Anba[79] .Bishoy. And my son is anxious to go there and to the Monastery of Anba Macarius. I have a long history with Mari Mina and many incidents." I inquired of him, "What are those incidents?" He said, "Many Sundays, I had decided to pray at specific Churches. But as I pass by the Church of Saint Mina, a nail gets into the tire, and I am forced to stop. Other times, the wheel-rotating axle breaks in front of the gate of Mari Mina's Church. So, please don't talk as such, and let us continue our trip peacefully." We laughed and continued on our way.

We didn't go further than several kilometers, about 5 to 6 kilometers, and the man shouted, "I told you, Abouna …. Oh Lord, what shall I do now?" As soon as he uttered those words, with extreme emotion, he stopped the car. We were astonished, and we all asked, "What happened?" He replied, "Mari Mina did it again." We asked, "How so, Mr. Aziz? He responded, "The car's Oil Pressure Gauge suddenly dropped to Zero." I asked, "What does this mean?" He said, "It means that the oil circulation in the engine ceased and that the engine will overheat if we drive the car."

"What is the solution?" I asked him while in a state of affection and astonishment. He said, "The solution is that a car tows us back to Alexandria." I asked, "Is it possible to drive at low speed?" He answered me, saying, "Abouna, this is impossible." I asked him again, "Is it possible to fix it here? Do you have tools?" He answered, "I have to rebuild the engine. This is not feasible except at the shop. Besides, that sort of work requires two full days." He said that and got out of the car, seeking a truck that would agree to tow us back to Alexandria.

As I recalled Mr. Aziz's words, his affection for Mari Mina, and the similar incidents that happened with him, I said, "If that is the case, why don't we return to Saint Mina's Monastery? If he restores the situation to its original status." And I also said, "The solution is to reconcile with Mari Mina, venerate him, and seek his prayers." We began praying the veneration …. My son Arsani held a small Symbols in his hands …. When we said 'Axios' to Mari Mina, I told Mr. Aziz, "Start the car." He turned the ignition key, and behold, everything was fine. All of the car Gauges were intact, and the oil circulation within the

---

[79] It is a Syrian word, means father or teacher.

engine was perfect. I told him, "Return us to the way of Mar Mina." Indeed, we turned and headed towards Alexandria …. We traveled a distance of 3 to 4 Kilometers …. I inquired, "Is all well?" …… The man was familiar with his car, him being an expert mechanic …. He replied, "Everything is perfect."

When he became confident in the car, he said, "I don't want my boy to feel bad; let us return and go to the Monastery of Anba Bishoy. Lest his psychological state worsens." I said to him, "As you wish. Are you assured that the car is okay?" He replied, "Absolutely perfect." So, as soon as he got a chance on the road, as he located a suitable spot for a U-turn, he turned the car around, and we were back on our way as before.

Stranger than fiction:

As the front of the car headed towards Cairo, the man shouted once more, pointing at the Oil Gauge for the second time, and said, "Look, look." I looked; behold, the Gauge indicator dropped speedily until it stopped at zero. He immediately slowed down the Car's speed and stopped at the side of the road. I said to him, "Mr. Aziz, we were doing fine. Why did you return, my brother?" He responded, "What shall we do now?"

I instructed Arsani and everyone in the car to "Chant 'Axios' to Mari Mina the Wonderworker." They did. Then I said to the man, "Start the car." Everything was fine, so he turned the car towards the Monastery of Mari Mina. Things became normal, as if nothing had happened.

One of the strangest things I have experienced in my life was what happened to us on that day. Because the incident was repeated three times in the same manner, we were shockingly surprised and in disbelief. It was as if Saint Mina was controlling the oil circulation of the car. If the vehicle headed towards the Monastery's route, everything stayed normal. But if it didn't, the oil circulation would cease entirely.

(May the reader believe me? If that account had not occurred in my presence as an eyewitness, I would have considered it an exaggeration. Or is that not true? But we were four adults and a little child witnessing that strange thing.)

Finally, because we had no choice, the man surrendered to that peculiar joke by Saint Mina and his insistence for us to be blessed by his Monetary on that day. Thus, we traveled down the road and reached the Monastery in about 50 minutes. At a distance of 200 meters from the Monastery, the car got stuck in a pool of mud since the road wasn't paved. We got out of the car and pushed it with our hands, and our clothes got dirty with Saint Mina's dust, which heals all diseases.

That day, we prayed the liturgy as usual and met with Abouna Mina Ava Mina[80]. He laughed, saying, "Why don't you come obediently? Is it necessary to use force, coercing you to come?"

(Truth be told, I delayed visiting the Monastery for a long time. And I felt that the saints rejoice when their loved ones are present at their homes, just as a generous man is pleased with the arrival of his visitors. They especially support our weakness by prayer so that we fulfill our mission and achieve our repentance, which brings joy to the heavenly beings.)

We returned back at the end of the day. On the way back, we were discussing that astounding, miraculous incident. My eyes, from one moment to the next, took a peek at the Gauge's indicator, which didn't change position the entire time, from the top position—giving the impression that everything was fine. Amazingly, that car stayed in Mr. Aziz's procession for more than a year, during which I was always inquiring about its condition. Every time, the man[81] recalled what had happened, he marveled and said, "Never in my life have I seen anything like this." And he was saying also, "This was because of the lack of my faith. But when I saw and believed. I feel that the Saints are not only alive in heaven but on earth as well. And they are very close to us, acknowledge us, and support our weakness." Mr. Aziz's words, whenever he met with me, were, "Believe me, Abouna, I love Christ so much from all my heart .... Pure unparalleled love .... But I am a sinner ... Tell me what I shall do to repent and be a good person?"

One time, he informed me, "Pope Kirollos (after his departure) gave me communion in a dream. Then he gave me the blood by his hand. Afterward, he gave me the Blood a second and a third time. Why is this Abouna, and I am a sinner and unworthy?"

I always felt that this man was blessed with a pure heart. I constantly recited the Lord's saying, "Blessed are the pure in heart, for they shall see God." As such, that simple man lived close to the hearts of the saints, and they were close to his mind and his heart. He was always manifesting God's acts in His saints. When he completed his good endeavor, he went to be with the Lord in good report.

---

[80] The Abbot of the Monastery.
[81] Mr. Aziz

"One should not say it is impossible to reach a virtuous life, but that it is not easy. Those who are devout and whose intellect enjoys the love of God participate in the life of virtue."

— St. Anthony the Great

25

The Lady "Mother of Mourad[82]" A Friend of the Angels

That pious lady lived amongst us for many years, and we became very familiar with her closely, for she was, truly, a beautiful icon depicting the sweetness of the fellowship with God. She combined the simplicity of the little children and the deep, trusting faith in God. And God has bestowed her with an astounding relationship with the saints. Especially the Commander of the army of the Lord, the Angel Michael. As she, from her youth, was attached to him. And her faithful relationship with him kept enhancing, as its experience[83] grew with the passing of days and the succession of events in her life. She was highly confident that if she asked him or interceded by him, her request would have to be granted and that she would obtain what she asked for, no matter how unattainable it seemed.

A strange account of acquaintance:

We were that day praying the Divine Liturgy at our beloved Church, the Church of St. George at Sporting in Alexandria, Abouna Bishoy and I. That

---
[82] She was known by the name of her eldest son. At that time, addressing older women by maiden name was not socially acceptable or common.
[83] Of that faith relationship.

was around the year 1969. After the Liturgy, a lady approached me. Modest in her appearance. She was, as she informed me, a widow and a mother of three young men. She was living in the governorate of Beni Suef before her husband's departure. On that day, she conveyed to me her desire to build a Church in the name of the venerated Archangel Michael.

(For the sake of truth, I admit that, back then, I didn't take her words seriously. The lady who was talking to me was not wealthy, and building a Church requires lots of money—large sums of money—not to mention the various obstacles that face such a task. Hence, I was just listening to her.)

Then, she took a folded and tied piece of fabric cloth out of her purse and presented it to me, saying, "Take these fifty pounds[84] and build me a Church in the name of the Angel[85]." I told her, "Ma'am, fifty pounds are not enough to purchase the Altar's Marble (By the prices of that era), but we are currently building a Church in the name of Saint Takla Haymanot, the Ethiopian at El Ibrahimiya. He is a friend of Angel Michael, so it is possible to allocate this sum of money for building a chapel at the Church in the name of Angel Michael. This will suffice the purpose, but building a Church is impossible." My words seemed uncomfortable to the lady …. She said while retrieving her money bundle from my hand, "Give it back; do you not have faith?" I said, "Faith in what?" She responded, "Faith that our Lord can work by the few." Then she began talking about all the wonders Angel Michael had done for her until she said, "Ask heaven for something, and believe me, I will bring it to you. Do not be unbelieving. The Angel had done many wonders for me. Keep the money with you until the Church gets built. Let this money be a leaven of blessing …. And the Church will be built. I never asked for anything, and I didn't receive it." That lady marveled at me.

I met with Abouna Bishoy, and I told him about that lady. He said to me, "Keep this good thing[86] with you, and wait and see what the Lord shall do." And so, it was.

Astonishingly, a week didn't pass by, and a respectable man, over sixty years of age, came to the Church …. He and his wife. He was an English professor …. They didn't have any children … We had no prior acquaintance of the man …. He was residing in a privately owned Villa near Mustafa Pasha[87]. He requested to meet with us.

---

[84] Equivalent to fifty Dollars.
[85] Archangel Michael.
[86] The lady's gift (50 Egyptian Pounds).
[87] "Pasha" was a higher rank in the Ottoman political and military system. It was an honorary

The Lady "Mother of Mourad." A Friend of the Angels

It happened that Abouna Bishoy and I were present at the Church. When the man met with us, he informed us that he wished to cede his villa to the Patriarchate because he has no offspring and refrains from acquiring possessions on earth. Abouna Bishoy asked him, "What shall we do with a villa?" The man replied, "Convert it into a Church." Abouna responded, "Let us pray and seek God's guidance for this matter."

After several days, we visited the English professor, Mr. Mikhaeel (Michael)[88]. At his villa in the region of Mustafa Pasha. It was a small villa on a narrow street.

(The regain is isolated and without movement nor lights during night hours …. Any person would fear walking its streets …… The region is not densely populated, and the number of Christians was limited …. Is it suitable to be a Church?)

We kept praying and presented the matter before God. The departed Pope Kirollos on the 6th was present in Alexandria, so we went to him and presented the matter. The Pope said, "In the future, things will change. It will be a perfect Church. Let him sign the waiver."

The next day, Mr. Mikhaeel was signing the concession form at the Patriarchate. He stated that he was ceding ownership of the villa to the Patriarchate to become a Church in the name of Archangel Michael. In the event, the Church was not built …. He recommences ownership of the villa. That day, Abouna Bishoy told me, "Bring the fifty pounds of that lady, friend of Angel Michael." I brought the money and paid the contractor to demolish the Villa and erect a modest building for the Church of Angel Michael in the region of Mustafa Pasha. As the construction workers dug to lay the foundations, they found a piece of limestone in the shape of the oblation bread portraying lots of Crosses. Hence, we became certain, beyond any doubt, that the work, from the beginning, was a Divine work.

At that time, I was assured that the lady "Mother of Mourad" 's desire to build a Church was driven by an invisible hand. God speaks in the hearts of His chosen and moves them to do the work of His delight.

---

title similar to the British peerage or knighthood.
[88] The fact that the man's name was Mikhaeel, which is the Arabic translation for Michael, declares the will of God the Pantocrator. And the deep unblemished and powerful faith of that pious lady.

Alms in many places:

I found out later that the lady "Mother of Mourad" traveled yearly to far places at various dioceses, villages, farms, and hamlets that were unknown to anyone. She did acts of mercy for many Churches and poor people, as much as her limited resources allowed and even more beyond her ability. She traveled to some villages in Faiyum[89], Beni Suef[90], and sometimes to certain areas belonging to Aswan[91].

When she became advanced in days and couldn't bear the hardship of travel, she continued sending[92] alms to those various places. She was delighted when she found places of worship in those areas and kept encouraging them. She often asked me for altar veils or altar vessels, which she delivered to those places. She was marvelous, for God put this care and this service in her heart.

From whence comes my help:

One day, she was sitting on the balcony of her apartment.(The feast of Angel Michael on the 12th of Baouna (June 18) was drawing near. During that time, her resources were very scarce. As her husband departed, leaving behind three children, she had no income except a modest pension[93].) Her heart was burning within her for almsgiving and for visiting some of the sick and needy.(But her resources are scarce, and she doesn't have the money in this world at all) She prayed, lifting her eyes towards heaven. She reproached Angel Michael, saying, "Why are you letting me reach this state where I have nothing to offer?" Immediately, the Angel appeared and consoled her with a splendid heavenly view. And before she got to move out of her seat, the mailman knocked on her door and delivered her a check from the pension bureau. Money was owed to her from previous transactions.

How much did she thank God, and her faith strengthened? After two days, she was on her way to Beni Suef, Faiyum, and all the places where she was accustomed to show acts of mercy and serve the Lord's brethren.

---

[89] A city in Middle Egypt.
[90] A city located 310 Km south of Alexandria.
[91] A city about 1,070 Km from Alexandria.
[92] By the help of other people.
[93] The pension of her late husband.

Instead of the housekeeper:

After God blessed her, her eldest son graduated from the engineering school. He hired a housekeeper to assist her, and he was paying her[94]. two pounds monthly.

However, since her resources were still limited, and she could still manage the burden of the housework by herself, she dispensed with the housekeeper. She said, "I will labor instead of the housekeeper, and I will donate her salary." And she also, at the same time, said, "My conscience bothers me because I dispensed with the housekeeper. I would have loved for her to have a source of income. But I am not concerned about the physical fatigue. The Lord helps me because I help His children."

My strength is made perfect in Weaknesses:

She suffered, one day, severe fatigue and a headache that she couldn't alleviate[95]. After several days, her children insisted that she see the doctor. And with persistence, she went, the following day, to the office of Dr. Aziz Zaki. (Professor of Internal Medicine. His office was located at Mehatet El-Ramal, Alexandria)

She waited for her turn while experiencing tremendous weariness, barely able to keep her eyes open. When it was her turn, she entered the examination room, and as soon as Dr. Aziz Zaki examined her, he was troubled. Her blood pressure was very high to the point that he feared for her life. He asked her, "Is there someone accompanying you?" She replied, "No one." He responded, "This is impossible. You won't be able to go back to your home on your own." (She was residing far from Mehatet El-Ramal. Her apartment was on Khaled Ibn El-Waleed Street, Sidi Besher)

---

[94] The housekeeper.
[95] Using over-the-counter medications.

The doctor advised her, saying, "Take this prescription, dispense it immediately, and then take a cap to your home as soon as possible. I ought to admit you to a hospital."

She thanked him, saying, "Doctor, by the Grace of God and the intercession of Angel Michael, I am fine[96]." She left the office, didn't dispense the medicine, and didn't take a cap. But she headed to the Church of the martyr St. Mark the Evangelist. Before the Icon of Archangel Michael, she stood praying[97] and crying for some time. Then she left the Church in total health as if she were never sick. She went back to her home, glorifying God.

When her son, a med school graduate, returned home, she said to him, "My son, take my blood pressure." When he did, they found it perfectly normal. She informed him about the doctor's visit. She glorified God and chanted a "Veneration" for Archangel Michael.

Archangel Rafael:

The following incident transpired in 1984 when the lady "Mother of Mourad" came to me as she was highly rejoicing. She talked about the acts of God with her and how He had done great things for her children and gave them all the desires of their hearts. The first is a successful engineer, and the second is a physician army officer. However, the most recent act of God was that her youngest son, a physician, wished to travel to Saudi Arabia to work there for some time. A year prior, he applied to one of the hospitals there. However, it didn't flourish, as he realized that the job requirements didn't suit him upon meeting with the Saudi delegation. A year passed, and that same Saudi delegation returned to conduct meetings with the physicians in Egypt. He met with them a second time and informed them of his conditions that suit him concerning the salary and otherwise. However, the delegation didn't accept the conditions. The son returned to Cairo, showing signs of distress. When she inquired, he told her the details of the meeting. They ended up rejecting him, and he didn't reach an agreement with them. Thus, he left the meeting and returned to Cairo.

---

[96] Notice that she said, "I am fine" and not "I shall be fine." This is "Faith." She

[97] Her prayer was directed to God only. And since the icon of Archangel Michael is consecrated with Myron. Therefore, it is no longer just an icon. But Archangel Michael himself present in the Church, helping and supporting God's children by praying to God on their behalf. Both the lady and Archangel Michael were praying to God.

The Lady "Mother of Mourad." A Friend of the Angels

That day was the 2nd of El-Nasea, September 7th, and the commemoration of Angel Raphael, "Rejoicer of the Hearts," falls on the following day, September 8th. At that moment, that pious lady prayed wholeheartedly and said to God's Angel Raphael, "O Rejoicer of the hearts, if you make my son's heart rejoice and put away his distress, I shall make your heart rejoice and build a Church in your name."

What is remarkable was that she stipulated of him, as such, saying, "If you let my son hear a report that delights his heart before midnight, I will then know that the Lord heard my petition through your acceptable intercession."

Astonishingly, the home phone rang several minutes before midnight; the speaker, on the other end, was the head of the Saudi delegation, informing her son of accepting all conditions and that he got the position. Later, she told me, "I shall bring you a large sum of money to build a Church in the name of Angel Raphael because he delighted my son's heart. Indeed, he is the 'Rejoicer of the Heats.'"

One of the most astounding Divine economies was that we were occupied, around that time, by searching for a lot of land suitable for building a Church in one of the vicinities. However, we didn't succeed to that day. Therefore, when we met with that virtuous mother, we anticipated good things and became assured that they came from the Lord. On that day, beloved servants surrounded us, along with Abouna Kirollos Dawood. I said to them humorously, "The previous time, the amount was 50 pounds, but this time, it will be 200 pounds."

After several days, I was surprised by her when she brought me an envelope with precisely 200 pounds. So, I preserved it for blessing, knowing that it was a little leaven that leavens the whole lump. Hence, within several weeks, we purchased land for 200,000 pounds for a Church to be built in the name of Angel Raphael, the "Rejoicer of the Hearts."

Saint Anba Macarius:

Her eldest son, the engineer Mourad, worked for Awlaad Makaar's company[98]. His work site was by "Cairo – Alexandria Desert Rd." Close to the Monastery of Saint Macarius at Natron Valley. Therefore, he would stay on-site, perhaps for a week or more, then go to Alexandria for a day or two, then return to his work site. When the time was convenient for him, he visited the monastery of Saint Macarius to seek blessing. And meeting some of the Monastic Fathers to hear a "Word of Benefit" and a "Word of Comfort." Once the rapport between them was strengthened, he extended a helping hand for repairing heavy equipment and the forklifts of the Monastery .... Because that was his specialty. Upon returning from his weekly time off, he told his mother his report with the Monastery and the Monastic Fathers. And she prayed for him to obtain benevolence and blessing. However, she was worried about him because he was working far away. She was praying that his work be in Alexandria, close to her. As she was preoccupied with that thought, entreating wholeheartedly .... Behold, Saint Macarius the Great appears and talks to her. He was, as she described him to me, an elderly man with a glorious countenance, tall and slim. She never heard about Anba Macarius before and didn't know anything about him. But astonishingly, history describes Anba Macarius by these traits exactly. When she saw and knew him, she confidently asked him, pleading to transfer her son from Desert Rd. to Alexandria. She told him, "The time he resided next to you is enough, during which he was serving your Monastery and repairing the Monastery's equipment." That same week, Mourad was transferred to the company's site in Alexandria.

As such, the life of that pious mother was a chain of wonders. The Lord's hand that supported her was vivid to all who were close to her, especially the intercession of Archangel Michael, who never disappointed her in one request all her life—until she went to the Lord in peace.

---

[98] The English translation is "Children of Macarius." A company founded and owned by Christians.

26

Overcoming Death

In the first days of our confinement in El-Marag prison in September 1981[99] The ambiance at that time was ambiguous from all directions. No one was expecting what occurred, and no one was aware of what was happening. As if darkness was closing in on all sides. But our hope in Christ was the only glimmer of light; the imprisoned fathers[100] were from all over Egypt, and many weren't acquainted with each other. Those first days passed slowly and were a heavy burden on the soul.

In the early morning daily, we were waking up to an ecclesiastical voice that brought forth great comfort. Praying parts of the Divine Liturgy …. We were listening to him praising with a spiritual melody that perished depression, which was emanating from the ambiance of the prison and the guards of the prison.

That father priest was from El Maragha, Sohag Governorate. As the days passed, his voice became like the rooster's crowing at dawn, always indicating the dissipation of darkness.

The dungeon I was in was amid the ward with three sides. And that father priest was in the dungeon at the edge of the first side. There was no chance to talk to him or see him. The ward's only bathroom was next to my dungeon. So, when it was his turn to shower, I saw him. He was greeting me, not knowing

---

[99] In September of 1981, former Egyptian president Anwar Sadat laid his defiled hands on the Church of God, arresting many of her Bishops and priests for political reasons. But since the Church is protected by God and since she doesn't get involved in secular politics or establish bonds of fellowship with the world, so our almighty God saved her. On October 6th, 1981, Sadat was assassinated in broad day light by the hand of his own people.
[100] Bishops, Hegumen, and Priests.

me personally, as I looked at him from the dungeon window, which was no bigger than a hand's fist. And because he was suffering from Asthma, he was permitted a shower every day. He, while in the shower, was praying, as well. But he was only praying the litany of peace and the litany of the fathers. When I listened closely to what he was praying, I heard him say, "The president, the armies, the counselors ... repose them all[101]." None of the officers or the guards comprehended anything ...... Some of the fathers responded, "Amen."

Only a few days passed until the Lord did His wondrous work and answered the prayer.

Afterward, we were transferred to a prison in Natron Valley, and we all got together in one Ambergris. Thus, we became closely acquainted with each other. Since we all lodged in the same dungeon for several months. As I closely became acquainted with that father priest, I found him a man with a simple heart and full of passion. He fathered, in the flesh, nine kids. He was abundantly affectionate and abundantly sensitive, and his tears were running down most of the time. Yet, on the other hand, there were pleasant times, when one can observe him smiling and laughing. His soul was simple .... His relationship with Christ was void of anxiety or complexity, as he loved the Lord from a simple heart, like the heart of a little child.

Our friendship has become very strong, and whenever we walk together for some time, talking about God's acts or contemplating God's words and faithful promises, the man cannot stop his eyes from shedding tears.

One time, he informed me, as we were speaking about the acts of God, of one of the astonishing accounts he encountered in his ministry. He was awakened on "Bright Saturday" after his vigil in the Church till the morning. Upon concluding the Divine Liturgy at seven o'clock, he went home to rest .... They woke him up with nuisance and said, "Rise. So that you pray the funeral prayers." He woke up from his deep sleep troubled and asked, "Who died?" They replied, "The kid ...." .... Who was about thirteen years of age and was not sick. But on the dawn of that day, they found him dead.

(The grief of Upper Egypt's people is harsh, and the funeral prayers are dire .... Especially if it is a sudden death or if the deceased person is a young boy.)

The father arose, trying to collect his thoughts, conquered by sleep, but the disturbing news shook him to the core ...... It was as if he was under the influence of an anesthetic. He didn't comprehend the situation .... He was functioning as if he was a machine working without logic. He washed his face,

---

[101] Instead of "Adorn them with all peace."

put on his clothes, and went to the Church. He found the people in a state of agitation, bold, and wailing. That meek priest entered the Church, weeping along with his congregation, and they placed the coffin before him.

(They had a custom in his city to open the coffin and pray upon the deceased while it remains open.)

He prayed the "Thanksgiving" prayer and then lifted his Cross, but instead of praying the "Litany of the Departed," he prayed the "Litany of the Sick." Unintentionally and without realization. As if he was still asleep. As he was praying, "You have visited them with mercies and compassions, heal them." Behold, the boy started shifting and moving inside the coffin. He said to me, "I couldn't believe my eyes …. My whole body shivered."

He froze in his place, but he continued the prayer. The boy's shifting increased …. The Priest cried out, "He is alive." The situation exploded around him …. They unwrapped the boy from the shrouds ……… HE IS ALIVE ……. The joy of life flowed and dissipated the sorrows of death …... It was the day of "Bright Saturday" …... The day on which Christ broke the sting of Death.

He was talking about that marvelous incident, which was more astonishing than imagination, as if he had nothing to do with it. But rather was an amazed spectator. The man didn't attribute anything to himself, and his soul was not considered, in his sight, worth anything. However, in actuality, he was a "Man of God." ….. He joined the chorus of the heavenly priests, departing from this fleeting world upon being released from prison by a few years. He suddenly suffered an instant heart attack. Thus, he departed the world within seconds. His praising spirit rose to the heavenly multitudes, those praising God without ceasing and without apathy.

27

The Angel of the Lord Encamps All Around Those Who Fear Him and Delivers Them

The First Account.

One of the most wonderful experiences regarding God's care and protection for His children is what they had experienced during wars. Some of them were exposed to inevitable death, but God saved them in an astounding, miraculous way. It was so, as they cried to the Lord, He saved them from all their troubles; He sent His angel at the precise time, pushing danger away from them.

During the war of the year 1973…... I met His Holiness Pope Shenouda the Third. He showed me something peculiar…. A Holy Bible …. The New Testament with a bullet piercing it and stopping in its midst. His Holiness said to me, "This Bible was in the pocket of one of our sons who went to the war; it was in his left pocket, covering his heart, and was hit by a bullet that pierced the Bible, and it stopped as you can see now. He was saved from death by a miracle."

How could the papers of the Bible stop a fired bullet? It was amazing. I answered His Holiness, "It was as if Jesus placed His hand on His son's chest, saying, 'Don't worry. My hand, which was pierced by the nail for you, is the one that will keep this danger away from you. '

Truly, it was said about the Lord, our pains He carried, and our aches He endured. I kept contemplating how that incident would be a reason for that brother to be saved, a testimony of God's love and care, and how he would love the Bible with all his heart, especially since it saved him from such death.

The Second Account.

That incident occurred in June of 1967...... to a colleague brother who served with us at the Church of the great martyr St. George in sporting, Alexandria.(He was spiritual, quiet by nature, loved God, and loved to serve His Name). When he served as a deacon, he prayed with an angelic, comforting voice......he experienced many astonishing miracles with God.

On the first day of June, unexpectedly, he was summoned, with many others, to the army. All left immediately to the Sinai desert.In a matter of hours, they found themselves in the depths of the desert.The signs of war manifested....... Nothing seemed normal……... Terror was all-round…. And without warning, Israel started the attack.

That brother hid in a small tent with a group of 15 individuals; all were in a state of fear and panic… They froze with scary stillness…. Stillness of death.They did not know each other, and their lives were about to end in sorrow and death.They stared at each other, ready to explode, yet they had no strength to talk.

Suddenly, they looked at that brother, It was evident that calmness was apparent on his features, and he seemed different, and one of them yelled at him, as if all placed their hope in him despite not knowing anything about him, and said, "Say something to us".All of them were not Christians.

The Brother answered, "I have a Bible, would you want me to read to you?"They all said, "Read!"He opened the Bible without specification, for he was not planning to read prior to that, saying, "I will read what I see."They all agreed.

And it was written, "Then, the same day at the evening, being the first day of the week, when the doors were shut where the disciples were assembled, for fear of the Jews, Jesus came and stood in the midst, and said to them, 'Peace be with you.'"When the brother read these words of grace and comfort and felt the peace of Christ within him, his eyes were overwhelmed with tears of joy. The same exact joy the disciples felt when they saw the Lord.

They noticed his affection and asked, "What are these sayings?" So, he opened his mouth and started telling them with all simplicity the news of Christ's resurrection from the dead and how He strengthened the disciples by standing in their midst and offering them His peace and eliminating their fear forever.

The hearts of all rejoiced, and they trusted that Emmanuel was standing in their midst despite not knowing Him. They didn't know how they felt this incredible peace that was not from this world. Nothing changed around them, but they felt the change within.

That situation reminded this blessed brother of St. Paul, who had been inside the struggling ship through winds, waves, and rain for 14 days. The Angel of the Lord who stood by him at night promised him safety and the safety of those who were on the ship. Therefore, St. Paul took bread, gave thanks to God, and ate. Everybody was joyful and ate food as well. God's promise was fulfilled, and all were saved—two hundred sixty-seven souls.

The Brother informed all, saying, "Trust. My brethren, God will save us all". They received that promise as if it were from God, and all believed it joyfully. God fulfilled His work; everyone was saved and not a hair was lost from anyone. That incident was a blessing for many.

The Third Account.

Another brother told me that during the war of the year 1973, he operated an anti-aircraft gun. That was a hazardous task, for the enemy targeted his attack against all who handled such weapons. Hence, the lives of numerous soldiers were lost.

That brother, a servant of Christ, always prayed without ceasing, entreating God through the intercessions of His Saints. He placed their images on the anti-aircraft gun he operated—a picture of the Resurrection, the Holy Virgin, and St. George. He felt safe and reassured.

And so, it happened that his battalion commander was a Fanatic one. Every time he entered the trench and saw the images on the anti-aircraft gun, he would utter some mocking words, sometimes implicitly and sometimes explicitly. However, that brother was meek, strong, and always looked unto His Master, who endured shame and disgrace for him and us. He was strong in faith and never feared or scared for a single moment; rather, he was strengthened by his trust in God.

As the attack increased, soldiers became in a state of panic and sorrow …… The number of victims increased, and the power of defense receded. They, from time to time, would hide in the trench with that brother. Some hid, avoiding the attack and seeking safety, while others were confident that this specific trench wouldn't be destroyed as long it had the image of the Lord, the Holy Virgin, and the great martyr St. George. Among those who hid, avoiding danger, was the Commander!

While they were hiding, the Commander asked the blessed brother, "Do you have a spell for your anti-aircraft gun?" The brother answered, with faith and joyful spirit, saying, "Thanks be to God, for He protects us through His Saints. This is not the power of man, but the power of God." The Commander was silent for a moment; then he uttered the unimaginable to anyone…………… He said: "I believe that you are right in all that you say and believe in." And from that moment, the Commander never left that trench till the war ended after six days.

All were saved in that fortified trench; no other trench spared destruction except that one.

That blessed brother glorified God, for He has manifested His wonders in His Saints.

The Fourth Account.

Another soldier, who loved the Virgin Saint Mary and was always seeking her intercessions, lived, during the early years of his life, in one of Upper Egypt's cities. His grandmother, on his mother's side, was a saintly woman who had a good testimony from all, and the Lord was working with her by signs and wonders. She raised and delivered him the "Life of Faith" and the "Trust in the Lord." Thus, he grew up in accordance with what he had received. On top of that, his heart was set upon the love of purity and the life of holiness. Therefore, he was copiously imploring the Mother Virgin to keep him in holiness, without which no one will see God[102].

---

[102] Hebrews 12:14

After graduating from High School, he studied engineering at the University of Alexandria. Upon graduation, he fulfilled the army's recruitment period, which was extended to four years due to the ongoing war.

During the war of 1973, and after "Operation Abirey-Halev[103]", which led to the besieging of the Egyptian third army; he was among a squad with whom a low-ranking officer belonged. That officer was a fanatic; he manifested intense hatred for Christians. He succeeded in turning the entire squad against that brother. Thus, he became almost an outcast among them.... But he was patient, longsuffering, interceding by the Holy Virgin to support him, and praying perpetually to God, esteeming the reproach of Christ as greater riches[104].

He woke up at midnight to find the tent and its surrounding trenches vacant from the soldiers. Where was the entire squad?! He called out with a mild voice .... No one responded .... He raised his voice until he started screaming .... No one was there!

Most definitely, they received an order to retreat from that site ... But where to? He couldn't tell which direction. He picked up some necessities that he could see in the dark, carried them on his back, and started running, hoping to catch up to them. (They deliberately didn't wake him up. That site was to be ambushed within several hours. So, it will be the end.)

He ran in a direction he didn't know where it would lead him. (In the desert, at night, all directions are identical.) He walked all night and most of the day. Finally, he encountered a different squad unit, as he was exhausted. He surrendered to the unit commander, who asked him, "Where are you from? And how did you get here?" When he informed him about all that had happened, the commander responded, "No way. Your deliverance is a miracle. The enemy had overtaken your unit, and it was eradicated."

The blessed brother said to himself, the exact words of Joseph's the Chaste to his brothers, "But as for you, you meant evil against me; but God meant it for good[105]."

---

[103] Also known as the "Gap."
[104] Hebrew 11:26
[105] Genesis 50:20

The new Barsoum:

I knew him as a young man in his early twenties, just graduated college. He was a servant at one of the Churches in Cairo.(That account occurred in the Sixties.)

A dispute arose among the ranks of servants in that Church, tearing the service apart.Those who became victims of that satanic dispute were many of the purest servants.Many of them, who were the most enthusiastic, lost their enthusiasm.For they were stumbled over whom they looked up to with great regard.However, that brother maintained his steadfastness, serenity, and marvelous peace.The storms didn't come upon his soul, nor his faith, nor upon his love for ministry, nor his zeal for the salvation of souls.He was like a dove of peace between the two opposing factions.Loved by all and respected by all.

As some of the brethren lost their enthusiasm, they began assembling, from time to time, at one of the houses.To exchange opinions and discuss aspects of disputes, offenses, and gossip. (Usually, these gatherings are not devoid of gossiping, judgments, criticism, or hurtful words.)Then, little by little, their gatherings became lacking in spirit and deficient in prayer.As they turned idle, they began occupying their time with games of entertainment, such as chess, backgammon, Etc.Many times, that brother would often surprise them with a visit. (For he was their colleague and was respected and loved by them all) And so it was, when he enters unto them, their status changes as if he were invoking the Spirit to their assemblies.Thus, the gathering turns towards good talks, valuable words, contemplation, and prayer …. As if he restored their spiritual consciousness and their first estate.

As such, he was disciplined without strictness, simple yet with depth, religious without hypocrisy, meek and humble without falsity.He had comprehended the history of the Church with spiritual awareness and depth as someone acquainted with the saints of the Church and contemporary to them, and the outcome of their lives was the greatest lesson of his life.He was an ecclesiastical man …. He loved everything concerning the Church … Her worship …. Her ritual …. Her prayers …. Her feasts …. Her structure, and its significance …. Oh, how much he loved the Church? ….. It is a marvelous thing.

Then, in the mid-sixties, he joined the army according to the mandatory draft.It was a new medium unfamiliar to him and a completely different life. He had spent his previous life in a religious house full of holiness and spiritual peace, fasting and praying.As well as worshipping, praying, vigil, and praising at the Church. But now, he was in the midst of an extraordinary milieu. However, by the grace of God, he became light amid darkness and became salt for the earth. He preserved his spirituality …. Perpetual prayers …. A heart elevated towards heaven, a chaste heart, a chaste mind, and an undefiled tongue that doesn't utter one idle word. He was the epitome of "Living by Christ." Thus, the Lord spread His mercy upon him and granted him favor in the sight of all who encountered him. These are God's promises.

Then, as the days passed, while stationed as a soldier in his unit, his superiors got to know him closely …. They trusted that he was a "Man of God." Therefore, if any of them quarreled, they would resort to him for reconciliation. And if their testimony differed before the unit commander, he requested his testimony, saying before everyone, "Brother so and so doesn't lie." Consequently, his presence in their midst glorified God.

I won't forget that on the Glorious Feast of Resurrection, I received a greeting card. And when I opened it …. I read words about the Resurrection written pleasantly and with Christian-greeting expressions. When I was done reading, I realized the signature belonged to a non-Christian person. That person was recruited by the army and served along with that blessed brother. When I met with him, and he introduced himself, I observed how that blessed brother has a spiritual impact on all who deal with him. Everyone who dealt with him was affected by him.

After the war of 1967, our army soldiers were camped by the shore of the Suez Canal on the Western side, while the Israeli soldiers were camped on the other side.

That blessed brother's squad was among the squads stationed on the borders of the canal. During that time, the soldiers stayed in trenches …. (The weather in summer is very hot, and the sun is burning.) One of his fellow soldiers was sharing with him the trench. While they both were inside, a vast snake entered into the trench quietly, seeking shade. When the soldier saw it, he panicked with fear. But the blessed brother calmed him, saying, "Do not be afraid of this. He has lived with us in peace for a whole year. It comes seeking shade, and we give it food … Eggs, or a piece of meat. Hence, it eats and rests. Then goes on its way." That scene reoccurred before non-Christian soldiers. So, they testified that man is living with God. And indeed, he was a "Man of God." Therefore, their love for him increased, and their reverence increased for his "Living Faith."

When I heard about that from his non-Christian friends, I glorified God, who doesn't fail to have witnessed in every generation and place for Himself. I say that the Church is alive and that Saint Barsoum, the naked who lived with a beastly snake, is not a dead history but a living history that can be repeated in our generation and all generations.

28

The Chastity of Joseph

Is it possible for a young man to live pure nowadays? Is it possible to resist seduction and temptation? With the increase in freedom, the spreading of sins, and all sorts of immorality, how can holiness and purity be preserved?

These questions and lots more confront man, especially the youth, on the path of "Spiritual Striving." These questions may remain ambiguous in the mind and the heart and without satisfactory answers. The life of purity and its related commandments may seem more theoretical than practical …. Or, more often than not, a person thinks it is impossible and that it is not within the ability of the average ordinary Christian …. Indeed, most of the time, the accounts of the saints seem as if fictional. As the person fails in his practical life to fulfill the demands of holiness.

But whenever a living and contemporary epitome exists, then it will be far greater than a thousand sermons. Also, life as such answers all ambiguous and puzzling questions altogether …. In short, we say, once we encounter a living epitome, even though the door is narrow, and the way is difficult according to the words of the lord. But as long as someone has walked on it and reached the target, then the way, even though difficult, is not impossible. Rather, "I can do all things through Christ who strengthens me[106]." This is similar to the advanced degrees physicians obtain in rare branches of medicine that amaze mankind. Or the researchers of engineering, electronics, and computers... until they reach what they have achieved …. It is vicious competition and tires

---
[106] Philippians 4:14

of knowledge that surpasses imagination, and the question is, how did they accomplish all this? The answer is through hard work, vigilance, perseverance, and strenuous effort.

The way is difficult …. But it is not impossible … As long as those who preceded us were humans precisely like us … Is it logical that the scientists are not like us?

According to this measure, our hope, then, is for a better life. The accounts of saints are the best support for us, as they walked the same paths and received the prize. The example that I recall that gives me comfort, the examples are many, and the witnesses for Christ are not subjected to census or enumeration at all times and in all places, is about that youth from amongst the hundreds I encountered, who tasted chastity, loved holiness, and preserved the purity of the soul along with the flesh.

That brother was one of those who attended the Church of St. George at Sporting regularly for confession and for attending the youth meeting …. His face was bright like the face of an angel, and the Lord endowed him with a special grace. He was very handsome according to the flesh and eye-catching by his angelic features. He was, naturally, meek and gentle …. Any onlooker who encounters him would wish to be in his presence.

Due to his tender nature and pleasant manners, he was loved in his home and was adored in the schools he attended, whether by his teachers or by his brethren, the students. No one ever heard his voice boisterous like the rest of his peers. He was also brilliant in his studies and faithful to his Christ …. Thus, he was always ahead.

He graduated high school, enrolled in med school, and was the "Head of the Class" for all his years of studying. He was also faithful in his daily-prayer canon, keeping its times and walking circumspectly with an astonishing discipline. Thus, his soul was pure, and his thoughts were chaste. He didn't allow the slightest impurities to roil the purity of his soul and heart. Therefore, he was rushing for confession with scrutiny and offering genuine repentance for matters that might not catch the attention of the average person for being a violation or a form of evil.

But as for him, he was vigilant and circumspect, and his love for Christ acquired all his passion and consumed all his emotions. Hence, he increased in holiness with a relaxed soul, free of trouble.

After finishing his studies and graduating from medical school, he was appointed an assistant professor at one of the university's branches …. He was obligated to spend most of his days and nights at a hospital according to the time schedule of his shifts.

From time to time, I would see him attending the youth meeting whenever his time permitted. As usual, he would hear the living Word of God wholeheartedly and partake in the mysteries the following day. Sometimes, he would allot time to inform me about his life status, especially since he was at the beginning of his practical life and about his dealings with people.

He was complaining to me about one of the nurses at the hospital. (A non-Christian young woman…. Beautiful …. She pays him more attention than she does with the other people. She tries to talk to him often during suitable and non-suitable times. And she talks inappropriately. As for him, his mind was clear, and his thoughts were pure. Neither concerned nor paid her any attention. However, he was cautious, alert, honest to his God, and adored holiness. I encouraged, strengthened, and advised him to pray copiously …. Especially, the "Jesus Prayer," the perpetual prayer because he is the name of Salvation …. The name of our Lord Jesus Christ with which they[107] defeated the demons and extinguished the power of fire.)

He was obedient and faithful in following the advice. Thus, he was acquainted with joy and gladness. He became assured and had inner peace without disturbance.

But as the days passed …. Her words and gestures increased …. She chased him everywhere. That was disturbing him, and whenever he was deliberately neglecting her, Satan pushed her further. IT BECAME A WAR.

One day, he came to me burdened and asked what he should do. I told him, "We have no weapon except the weapon of prayer and fasting …. This strengthens us and supports us by the Grace. At the same time, the words of the Lord, 'This kind can come out by nothing but prayer and fasting[108]." Heavens and earth will pass away, but His words will by no means pass away[109]. I asked him, "Do you fast Wednesdays and Fridays?" He replied, "Yes." I said, "Let us[110] fast a third day." So, he began fasting on Wednesday, Thursday, and Friday of every week, abstaining from food for some time and continuing steadfastly in fervent prayers.

---

[107] All the Saints of the Old and the New Testament.
[108] Mark 9:29
[109] Luke 21:33
[110] "Let us." Meaning that Abouna will join him in fasting. He will not let him fight alone. This is the depiction of the true religion.

Several weeks passed …. He was working overnight, and so was that nurse. After midnight, as the workload eased, he entered his private room, prayed some of the night Psalms, and fell on his bed. He hoped to get some sleep before getting called to see a patient or an emergency. He fell into a calm sleep, hedged by the Angel of peace. Suddenly, he was awakened by screams. So, he got up disturbed, jumped out of bed, and ran towards the sound. He heard a woman screaming from one of the rooms; he rushed into the room to find that nurse, alone by herself, fully undressed.

(Satan had set his snare to catch him; he occupied her heart and inflamed her thoughts with evil. She pursued him with every possible method but didn't succeed. She tried luring him for several months by all methods of temptation, but he didn't pay her any attention. When someone defeats Satan, he goes berserk. And Satan was defeated by him, so he planned this dirty trick. But the power of fasting and prayer, the grace of vigilance, and the love of Christ …. "How then can I do this great wickedness and sin against God[111]?. Sin is not attractive; it is hated.)

He crossed himself with the sign of the life-giving Cross; he received great power and pushed her with his hand. She had closed the door and blocked it, preventing him from leaving, but his push was not strong. But he doesn't know how she fell to the ground. There was an unseen force …… something extraordinary … something supernatural …. He opened the door and went out hastily, glorifying God, the almighty God …. And glorifying the Cross which is foolishness to those who are perishing, but to us who are being saved is the power of God[112].

He left the hospital and came to me before dawn; I was surprised by his knocking on my door …. He couldn't wait until the morning …. He was troubled and sorry that he came to me at such an early time. I rejoiced when he told me what happened and how I glorified God, the wonderful and the capable of all things. We prayed the Matins' Psalms together with joy and with sweet victory. The taste of victory and triumph is inexpressible. As much as falling into sin is bitter, it is as much the joy of triumphing over sin. It is a joy that satiates the soul because the person acknowledges and feels the arm of Christ. I prayed for him wholeheartedly and said, "The angel of the Lord

---

[111] Genesis 39:9
[112] I Corinthians 1:18

encamps all around those who fear Him and delivers them[113]." "Oh, taste and see that the Lord is good; blessed is the man who trusts in Him![114].

---

[113] Psalm 34:7
[114] Psalm 34:8

29

The Lord Answers You in the Day of Trouble

He was a good-hearted Christian youth. He was raised by a religious family who lived in one of the cities belonging to the Governorate of Elmenia, Egypt. He was the epitome of obedience and pleasant manners. His high grades granted him acceptance into the College of Medicine in Cairo during the early fifties of the past Century.

Despite the family's poverty and the lack of resources, they were adamant about letting their son travel to Cairo and pursue his college education.

Accompanied by his older sister, who was unmarried, they rented a small room in a city known as El-Giza. He attended all his classes regularly.

While depriving themselves, the family sent 3 Egyptian Pounds monthly to cover rent, provisions, and college tuition. That was a significant burden for them, yet they continued thanking God and looking unto their son's future. (This was the situation of most Coptic families regarding their children's education.)

The youth was firmly attached to the Church in El-Giza, for, in her, he found what the Psalm says, "The sparrow has found for himself a home, and the turtledove for herself a nest, where she may lay her young....... Your altars, O Lord....... Blessed are all who dwell in Your House."Hence, he attended all the liturgies, all the youth meetings, and all the servants' meetings.And in the departed Hegumen Saleeb Soreial, he found a faithful, compassionate father. So, he held on to him, seeking his consultation in every small and large aspect and not taking one step without his fatherly advice.Months passed; the youth adjusted to his new life in college, Church, and the new home with his sister. He gave himself to many prayers and much thanksgiving.

The allowance continued to be sent monthly by his family from Upper Egypt. At the beginning of one of the months, it was delayed. The youth waited two days…one week…to no avail. The food supply was shrinking, almost gone. There was no solution…for he had no relatives in Cairo…… too ashamed to ask anything from anyone, for he was timid.

He and his sister reduced their consumption of the little food left in the house; however, they continued praying with persistence.

All the food was gone; they did not have a single loaf of bread. That situation aggravated the sister. One morning, before the youth left for college, she told him, "Take heed, do not come back home without finding a solution; otherwise, we will die of hunger."

He lifted his eyes toward heaven while walking to the university, for his home was close by, crying profusely, saying, "You give food to the young ravens that cry to You…. You open Your hand and satisfy the desire of every living thing." He then prayed Psalm, "The Lord answers you in the day of trouble," finding great comfort in its words.

The youth was perplexed; what shall he do? With a broken heart, he entreated God's advice. Shall he go to school and ask one of his colleagues for help or borrow money? Shall he send a telex[115] To his family? But where was the money to pay for the telex service? Finally, it came to his mind to go to Abouna Saleeb and ask him….it was very embarrassing, but what was the other option?

He reached, while contemplating on all those thoughts, to El-Giza Square. He stood in the middle of the square as if facing a crossroads. Where was he heading? He looked up toward heaven again with eyes full of tears, saying, "How long, O Lord?" When he lowered his eyes, a flying paper, driven by the wind, for it was winter, flew and reached his leg and stuck to it. He reached down to remove it…. Behold, what an astonishing surprise for the mind. No, it surpassed all logic. It was not a paper but a paper currency. It was one Egyptian Pound.

Not believing his eyes, he was shocked for some time. Maybe that pound has slipped out of someone's hand? Hence, he held it and raised it above his head, hoping that the person who might have lost it would come and claim it. No one came; he stood there for several minutes. No one came….no one

---

[115] A method of communication during that era.

inquired. He feared continuing to stand as such, for people might consider him foolish. God had immediately answered him in a miraculous way.

Thanks be to God. With tremendous reverence, the youth's heart kept offering gratitude. Unable to control his tears, the words in his mouth were muted. (For the heart was overabundant with inexpressible thanksgiving.) He continued his walk……. where to? To the Church, "I have to pay the tithes," that was what he thought of. He went to a deli, purchased some necessities, and headed towards the Church to place ten piasters in the donation box.

When he was entering the Church, he encountered Abouna Saleeb. Seeing him in that condition, Abouna hugged him and asked, "What is it, my son?" The Youth told him everything until he said, "I am here to pay the tithes." To which Abouna responded, "What tithes my son, keep this little for yourself till the Lord brings relief." The Youth insisted, saying, "Abouna, let my conscience rest and allow me." Abouna was surprised by that profound faith. He allowed him to do what he willed.

He headed home, glorifying God.… He informed his sister about the Lord's extraordinary act …. Since that day, the youth has never been destitute for anything, for the hand of the Lord is with him.

He graduated from the College of Medicine, becoming a Medical Doctor. As he was, he continued to give liberally and have compassion for the poor. The Lord blessed that brother abundantly and performed numerous miracles for him throughout his entire life's journey.

30

Mikhaeel[116] the Simple

Among those waiting for confession, I would see him from time to time, sitting silent. He was indeed a man of prayer. He was delaying himself, deliberately, until the last of the confessors, which required him to be in the Church for two or three hours before he came in for his confession. The man was simple in appearance; any onlooker would pity him and wish to give him alms, for he was a construction worker.

From his repeated confessions, I found him a simple soul yet enlightened. According to his outward appearance, he labored from morning till evening carrying a kuphar[117] filled with sand and gravel. Or carry a large metal container filled with concrete during all work hours.

(It is a known fact that the construction milieu is harsh. The workers' morals, expressions, and dealings with them are very tough. Not to mention their altercations, which are not devoid of violence, wrath, shouts, and even fistfights; sometimes, with the construction tools, it may not be possible for someone to live and maintain his peace and his spirituality.)

As for that man Mikhaeel, he was able, by the Grace of God, not only to survive in such a milieu. But also grew in Grace and spiritual stature, for he practiced the life of perpetual prayer within that strange environment. He was, despite the modesty of his appearance, deep in his relationship with God and his love for Christ. He knew the Agpya by heart, for he had memorized it at the village's Kuttab[118] in Upper Egypt. He was happy and joyful, keeping

---

[116] The Arabic translation for "Michael."
[117] A basket woven from reeds and leaves.
[118] A type of elementary school. Primarily used for teaching children in reading, writing,

his secret prayers and solitude with God. He wasn't concerned about people's perception of him. Rather, he was peaceful to all people and serving all with such an astounding humility. Prayer imbued his life with a wondrous hue.

He came to me one day as the thoughts of leaving the world behind pressed upon him. His presence among people had become a burden that he could no longer bear, and he felt that the time consumed in daily work was a waste and useless.

(Why doesn't he spend all his time in prayer without anything disturbing his peace? He desires nothing from the world, seeks nothing, and hopes for nothing, so why is he in the world?) All those thoughts pursued him for a long time, but at that time, they persisted and didn't depart his mind. I always emphasized to him that exodus from the world requires full intention, an undivided heart, and a vivid target. Also, he ought to test his own self and count the cost. I advised him with such advice which was given by the fathers[119], as they defined the milestones of the pathway for those wishing to walk it. He was submissive in serenity and obedient without argument or discussion.

But that time, he was pleading with tears. The world had become, to him, a heavy burden he was no longer able to handle. Once I sensed his genuine intent, I wrote him a recommendation letter to give to our father, Mina Ava Mina, the abbot of St. Mina's Wonderworker monastery. I explained his circumstances and clarified his desire to live in the monastery.

The man's intention was devoid of any desire for a status, a name, or a specific outward appearance. He didn't want to wear monk's apparel or receive a new name[120]. Or...... etc. He wanted to be just a servant at the monastery and nothing more. Thus, our father Mina accepted him and, according to his wish, granted him a small room by the monastery gate.

How overwhelming was the man's happiness? He got what he wished for. How much was his joy by the prayers and praises at the dawn of every day? How much was his consolation by the daily Liturgies? Indeed, this is Paradise on earth.

One night, after Vespers' conclusion, he returned to his modest room, lit a candle, and prayed the Psalms of the "Midnight Prayer" until late in the night .... He was overcome by sleep while he was still holding the candle. He kneeled on his small cotton mattress. And as he was entirely overcome by sleepiness, he

---

Grammar, memorizing, and reciting.
[119] "The Paradise of the Monks."
[120] Once a person becomes a monk, he receives a new name on the day of his ordination.

laid down on the cotton mattress …. The lit candle fell out of his hand, and the fire reached the mattress. (One can imagine how fire consumes cotton in seconds and with frightening speed.) That was happening, yet he didn't sense the danger ….He was asleep.

The odor of the fire and smoke spread was smelt by some people from afar, so they rushed to the room. And what a surprise …. The place was filled with smoke. They called out the name of Brother Mikhaeel with a loud voice, and he woke up. Later, when they brought a flashlight and entered the room, they discovered that the fire was extinguished on its own… The entire mattress was burned except the part which he was lying on. The fire did not touch it, as if it were defined by boundaries that the fire couldn't cross …. His clothes weren't burned, and the smell of fire didn't even emanate from them. Not a hair of his was burned …. What a marvelous thing. Everyone was astonished by that miracle as if he were one of the men in the burning fiery furnace and the fire didn't harm him. Thus, they thanked God.

He blamed himself. How did his negligence and sleepiness cause all that damage? Some feared his negligence might cause them trouble or harm, so they sent him back to Alexandria. He came to me sad, but I comforted and enrolled him in the Church of Archangel Michael service as an intendant.

After several years, the Lord reposed him from the labors of this fleeting world, and he joined the ranks of the righteous of whom the world was not worthy.

31

The Cross Is the Power of God

One of the touching scenes that arouses pity within the soul is the scene of those tormented by unclean spirits. Truly, how precise and astonishing is what was written about he who was crying out, cutting himself with stones, and those who had their dwellings among the tombs. Or that who Satan threw him down and was foaming at the mouth …. This is the "Tormented Humanity" under the weight of the One who was a murderer of people from the beginning.

Since man, during vintage times, was primitive in his thinking and primitive in his life economy, he was confined within the boundaries of the flesh[121]..So, Satan, in order to control man, would then take possession of his body and dwell in it. Destroying it and leading him to destruction. However, in civilized societies, as man's understanding enhanced and his mind became innovative, satanic wars have become focused on the "Thought." If Satan succeeds in captivating the mind of man, he then has taken control of his entire being. Therefore, it is rare to encounter, within the civilized milieus, a person possessed with an unclean spirit, dwelling in him and acting within him. Rather, you will observe him controlling man's mind. Thus, he leads the whole person to all sorts of evil without the violent control of the body.

In the late sixties, I was with some of the servants in the Church on the first floor during a day designated for a specific category of servants. At approximately six o'clock in the evening, four men entered the Church. At first glance, it was apparent that they were not from the Church's neighborhood.

---

[121] Survival was man's primary concern.

And they were non-Christians. Upon their inquiry, one of the servants led them inside the Church. They were accompanying an exhausted elderly man, about seventy years old. He was manifesting extreme fatigue and was about to fall unconscious. I hastily approached them, inquired about their request, and asked if there was any help I could give them. They said that they were not Christians, and they heard about the great martyr St. George. And that the old man was possessed with an unclean spirit that had been torturing him for years. But in these last days, he began killing him by preventing him from food and water.

(I have never seen anything as such in my life …. I have never seen a man possessed with an unclean spirit.)

I asked them, "How can this be?" They replied, "He speaks with strange voices and a foreign language that we can't understand." I asked them, "Why doesn't he eat since he is that weak?"

They said, "He had not eaten anything in three days." I inquired, "Why?" They explained, "When we bring him food, the demon grinds his teeth, and his stomach swells. No one can help him open his mouth or feed him anything, and here he is, as you can tell, in misery and anguish."

I looked at the man …. His appearance arouses pity and sorrow in the soul. (O Lord, is it to that extent that man becomes a prey to this cruel enemy …… Is it to this extent that he destroys your creation and humiliates the work of Your hands …. The one who has been a murderer of people since the beginning!)

However, I listened to the words of those people with caution and fear, and I wondered within, saying, "What shall I do, Lord? For I am small and with minimal experience in such matters. I requested from one of the servants standing around me listening to the conversation, "Go and buy some sandwiches from the shop next to the Church." The servant went quickly, and within minutes, he returned with the food. I offered a sandwich to that man, saying, "Take this, and eat it." I was astonished by the sight that I witnessed…. The man's teeth chattered fearfully for a moment with a loud, strong sound. And his stomach swelled, as an inflating of a balloon …. What a terrifying thing …. The servants were stunned, overtaken by astonishment and fear. I was holding a small Cross in my hand …. So I, with a spontaneous movement due to my panicking from the sudden sight, placed the Cross on the man's stomach quickly, and without thinking …. And Behold, The man's stomach returned to its normal state, and he opened his eyes and mouth. I presented him with the food again, and the helpless man pleaded, "Keep whatever you placed on top of his stomach – he doesn't know the Cross – and do not remove it, please." The man devoured the food like a madman, as he almost died of hunger. When he was done eating, I showed him the Cross and informed him about our dogma of the Cross. "The Cross is foolishness to those who are perishing, but to us who are being saved is the power of God[122]". I handed him a small Cross, saying, "Wear this around your neck and on your chest. Hold on to it, so Satan will not be able to harm you."

One of the servants was reciting the name of Salvation of our Lord Jesus Christ, saying, "O Lord Jesus .... O Lord Jesus ......O Lord Jesus ...." Then the man spoke with a hoarse voice different than his normal voice and said, "O Jesus." I rebuked him, asking, "Be quiet. Do you know Jesus?" He answered and said, "How can I not know Him? I know Jesus Christ very well."

Truly indeed, what is written, "And He, was rebuking them, did not allow them to speak, for they knew that He was the Christ[123]". They knew He was the Holy One of God, and He defeated them on the Cross when He made a public spectacle of them.[124]

A Second Account:

Once again, a taxi stopped at the Church's gate. We had just concluded the Divine Liturgy and were greeting the people at the church's door. Three men got out of the taxi, looking very exhausted and suffering from bleeding wounds. (They opened the taxi doors and got out hastily as if fleeing from a great danger.)

Their actions terrified the people, as they were gathered around the taxi, wondering what it[125] might be. I approached the taxi, as well, and I found a lady in a strange state of agitation. They said a demon possessed her. She had hurt, by her nails and teeth, the three men. Until she caused them severe injuries, as they were unable, with all their strength, to subdue her. The taxi driver was the most terrified person, for he wasn't aware of her condition until after she got into the cap.

As I approached the taxi, the oblation baker came quickly after me. He feared, upon witnessing the commotion, that harm might befall me. He tried

---

[122] I Corinthians 1:18
[123] Luke 4:41
[124] Colossians 2:15
[125] The ongoing current situation at that moment.

to prevent me from approaching. I said to him, "Mr. Pishaay, Satan fears the Cross." I extended my hand with the holy Cross toward that poor lady, as she was behaving exactly like a rabid dog. As soon as she saw the Cross, she lowered her gaze downwards and manifested remarkable calmness in a moment, in the twinkling of an eye.

I extended my hand …. Held her, got her out of the taxi, and brought her into the Church. She knelt on the ground and began crawling on her knees …. Those accompanying her became astonished. I told them, "The Cross is frightening to the devils." I explained to them the parable mentioned in the book "The Paradise of the Monks" about the dog that was accustomed to snatching meat from the butcher. So, the butcher grabbed a wooden stick and beat the dog severely with it, almost killing him. Then, after a day, the dog returned, approaching the shop. So, the butcher grabbed the wooden stick, and as soon as the dog saw it, he ran away howling. The dog remembered the beating it received from the wooden stick, and whenever he saw the butcher reaching out to grab the wooden stick, he ran in panic and fear. They asked, "What does this mean?" I answered them, "Satan has not and will not forget that day Christ crushed him by the Cross, humiliated and insulted him, stripped his power, and defeated death by death. He was risen, destroying the sting of death. Since that day, Satan fears the cross, fears the name of the Cross, and fears the sign of the Cross."

A Third Account:

One of the solitary Fathers told me that they brought a person with an unclean spirit to the Monastery, and the spirit was tormenting and destroying him. Those who brought him to the Monastery's Church waited until it was time for Vespers so the fathers would be present. In fact, they brought him to one of the Fathers after the conclusion of Vesper's prayer. They said, "He had not drunk water for two days."

So, they got a jug of water, and when the father blessed the jug with the sign of the life-giving Cross and handed it to the man, he didn't see the father blessing the jug; he took the jug and threw it to the ground. Thus breaking it. He did not drink at all. The father requested, saying, "Bring another jug of water." The father got the jug and, in concealment, blessed it with the sign of the Cross. The man did as before. The father said, "Bring another jug." Which he didn't bless. But when he handed it to the man, he drank.

The father became certain that it was Satan who feared the sign of the Cross. Thus, the father asked him with authority, "How did you dare to enter and dwell in this man, and him being a Christian? Do you have authority over him?" The unclean spirit answered, "Because he doesn't receive Communion." The father asked, "Since when?" The spirit answered him, saying, "More than forty days." The father asked the spirit again, "Does this mean that you are familiar with the canons of the Church?" The spirit replied, "Yes." The father said, "How about the non-Christians?" He replied, "Oh, as for these, I enter them as soon as they are born."

To this extent, Satan knows the points of weakness within us and understands the power of fortifying ourselves by the Divine Mysteries .... And he is terrified by the sign of the Cross, which is the pride of the Christians.

A Fourth Account:

Our father, Bishoy Kamel, told me that at the beginning of his ministry at the Church of St. George of Sporting[126], during that time, he wasn't acquainted with his congregation, and his name was not widely known. The Church was a small red clay brick building roofed with inexpensive material (Asbestos.) At the entrance, there was an icon of the great martyr St. George with an oil lantern[127] Hanging in front of it, a man and a woman who appeared wealthy came to the Church. They entered the Church very shyly and politely. They inquired, "Is there a person here named Father Bishoy?"

Our father, Bishoy, met with them, welcomed them, and informed them he was the one they sought. Then, he inquired about the reason for their visit to the Church. It turned out that they were one of the affluent families in the neighborhood and that their residence was not far from the Church. They were not Christians, and that an unclean spirit had attacked their young son some time ago. They were baffled by his condition; thus, they didn't neglect any method or remedy in hopes of their son's healing. They even went to fortune-tellers and summoned some Sheikhs[128]. However, the young man's condition was deteriorating day by day. They were in a state of great sorrow

---

[126] Sporting is a compact district known for its Corniche seafront promenade.
[127] A source of light. An oil lamp with multiple cotton wicks
[128] Sheikh: Is an authorized person to officiate prayers at the mosque. Muslims believe that the Sheikh is able to cast out demons.

and heartbroken. They heard the devil inside him say, "I won't leave unless Abouna Bishoy brings an oiled cotton from St. George's lantern."

They asked Abouna, "What is a lantern, and who St. George is?" So, Abouna told them about the wonders of St. George. Then they asked him, "What about the spear he is holding? He explained to them that it is a symbol of the Cross, which is the power of God. By this power, we overcome Satan.

They, tearfully, pleaded with Abouna to accompany them …. Abouna got a piece of cotton, immersed it in the oil of St. George's lantern, then he went and singed, with it, the young man's forehead with a sign of the life-giving Cross. He was instantly healed, and everyone glorified God for his wonders through His saints.

32

Poor, Yet Rich in Faith

My faith was increased and strengthened in the words of the Apostle James, "Has God not chosen the poor of this world to be rich in faith and heirs of the kingdom[129],"after the Grace permitted me to see and come in contact with many of these blessed people …… I loved, about them, the pure faith manifested without affectation or hypocrisy …. And that the lack of money was not of an issue, and didn't harm their souls which mimicked their Savior who was born in a manger, and had nowhere to lay His head.

A poor widow in her mid-sixties used to come to Church every Monday to attend the Divine Liturgy …. (Abouna Bishoy bestowed the "Poor" with special care. Thus, he allocated Monday to minister to them. After the Liturgy, he divided them into classes similar to Sunday school classes. And he appointed some female servants to help them, chant praises with them, teach them hymns, and read, with them, the Holy Bible.) That poor widow was coming regularly to Church to partake in the Divine Sacrament, as her life in Christ was as calm and peaceful as the breeze. Every Monday, she received a blessing from the Church …. A small sum of money, 25 piasters. In addition to what was available at the Church, in terms of produce, fruits, oil, butter, or other items according to what the Lord had given. All those items were distributed amongst them.

Abouna Bishoy approached me one day, as he was deeply affected and moved, saying, "Do you know the mother of 'So and so,' the poor widow?" I

---

[129] James 2:5

said, "Of course, I know her." He said, "Well, I was visiting some homes at Al Hadrah[130], and some people led me to a very poor tin shack that housed an elderly disabled man. It was a heartbreaking sight. I asked everyone to step outside the shack, offered him money, and suggested assigning someone to bring him whatever he needed every week. Would you believe it? The man said, 'No, Abouna. I thank God. The Lord sends me the lady mother of 'So and So,' she gives me 15 piasters and plenty of food every week." Abouna Bishoy continued, "I couldn't believe what I was hearing. How can this poor widow give more than half of what she receives for the Church? This widow has no income; she receives alms from the Church, yet she is capable of doing 'Good.'"

Doing 'Good' cannot be bounded by limits. "Has God not chosen the poor of this world to be rich in faith?" Truly, she was wealthier than the rich.

A Second Account:

One morning …… Abouna Bishoy met me with his bright smile and said, "Yesterday, at our home, there was a sight you would have loved to witness." I asked, "What is it?" He replied, "Do you know Shamas?[131]" I said, "I know her. She is this poor woman who sells produce at the Zananiri market[132]." He said, "Her apartment building collapsed. All the tenants became homeless and were taken to the mosque on Zananiri Street for shelter. All of that occurred the night before last. She, along with her children, spent the night there. The Imam[133] Of the mosque said to her, 'You are Christian. Are you willing to sleep here tonight?' She replied, 'I am the daughter of Abouna Bishoy. He taught us to love all people. We are all brothers and sisters.' (The man thanked her, thanked Abouna Bishoy, and said, 'It is indeed so. We all ought to live by such love and peace.') The following night –yesterday evening – she came to us after the market closed and informed us of what had transpired with her. And that all her possessions got buried under piles of debris. However, she said, 'All these things are fleeting, and I thank God for His gift.' Angaeel (Abouna Bishoy's wife) insisted that she spend the night in our home, and she offered her provisions. She ate and thanked God. Then, it was time for sleep. Angaeel asked her to climb into bed to sleep …. But she ultimately refused …. (How

---

[130] A poor neighborhood that lacks water, sewer, and electricity.
[131] The person's name. "Shamas" means "Sun."
[132] It is a market located at Sidi Gaber, Alexandria. It is a market for the sale of fruits and vegetables, fresh seafood, and meats.
[133] The person who leads prayers in a mosque.

dare she get the bed dirty?Her garments are filthy, and her feet are also from walking barefoot on the muddy streets of the market.How could this be?No, this will never happen) ... At that moment, a quarrel and altercation began .... She was adamant not to climb into bed, while Angaeel was dragging her towards it."I asked, "What was the final result?"He replied, "Both of them slept on the floor all night.Angaeel tried to give her certain necessities in the morning, but the woman was astoundingly content."

She was destitute ... No home, no possessions, and she even lost the basic necessary things.However, she didn't lose her contentment and her satiety in Christ ... She was satisfied, and her satisfaction was from God.At that moment, I remembered the complaining rich people who were unthankful.And realized how greed has corrupted the lives of numerous souls.I recalled the words of the Holy Book, "There is one who makes himself rich, yet has nothing; and one who makes himself poor, yet has great riches."[134]

A Third Account:

Another person, poor in appearance and capabilities, was a young man born with specific disabilities. He was slow of tongue, uttering only a few words, and people can barely grasp what he wants to express. His clothes were very filthy, and his saliva dripped down from his mouth onto them. Thus, some people were disgusted by his appearance.

Although his capabilities were limited, and his countenance mimicked an old man's, that poor young man had a fervent heart for the service of the destitute. (It is incredible and unbelievable.)He loved Christ and loved the poor brethren of the Lord. Many people, upon encountering him, offered him money, which he didn't refuse to accept. Furthermore, he often approached the fathers (Priests) asking for money.

(We later learned that he was the son of a wealthy man and a produce wholesaler and didn't lack anything.Rather, we learned that that chaste young man was generous in almsgiving.He took large sums of money from his kind-hearted father to serve the poor.The father was pleased that the Lord had blessed his son, compensating for his physical deficiency.That was an increase of the Spirit and service of Christ.)

The blessed young man knew many destitute families .... He knew them by name .... If someone happened to be present in the Church to receive their

---
[134] Proverbs 13:7

needs, he would approach the priest and whisper in his ear, "This lady is in great need. Just give her a small portion ....This one can survive on her own."

I was surprised, one day while I was at St. Mar Mina's monastery, by a colossal bus fully occupied by poor people ....Women and Children exited the bus with joy and exaltation ... That young man had arranged a trip for the poor ... He raised the funds required for the bus rental and asked one of the brethren from the Church to rent the bus for him since he didn't know how ....He directed the poor women, along with their children, to convene at the Church. Then, he accompanied them to St. Mina's Monastery. None of them paid one penny .... He took care of all the expenses ....He was always saying, "They are all poor. Jesus loves them." "Jesus loves His poor children."

Those trips, arranged by that marvelous brother for the poor women and their children, were repeated dozens of times. Yet every time, he took a different group than the previous one. He, with childish simplicity, with wisdom that descends from above, and with a loving, fiery heart, carried their provisions. He walked for long distances, knocking at their doors, delivering to them crates of fruits and crates of food. He wandered the streets all day, serving Christ with those modest resources.

The sight of that brother convicts the greatest servants and priests ... And teaches a lesson, ""Not by might nor by power, but by My Spirit, Says the Lord of hosts[135]."

Bliss in Almsgiving:

Another account that I recall is about a destitute poor man. He was accustomed to praying at the Church of the Lady Virgin of Cleopatra, Alexandria. He was modest in all things ... including his conduct and appearance. He wore cheap, mended clothing .... He labored with his hands to earn his living. However, he was injured in one of his eyes and suffered heart problems. Thus, he was no longer able to perform manual labor. He had no choice but to ask people for alms.

The amazing thing was that as soon as he entered the Church for prayers, he would enter the Altar, shedding his tears and pouring out his supplications to God. He would pray the Liturgy with all his soul and mind and participate in the responses with a soft voice .... He memorized them, for he was a pious man who loved Christ.

---

[135] Zechariah 4:6

Poor, Yet Rich in Faith

Despite the magnitude of his need, he didn't accept to be given anything by anyone from the Church. The Church, to him, is a house of prayer. Barely do I give him anything after the conclusion of the Liturgy. For the man's, despite his tremendous need, faith in Christ made him in perpetual sufficiency.

I saw him, upon the conclusion of one of the Liturgies, standing perplexed, trying to find his shoes. (The Church was almost empty of worshippers. Nearly everyone had left, and he remained, trying to find his shoes.) I asked him, "Is everything alright with you?" He answered, "I can't find my shoes." I looked around … I only saw one pair of new shoes. I said to him, "Maybe this is your shoes." He said, "No." I told him, "Everyone has left. This is the only pair of shoes remaining …. Wear it, then, and go!" He responded, "I can't. My shoes are worn out and deteriorated, and this new pair does not belong to me." I insisted that he wear it, but he adamantly refused. I suggested, "Wait a bit more; perhaps someone wore your shoes unintentionally, and once he discovers it, he will return to the Church." The man continued to wait, standing, for more than half an hour. But no one returned. Afterward, he said to me, "Absolve me, Abouna. I will go." When I peaked at him, I found him barefoot …. I asked him, "Why didn't you wear the shoes?" He replied, "I couldn't." At that moment, I grabbed[136] the pair of shoes and pressured him until he was forced to wear them and left troubled. However, I comforted his conscience and assured him, saying, "I will find out who did this, and I will resolve the issue." After a few days, one of the deacons informed me that he saw Mr. (……) wearing the poor man's shoes after the communion and left hastily. I told the deacon, "Perhaps he wore it by mistake."

I went to visit Brother (….) at his home. I took him aside privately and asked him, "What transpired so that you wore the shoes of the poor man?" He responded, "Who informed you?" I replied, "I found out!"

He said, "I am perplexed concerning this man, for he was destitute … I tried, several times, to offer him something, but he adamantly refused. I offered him, after the conclusion of the Church's service, some food. But he declined and thanked me, saying, 'Thank you, my beloved, Jesus Christ cares even for the little ravens … Feeding them.' So, I kept silent, yet marveled and with all my heart wished that I could give him alms. Last Sunday, the opportunity was favorable. After partaking in communion, I found his old, worn-out pair of

---

[136] True humility and meekness, fitting for the **"Man of God."**

shoes[137]..So, I wore them quickly and left my new pair of shoes which I had only used for several days …. I left the Church joyfully because I offered the brother of Christ this simple and worthless thing."

That day, I glorified Christ and His Spirit, who is working within us. He motivates the "Giver" to give alms and works in the heart of the "Needy" to be content. Thus, the Church ought to be rich by the "Faith[138]." Of her children.

---

[137] Truly our Church is a Church of discipleship. That blessed brother practically applied what he had learnt from the Church. Few years prior, another blessed man of God, after communion, replaced Pope Kirollos' old and worn-out shoes with a new pair. Pope Kirollos refused to accept as well.

[138] "For in Christ Jesus neither circumcision nor uncircumcision avails anything, but faith working through love." Galatians 5:6

33

Drink of the Spirit

Brother (W) and sister (N), his wife, were one of the examples of religious, devout Christian families. We always felt that their household was a Church in every sense of the word. The "Spiritual Peace" was the ambiance in which that blessed family lived. All ministers of the Lord .... Bishops, Priests, and deacons were obtaining their rest there. Especially H.G. Bishop Yoannis, the departed Bishop of El-Gharbia diocese, and Abouna Bishoy Kamel. The "Word of God" was the focus of the assembled during every visit, "Praises and Hymns" filled all corners of the house: true joy and happiness beyond expressions.

They[139], from time to time, were visiting Papa Sadiq[140]. There, at his house, their souls rested in the abundance of the "Fountain of Grace" from the table of the "Word of God," as the "Grace" was bestowing her gifts upon everyone. Mr. Sadiq was considering them his own children because they, having heard the word, kept it in a noble and good heart. Thus, they were bearing the "Fruit of the Spirit." They resided on the same street as Mr. Sadiq, so they were confident that the Grace bestowed them with supernatural heavenly blessings.

They had two children, a girl and a boy, who grew up in that spiritual ambiance. Thus, they emerged amazingly calm, as the children's meekness and purity remained their permanent traits even after they grew up and graduated college.

---
[139] Brother "W", and his spouse.
[140] "The Sweet Fragrance of Christ in the Lives of Contemporary Saints." Volume 1

Due to household burdens and caring for the children, sister (N) had a maid. (A young girl residing with them, full board. She was a non-Christian, about 12 years old, and from a poor rural family.) Sister (N) and her husband bestowed her with the utmost care and treated her with inexpressible love. Rather, from their perspective, she was their eldest daughter.

As she received that extraordinary kindness, she became a family member without distinction or discrimination. She was dressed as one of the family, and whenever they sat at the dining table.... Sister (N) would prepare the table and serve her maid before serving herself. In going out and coming in, she kept her company. Once the maid grew into a young woman, she had already assimilated the family's spirit and was living this by her will[141]. Holy life.

She was fasting a lot, sharing her lady's personal fasts, along with all the fasting of the Church, including Wednesdays and Fridays. In vain, her lady tried to dissuade her. Rather, she told her, "These fasts and prayers are not for you; this is not your Dogma, nor the faith of your parents!" However, she was insisting with such an astonishing will and sincere intent, for her heart got attached to the Lord, whom she had heard so much about, rather, whom she had seen by her eyes in the life of her lady.

(There was no comparison between what she saw in the world and what she saw within the family with whom she lived under their roof ... She was living in Heaven, an atmosphere scarce to encounter in the world. Rather, it was beyond imagination that pure life filled with joy.)

One of the scenes that lingered in my mind, despite the passage of more than a quarter century, was the argument scene that transpired between that maid and her lady. On that day, the departed Bishop Yoannis was visiting them with Abouna Bishoy Kamel. And I was with them, along with some beloved brethren. Sister (N) got up to serve in the kitchen and prepare a "Welcome offering" for her beloved guests. Her maid quickly got up, preventing her from doing that, so she would serve instead. Sister (N) said, "No, you go sit and listen to the words of God, and I will prepare everything." Her maid objected, saying, "No, you sit and rest now because this is my job." Lady (N) refused. When Bishop Anba Yoannis heard them, he rose quickly and went to the kitchen. He found them in such a state. He marveled and said, "Neither you nor her .... Come, all of us, let us pray and read the Gospel, and when we finish that, you two can prepare whatever you want."

---

[141] The holy life is a perpetual one, and not subject to time. The past, the present, and the future are all one continuous unit.

It is a scene that may not be repeated … To this extent, humility and love were practical in that home.

One of the fantastic economies was that the maid's parents died, and some of her relatives came seeking her to be the wife of one of their sons. However, she adamantly refused and informed them, "I have chosen my path." They said to her, "Your parents died." She turned and looked at brother (W) and sister (N) and said, "No, they are my parents, and in their shadow[142] I live the happiest and most pleasant life. Thus, they let her be. As the Lord bestowed upon that bondservant the grace of "Sonship," her joy was fulfilled in Christ. She became one of the distinguished marks in the rows of those partaking in the Sacrament of Holy Communion because she was thirsty for the "Fountain of Life."

Truly, the Spirit is like a drink of water, "All have been made to drink into one Spirit[143]", and flows like water. This is the secret of "Living by the Spirit," it is a life that flows without artificiality, faith that drifts without hindrance, and righteousness, which is like a seed that falls on good ground; thus, it yields some thirtyfold, sixty, and a hundred. Did the Spirit not fall upon and flow from Cornelius to all those who were around him and even the soldiers who waited on him?

Then, the Grace further blessed that sister. She bonded, by the bond of Holy matrimony, to a devout Christian young man. Thus, she, in turn, established a Church, according to the example that she had seen and lived in the bosom of her beloved family.

---

[142] Beneath their wings.
[143] I Corinthians 12:13

34

A Ceremonial Reception in Heaven

Mr. Ghobrial[144], whom I had known since 1967, was an army officer with the high rank of "Colonel." He was kind-hearted ... A simple man who knew no double-dealing, deceit, or cunning ... His voice tone was loud ... He explicitly behaved spontaneously with everyone ... His life, upon his retirement, was almost totally consecrated and devoted to the "Life with God." .... Bible study, reading of spiritual books, perpetual partaking of the Mysteries, attending Vespers on a regular basis, and rendering acts of love within the scope of the family and the scope of the Church. He was beloved by Abouna Bishoy Kamel and by many Priests of the Church.

And so it happened, towards the end of the year 1971 and after Pope Shenouda was seated on the See of Saint Mark, he[145] Scheduled his first visit to Alexandria to be at the Church of Saint George in Sporting. It was a memorable day, as the Church, all her entrances, the first floor, and all the streets surrounding the Church were crowded. A plethora of people[146] Came to celebrate the Pope's first visit to Alexandria and seek his apostolic blessing.

(During that time, Abouna Tadros[147] was serving in Los Angelos. We hoped his return to resume his ministry in the Church of St. George at Sporting.

---

[144] Arabic name for the English "Gabriel."
[145] Pope Shenouda
[146] Almost 15,000 people attended.
[147] Father Tadros Yacoob Malaty.

Abouna Bishoy Kamel, may the Lord repose his soul, was intending to request that matter, in the name of the congregation, from the Pope.)

Many people requested to say a brief rhetoric, expressing love and greetings for Pope Shenouda. Colonel Ghobrial was among those who asked to speak. (His son was living in Los Angeles. Thus, Abouna Bishoy feared that the man would say and justify, before the Pope, the ministry of Abouna Tadros in Los Angeles and express the crucial need of him there because of his fruitful service. Especially since he was aware of the current events and news from his son.)

Abouna Bishoy said to me, "I am worried that Mr. Ghobrial speaks!" Therefore, since I was the presenter that day, I whispered in the Pope's ear, saying, "Those who wish to speak are many. Shall we allow just a few due to time constraints?" The Pope replied, "Do as you see fit." Thus, I approached Colonel Ghobrial and said to him, "Due to time constraints, the speech will be limited to three people. A certain person, followed by Abouna Bishoy, then the sermon by the Pope." He asked me, "Am I going to speak?" I replied to him, "No, you won't speak." He said with a loud voice, "I will ask permission from the Pope. I must speak." I responded to him harshly, "I told you not to speak, and you won't speak." The man got angry, rose from his seat, and left the Church shouting with a loud voice. The situation influenced him.

The scene caught the Pope's attention, so he asked me, "What is going on?" I told him, "The man requested to speak, but I informed him, 'Due to time constraints, we will suffice with three.' So he got angry and left the Church." The Pope responded, "That is okay. Reason with him afterward."

The speakers delivered their speeches, and Abouna Bishoy mentioned Abouna Tadros's situation during his speech. Then the Pope spoke, indicating Abouna Tadros's return, and uttered spiritual words of grace to the congregation. The people rejoiced and were blessed by the Pope, and the evening passed peacefully without disturbance except for that issue.

In the morning, I felt that I must go and meet with the man ... I actually insulted him and inappropriately spoke to him... perhaps with some sort of harshness that was not suitable for either our bond of love or his age as an elderly person. I felt great remorse for what I had done, especially when he walked out of the Church. Thus, I decided to visit him, apologize, and ask for his forgiveness.

I went to his house, knocked at the door, and when he opened the door and saw me .... Behold, I was surprised by him falling to the ground prostrating

A Ceremonial Reception in Heaven

…. Offering a Metanoia[148]., I fell to the ground, kissing his head and asking him to forgive me. He was crying and saying, "It is my fault." (How small I felt t before that wondrous heat.) He said, "Abouna, you come to me? I am the one who dared, with ego, to speak. I should not have justified myself. I am the one who raised his voice in the Church and didn't obey. I am at fault, and you are coming to me!"

That day, we spent a pleasant time in pure love. We read chapters from the Holy Bible and prayed the Psalms. I left with gained benefit, ashamed of myself, and increasingly respected the kind-hearted man who repaid my sin with goodness and blamed himself.

(Years passed, as that good man lived in the fear of God. Then, he became ill and was admitted to the hospital. He suffered kidney failure. As the Urea levels became elevated, he fell into a deep coma. I went to give him the Mysteries. It was on the first day of Jonah's fast. I went in haste because I was informed that he was in critical condition. And it was only a matter of an hour or less to his departure from this fleeting world. Three days had passed as he was utterly unconscious, unaware of anyone, and didn't open his eyes or talk. I went, as I was very emotional, to him. The man was dear to my heart. I loved him sincerely, like a father. I loved, in him, his kind heart and his willing, Christ-devoted spirit.)

I entered the room where he was lying, and his family members were surrounding his bed. Behold, the man opened his eyes and said, "Blessed is he who comes in the name of the Lord. My son, bring a chair for Abouna to sit and rest. Welcome Abouna." (My heart rejoiced as the light of God's grace shone on the man's face.) I gave him the Divine Mysteries and dismissed the angel of the sacrifice. Then I stood next to his bed, and behold, the man opened his mouth speaking with astonishing words: "What is this? A great celebration ….All of this …. No, I don't deserve …. Who? David the Prophet …. Job the righteous …. Our father Abraham, Oh, who is this who is organizing the seats? …. Is this you, Abouna Bishoy? It is not possible, Abouna; I am not worthy of all this. No …. No …. It is not possible …. It is not possible."

And it was only moments … Until that good soul went to enjoy that beautiful ceremony, which the saints prepared for his reception. YES. He saw them with his eyes, and in his humility, he cried out that he was not worthy. Indeed … The soul during the time of its departure, as the dense body already

---

[148] A Greek word that means repentance. Expressed by a prostration to the ground.

collapsed and begun to disintegrate ... Allowing the Spiritual eye to see, though it, as it is torn apart, discovers the heavenly things, and sees and hears with the spiritual inner eye and ear through the circumcision by Christ[149]. "Blessed are your eyes for they see, and your ears for they hear[150]." And "Blessed are the dead who die in the Lord."[151]

---

[149] Deuteronomy 30:6; 10:16; Jeremiah 4:4
[150] Matthew 13:16
[151] Revelation 14:13

35

"Epitome" of the Christian Family

"Behold, how good and how pleasant it is for the brethren to dwell together in unity!It is like the precious oil upon the head, running down on the beard[152]." Thus, the Holy Spirit spoke through the mouth of the Psalmist, praising Christian love. For if the brethren dwell together in spiritual love, they, then, will be like the precious oil upon the head of Christ, running down to the feet, anointing, every day, the elders and the young men—those whom the Spirit has attuned together as a stringed instrument. According to the words of the "Morning Doxology," the Church prays during Matins daily.

The Church has lived, in all her generations, this profound and genuine experience, the experience of sincere love, so she became united by the spirit of Divine love and tenderness as members of the "One Body."Because love is the backbone of the Church, as Abouna Bishoy Kamel labeled it, we encountered this blessed epitome in one of the families of our Church at Sporting.(Since the founding of the Church in the year 1959.)One of the homes of that family was adjacent to the Church, and most members of that family lived within the Church's visitation area.Hence, they were considered one of the first building blocks, especially since their numbers as one family exceeded fifty at that time. Most of the family members were related to each other, for most marriages

---

[152] Psalm 133:1

occurred between cousins. As the days passed, the Lord's blessing was abundant for them in all aspects of life. And as their numbers multiplied and increased, they preserved the bond of love. That family used to assemble once a week, at a different house every time, on Sunday. They would pray together, the men and their wives, their young lads and gals, and their children, chant praises, hymns, and Church melodies, recite the Psalms, read chapters from the Bible, and share an Agape[153]. Meal together.

The primary prevalent trait, among them, was love. In contrast to what is common amongst other families, whose social life is not devoid of gossip, jealousy, estrangement, quarreling, words of criticism and condemnation, and all the rest of these unpleasant traits. On the contrary, we were pleased by that blessed family. These repugnant traits were non-existent; in contrast, love bore delicious fruits. They became an authentic and genuine example of the Christian life.

Roots of Origin:

If we were to delve into the motives of this wonderful phenomenon, which we wish would prevail all over our ecclesiastical milieu, we would find that the roots of spiritual love had previously been established in the great-grandmothers and the grandmothers.

They were biological sisters who grew up in one of Upper Egypt's villages. The bonds of love were established between them, at the spiritual level, since their childhood. Hence, they were fed the "Living Faith" and simplicity without philosophical ideologies. For it was not yet the era of knowledge[154], But rather purity, virtue, holiness, love, and humility of little children. Once they moved to Cairo, they brought the "Leaven of Faith" and the core of the "Ecclesiastical Life," as well as fasting and prayers, with them. Then, they finally settled in Alexandria.

They instilled in their children the transcendent love of Christ and delivered, to the generations, the epitome of the Christian life. (How much the Church is in need of these mothers?)

---

[153] Love without self-benefit.
[154] Secular knowledge and science are indirectly proportional to Faith. Any attempt to reconcile faith with secular science, will render lukewarmness. "So then because you are lukewarm, and neither cold nor hot, I will vomit you out of My mouth." Revelation 3:15

"Epitome" of the Christian Family

One of the elderly sisters' house, the lady "Mother of Nouzmi[155]" was adjacent to the Church.She was indeed a pious woman ... Living by simplicity and depth of the Christian love.She possessed a broad, humble heart.She lived with her eldest son, his wife, and his children, her middle son (Unmarried at that time), a third son, and a daughter.She hosted one of their relatives, an old man, permanently.(That was not a "Breadth of space" as much as it was a "Breadth of heart and love.")She encountered trials and tribulations in the course of her life that caused her early widowhood. However, the hand of the Almighty was supporting her.Her youngest son graduated medical school and was employed, for some time, as a medical officer in army hospitals.But he was inclined, since his childhood, toward a life of solitude and worship.He was a caring person, well-spoken of by adults and kids.Not only within the scope of the family but even by outsiders.

The Lord had bestowed him with abundant blessings, as he occasionally frequented the holy monasteries to obtain times of serenity and worship. He was a close friend to some of the consecrated individuals, enjoying their fellowship and spending with them nights of prayers and times of solitude. Among them was H. G. Anba Arsanious, Bishop of El-Minya.Once, his soul was delighted with the monastic consecration and was determined to abandon the world.He went home that day in the company of one of the monks of Saint Macarius, at which he was ordained.He informed his mother about his decision and asked her to bless him and to bless his path. (How wonderful is the behavior of the righteous.)She placed her hand on her son's head, blessed him, and prayed for him that the Lord would support his way and complete his salvation while her eyes overflowed with tears.

This is "Motherhood" .... Spiritual .... Provides the Church with fruits[156]Without selfishness, and doesn't hinder nor restrict the economy of consecration ... Rather, encourages it.

As such, the holy mothers offered their sons and daughters to Christ as a sacrifice and pure offering with all the contentment of the heart. This is an example we scarcely encounter these days.

---

[155] **Nouzmi** is the name of her eldest son.
[156] Sons and daughters.

"Falling Asleep" of the Righteous:

When that pious lady peacefully completed the days of her endeavor, she fell ill for a little while; then she fell asleep in the Lord … Her face was like the face of an Angel. "Let me die the death of the righteous[157]." …. "Precious in the sight of the Lord is the death of his saints[158]"…… How truthful are these words?

The day of her departure was on a Wednesday ….We were at the house as her children, grandchildren, and loved ones gathered around her in humility, serenity, and prayer. The only brother of that righteous woman, El Mallem Labeeb[159], the cantor of the Church of Mari Mina in Fleming, Alexandria, was attending the Liturgy. As soon as he was done praying the Divine Liturgy, they brought him home and didn't inform him of the news until he entered the house. He was also a pious man, well-spoken of by all people. So when they told him …. The man groaned in the spirit and was troubled …. But as he felt the presence of the Church fathers in the house, he removed his Fez[160], bowed his head before the fathers, and said, "Pray for me, and entreat on my behalf …. I just received the Holy Communion and do not wish to be troubled …. I don't want to weep, for I just partook Christ." The man kept entreating Christ to support him and interceding the Virgin Mary and Mari Mina to be by his side, lest his faith weaken. As such, he remained, the whole time, lifting his heart in prayer … His conduct was a valuable lesson for many people who sorrow as others who have no hope[161].

---

[157] Numbers 23:10
[158] Psalm 116:15
[159] A title given to the "Cantor" of the Church. One of his responsibilities is to deliver hymns and praises to children, and youth. Therefore, "El Mallem" literally means "The Instructor."
[160] Hat.
[161] I Thessalonians 4:13

Impressive Procession:

The farewell procession for the lady "Mother of Nouzmi" was truly an impressive procession. Her middle son was a high-ranked Navy officer and a professor at the Academy. He was admired by everyone. Therefore, several units were commissioned by the Army and the Navy to conduct the funeral militarily. As such, that was a glimpse of honor to that lady whose life was simple and modest. Yet, it developed a profound, deep fellowship with God. People were astonished by that solemn procession …. I recalled the saying of the Lord, "Far be it from Me; for those who honor Me I will honor, and those who despise Me shall be lightly esteemed[162]."

El-Mallem[163] Labeeb:

As for El-Mallem Labeeb, her brother was a man of the "Pillars of the ecclesiastical life" in his generation. He was knowledgeable of the Church sciences …… Living them. He was a master in ecclesiastical hymns, which he had received from an early age. And began to deliver them faithfully to Bishops, Monks, Priests, and deacons. He was faithful to the "Ritual" without manipulation, deletion, or additions. Rather, he was always teaching, at every assembly, what was beyond the visible ritual of richness, depth, and spiritual meanings.

Those who were his contemporaries saw a unique example of the Church cantor; all the times he ministered the holies, he was a partaker of the Holy Communion …. No one had ever seen him praying the Liturgy and not receive Communion …. He was like the officiating Priest …. He never attended a Liturgy without being prepared to partake in the Eucharist …. Partaking in the Sacrifice was his life, his joy, and the desire of his heart.

---

[162] I Samuel 2:30
[163] A title given to the **"Cantor"** of the Church. One of his responsibilities is to deliver and teach hymns and praises to the children, youth, adults, and Clergy. Therefore, **"El Mallem"** literally means **"The Instructor."**

On the Deathbed:

As El-Mallem Labeeb reached a good old age, and as his health declined ...... He was transferred to the "El-keptie[164]" hospital. He was in a semi-coma. (There is a small Church inside the hospital.) On Wednesday morning, El-Mallem Labeeb asked, "What is today?" They answered him, "It is Wednesday, Mallem." He said, "Tell Abouna to bring me the Eucharist." Those around him replied, "We informed Abouna, and he will bring you the Eucharist." Then, after a few minutes, he opened his eyes and said, "Where is Abouna?" They answered, "Mallem ... He is still in the Liturgy." He said, "He will be late then." They assured him, saying, "He will bring the Eucharist after the conclusion of the Liturgy." Then he, again, asked for the second time, and they answered him with the same response. They said to him, "Be patient, Mallem."

After a short while, they heard him recite the "Before Communion" prayers and say, "Blessed is he who comes in the name of the Lord." Then he appeared as if eating and chewing...... Then, praying the thanksgiving prayer post Communion. So they woke him up saying, "Wake up, Mallem. Abouna brought you the Communion." He said, "Thank you, Abouna; I already received Communion. Thanks be to God." They thought he was delusional. But he insisted, "Believe me, Abouna, Pope Kirollos came to me. He brought the Eucharist and gave me Communion. The taste of the water is still lingering in my mouth." When he uttered those words, all present were astonished and confident that what he said was true, and they glorified the wonderful God in His saints. Shortly after, that righteous man rested in the Lord peacefully ......Upon the departure of el-Mallem Labeeb, his relatives and all the family wondered about a strange scene they witnessed every day ....Whenever they opened his bedroom window, a Dove entered and rested on his bed, his closet. From the morning till evening, daily. In vain, they tried to get it out or catch it ....Then, after forty days, it disappeared, and they did not see it again.

The Lady, "Mother of Adlee":

Their eldest sister ... was a marvels person for her fervent prayer and profound faith. She taught and delivered her children the "Life of piety," as she always told them, "Whoever prays the Psalms in the morning .... Cannot

---

[164] The Coptic.

be overcome by trials." Her Children live by that wisdom and experience it. His eldest son, CEO of a huge corporation, always told me, "My mother taught me to pray. The day that I don't pray Psalms in the morning, Satan bounces around me all day." Thus, as he received the life of purity, humility, and love from his mother, he lived by it … The Lord prospered his way. Hence, he was constantly promoted and admired by everyone. And wherever institution he went, he preached love and peace among the people. If an issue arose in a place, or disagreements and conflicts prevailed …. They sent for him, Mr. Adlee, to resolve the dispute. Once he dwells in their midst, peace prevails instead of strife. (How wonderful is the practical Christian life.)

Everyone testified and witnessed that the lady "Mother of Adlee" was never upset with any person or quarreled with anyone in her life ….She was doing "Good" with everyone and didn't neglect the service of the poor. She showered them with generosity and love—especially the peddlers whom she insisted on feeding whenever they knocked on her door.

In December 1967, during the month of Kiahk, she fell ill. Her children and grandchildren were gathering around her, praising, chanting, and praying the Psalms. I was next to her bed as they were around her singing a hymn. She said, "Children, is nowadays not the month of Kiahk? Recite one of Kiahk's praises."

As they were praising, her soul departed so that she could continue with the eternal praises, living in the delights of the righteous.

PART 3

36

The Wonder Worker

There was a profound fondness between the departed His Holiness Pope Kirollos the Sixth and the great martyr St. Mina the Wonderworker. Such profoundness couldn't be perceived by the people, for the spirits of the prophets are subject to the prophets. The depth of the communion with the saints in Christ Jesus is real and is not an illusion or exaggeration of speech. Those who were close to His Holiness realized that fondness. They marveled as they circulated, amongst themselves, those fantastic accounts in the daily life of the Patriarch as he was shepherding and caring for the flock of Christ, supported by the great martyr St. Mina the Wonderworker.

I know a pious lady who belongs to a religious family from a city called Gena (A city in Upper Egypt). They were living a true Christian life adorned by pleasant virtues and were living in the fear of God with steadfastness in faith and a life of holiness. They, as a family, were known to His Holiness Pope Kirollos and were close to him. For he realized, by his transcendental discernment, the extent of their love of Christ and their adherence to the virtuous life.

That pious lady was one of those people who persevered in attending the liturgies daily, especially during the times when His Holiness was present in Alexandria. She was eager to receive his blessings daily, along with some members of her family.

It happened one day after His Holiness concluded the liturgy prayer, blessed the congregation and distributed the "Eulogia." As he was on his way to his cell, a woman grasped onto him while crying profusely and pleading for help. She was going through a harsh trial. I was present that day, for I prayed the Holy Liturgy with His Holiness. In vain, I tried to calm her; she was emotional because of excessive crying. Her appearance and persistence reminded me of the Canaanite woman who kept asking for help for her daughter till she received, from the Lord, the healing for her.

All those who were gathered around His holiness witnessed that scene. Truth be told, that scene was frequently occurring among those who were in need, sick, and under tribulations and trials. They had the trust that their compassionate father could, by the Grace of Christ, give them comfort.

His Holiness turned toward that poor lady and told her in his fatherly, sweet manner, "Fine, my daughter, we will send you Mar Mina…. Enough…. Enough …. We will send you Mar Mina".

Standing beside me, on my other side, was that lady from Upper Egypt and her niece. Observing the persistence of the woman, His Holiness' response, and his promise to send Mar Mina to her. All of a sudden, she hollered toward the Patriarch saying, "Me too Sayedna... Me too Sayedna."

His Holiness turned toward her and asked, "What do you want?" She answered in a childish naivety, "Send me Mar Mina Sayedna…. Send me Mar Mina." He said to her, smiling, "Fine… You too, as well."

We left as soon as His Holiness went into his cell. Everyone went their way. The pious lady went to her school, for she was an elementary school teacher.…... In the afternoon, she took care of some housework and prepared dinner for her husband. When he came home after work, they ate dinner together. They didn't have children. Afterward, they were visited by some of their relatives, and as usual, they spent pleasant time in spiritual talk, prayers, and contemplation on the lives of the saints. Due to her daily routine, the lady forgot entirely what took place with His Holiness that morning, as she didn't take the matter into account or give it any attention.

After praying the midnight prayer along with her pious husband, they went to sleep around eleven PM. At two in the morning, the lady was awakened by the opening sound of the bedroom door. She was appalled by a magnificent spiritual spectacle. Mar Mina, in his traditional appearance, lifting both his arms and wearing his short tunic, enters with an astounding calmness and approaches her as a subtle, luminous spectrum. She stopped breathing in panic…. She was overwhelmed by a feeling of fear and unworthiness. She was unable to contain herself or comprehend what she was witnessing. She wanted to wake her husband up at that moment, so she tried with all her might to use her arm to wake him up but could not move it. She tried to speak to him, but she didn't have the ability to do so. She was completely frozen. After tremendous effort, she was able to pull the blanket and cover her face, and she fell asleep!

She got up in the early morning, more than an hour later than usual. Realizing that she was late for the liturgy, she hastily got ready and headed to the Church. When she arrived at St. Mark Patriarchate, His Holiness Pope Kirollos was already done praying the liturgy, dismissed the congregation, and went up to his cell. Due to her hastens and her efforts to get to the church as fast as possible despite tardiness and traffic, she forgot the vision she saw earlier that day. She inquired about His Holiness and was told that he went up to his cell. She went up to the upper floor and knocked on the door, and when it was opened, she was known to the secretaries; she asked, "Is Sayedna available?" They answered, "Yes." She asked to receive his blessings, and they permitted her to enter.

His Holiness was sitting on a chair right outside his cell. She prostrated while saying, "Peace to you, Sayedna." His Holiness shocked her by responding loudly and harshly, saying, "Don't you have any manners? Haven't you learned any etiquette?" She was exceedingly surprised.... Why such words? It was her first time hearing rebuke from His Holiness. She pleaded, "What happened, Sayedna? Why such words, Sayedna? He said to her, "We sent you the man, and you mistreated him." At that moment, the lady remembered the vision of Mar Mina.... She yelped, apologizing... "I got scared, Sayedna.... I am sorry... I was afraid and did not know what I was supposed to do.... I have sinned... absolve me and forgive me."

His Holiness resumed to smile telling her, "If you can't handle such matters, you should not ask and keep silent." She asked him to pray for her and to place his hand above her head and bless her while pleading to him, "I am afraid that Mar Mina may be upset with me, Sayedna." His Holiness laughed and said to her; "Saints don't know how to be upset my daughter."

The lady came back to me, the same day, and informed me about that beautiful account. His Holiness had sent her Mar Mina indeed, and Mar Mina got back and told him precisely what took place with her. I was greatly astonished.... Was it up to that level of friendship and familiarity between the Patriarch and Mar Mina?

I felt that we were living heavenly days on earth.... No difference.... No time.... No boundaries... Heavens were opened. People were in the time of Grace descending from heaven because of that spiritual Pope, the man of prayers and the friend of Mar Mina.

37

St. George Abolished the Trouble

One of many humorous accounts occurred almost 30 years ago when a young girl about ten years of age came to our Father, Bishoy Kamel. She sat down next to him and asked him a strange question. She asked, "If I found money in the Church and I took it, is this wrong?"

Abouna Bishoy answered her with his typical wisdom, for he is genuinely acquainted with the girl and her family, and he acknowledges her purity and her love for the Church where she was raised along with her siblings[165], Saying, "Why are you asking me this question? What happened?"

The girl recited to him an exciting story ...... Two days prior, her father came back home around noon. And after several minutes, there was an intense argument between him and her mother that escalated to screams. The girl usually panics when those hearted arguments begin, as they always end up in violence by the father and screams by the mother. Even though the girl and her siblings apprehended those situations, however, the images that adhered to their memories of humiliation – beatings – and insults had the most damaging effects on their innocent souls.

The leading cause for such disputes was "The Money." The man accused his wife of excessive expenditure and lack of wisdom in finances. Yet the wife, who was kindhearted, did not take any initiative without her husband's permission,

---

[165] Abouna Loka uses often the **"Present tense"** when mentioning the **departed** Abouna Bishoy.

except within the narrow limits of daily living and according to the need. Abouna Bishoy was aware of their problems, and he intervened to resolve them. He continued consoling that lady and extending her power through prayers for endurance and thanksgiving. He was guiding her to acquire the "Wisdom that has built her house[166]." On the contrary, in vain were Abouna's efforts with the man. For he (The man) was always busy, finding excuses for himself not to attend Church. Thus, Abouna Bishoy continued his support for the man's wife so that she could abode in faith for the sake of her children and the peace of the household. The wife obediently followed Abouna Bishoy's advice; therefore, many problems were eliminated before they started because she was careful to avoid the elements that caused them. And so it was; the family spent their days in almost perfect peace. Except for what took place two days prior!

There was a certain amount of money that the husband had kept in the house for a couple of months. When he retrieved it, it was short three pounds[167]! He counted the money twice to make sure. The man was enraged as he was calling out his wife asking her about the missing money.

During the past two months, the wife needed to purchase specific necessities. So, she used that money without her husband's knowledge. She was waiting for a proper time to inform him, but she forgot about it and never got the chance to do so.

She realized as she heard the screams of her husband that a stormy whirlwind was about to shock her life, and there was a significant problem apparent through his angry voice tone. She signed herself with the sign of the Cross and lifted her heart toward heaven, praying, "Lord have mercy." And requested wisdom from above; "How should I deal with this? It is tough.... Any words won't be feasible at this time .... St. George, help me and intercede on my behalf." She drew near her husband, saying, "Why are you upset?" He answered, "The money is missing three pounds." She responded immediately without thinking, "Yes, the three pounds. I gave them to Abouna Bishoy." – Abouna Bishoy had advised her to say so regarding any missing money – The man revolted; "What? Abouna Bishoy! You are a liar." The lady calmly said, "I will bring the three pounds now, so calm down and be quiet." She called out her little daughter, saying, "Go to the Church of St. George and get the three pounds from Abouna Bishoy." Then she said to her husband, "Don't say anything, and don't get angry."

---

[166] Proverbs 9:1
[167] 1 Egyptian pound is as 1 US Dollar.

St. George Abolished the Trouble

The little girl, with a fast pace, headed towards the Church; she must get that money to calm the storm. With childish innocence, which was troubled by screams and insults, she kept praying all the time while running to the Church. Her house was about ten minutes away from the church, which she spent praying to God interceding by St. George. And as if she were on a rescue mission, she neither turned right nor left nor slowed down. The situation can't tolerate delay. Minutes later, she was in the Church. It was noon, and no prayers, liturgies, or assemblies were going on. No one at the Church but the watchmen. Anxiously, she asked one of them, "Is Abouna Bishoy available." He answered, "He is not present now at the Church."

She was struck by fear and loss of hope. However, she entered the Church and stood in front of St. George's Icon, praying in simplicity and by faith. She looked down and saw a strange article next to her foot. It was a paper currency...... It was one pound....She picked it up off the floor.... It was rolled up ... She unrolled it quickly.... Behold, it was two pounds.... No.... Three pounds....... Amazing....Thank you so much, St. George.

She returned running while being in a state of thanksgiving and an inexpressible joy. She entered into her mother, placing the money into her hand, saying, "Here are the three pounds, Mom." The lady took the money and gave it to her husband and said, "Here.... Believe and be calm." The man didn't respond nor inquire about anything; all his concern was the money. So, the Lady was spared the wrath and the fights.

After the situation settled, the mother asked her daughter; "What did you say to Abouna Bishoy?" The girl answered, "I didn't meet Abouna Bishoy." "What happened then?" The mother inquired. The girl told her all that had transpired. The mother glorified God and said, "My beloved, this is the Church's money. But go and ask Abouna Bishoy about your actions whether they are right or wrong?"

That was why the girl asked Abouna Bishoy such a question. So, when he inquired about the significance of her question and she informed him, in detail, everything, he said to her; "My beloved, St. George knew that I wouldn't be present at the Church at that time to fix the problem. So, he immediately came and fixed it himself by placing the three pounds by his Icon. And directed you toward it.[168] As the Icon of the saint resembles him personally.[169] When we ask for the saints' intercessions, they hear us, and they help us. Because they

---

[168] This is done by the will of God and by His permission.

[169] All Icons in our Coptic Church are inaugurated with Holy Myron. Therefore, when we seek the saints' prayers, they are present in person, and they hear us. They entreat God on our behalf.

are servants of Christ whom we worship. Because of this, what you did was perfectly right and not wrong at all."

The little Girl was happy. Abouna Bishoy came to tell me the details of that charming story. We were glorifying God for all his wonderful works, for He is glorified with His saints everywhere and at all times.

38

In the Last Watch

A virtuous lady living a Christian life, along with her husband and children, was a good religious family who persevered in worship and service; approached me one day, crying and saying, "My neighbor, who is not Christian, is sick with a deadly disease. She has cancer, and it is at its final stage." I said to her, "God's mercy is infinite, and the human flesh is weak and limited. What would humans do in such circumstances as they are deprived of Christ? How could they be comforted or have hope, for they don't have a part in Christ."

The virtuous lady responded, "But she would like to meet you."
I asked, "How do you know?!"
"She requested this." The Lady answered. I asked, "Does she know me?!" She said, "Yes." I asked. "How?"
"I don't know, but she knows you by name." She answered.
"If time permits, I will visit her," I spoke.
A week passed, I was swamped, and I met that virtuous lady again. She pleaded, "Why didn't you visit her? She, the sick woman, is eagerly waiting, and her condition is deteriorating".
I responded by asking, "How can I help her? My hands are tied; how can I visit a non-Christian home? Why didn't her husband invite me to visit them?
The virtuous lady explained that the sick woman's husband was out of town most of the time because of his work. And he comes back home once every several days. He was present when his wife requested my visit. He did not object, on the contrary, he welcomed it.

I had to, because of her persistence, accompany her and visit that sick neighbor. She unlocked and opened the door; she was given a key since her neighbor was bedridden. Once we entered inside, I was shocked by an overwhelming stench. It was unbearable.

I endured the odor and stepped into the room where the sick woman was. She was in her fifties, and despite her sickness, she appeared pretty. I was informed that she had a bilateral mastectomy about a year ago, and she was treated with radiation, which burned her skin. So, that stench in the whole house was because of her unhealed, festered wounds. The odor did not subside from the home or her bed, regardless of the copious quantities of air fresheners used. Very painful thing!

I sat next to her bed ……….. greeted her…….. She kissed my hand, and her eyes teared up. I was so much affected, so I talked to her concerning God's mercy and explained that God uses sickness for one's own good, and that all saints suffered, yet they were patient. I also talked about Job briefly. She was listening without commenting, but she was fully alert and conscious.

She waited till I finished my talk, then she said to the virtuous lady and her daughter, who were present in the room, saying; "Can I talk with Abouna in private for several minutes?" They agreed immediately and left the room.

The sick woman turned her face toward me and stared deeply, then burst into tears of bitterness. I have never seen in all my life a person confined by sorrow during intense sickness as she was. My heart was broken seeing her in such agony. I could not do anything, for I did not know the reason she burst into tears like this. I tried to calm her with words of comfort, as she was crying, and barely managed to quiet her by saying, "Speak without crying so I can understand and be able to answer you." The poor lady contained herself and said, "Abouna, I am Christian." Those words fell on my soul like a thunderbolt. So, I directed my vision toward the floor of the room and said, "Pardon?"

She went on to say, "I am the sister of Dr. (……).(I know him personally). I was 16 years old when my dad permitted my marriage to a wealthy Lebanese man who was in his fifties. I was young and beautiful, but I lacked wisdom. That marriage was not successful at all due to numerous differences in many aspects. I was surrounded by some friends who encouraged me to run away. I did so and married my current Muslim husband. I did everything without thinking. That happened more than 30 years ago. She started again to cry bitterly saying; "Jesus was never absent from my sight, my heart, and my life nor His

Cross was absent from my thoughts, believe me, Abouna, not a single day of the days of my life."

I gave birth to two boys whom I secretly baptized. I taught them the Christian Faith from childhood. Now, they live abroad a virtuous Christian life. And here I am bedridden, awaiting death, as you can see, decomposing while I am still alive......... I deserve this and more.... I disowned my Faith.... I denounced my Christ.

Truth be told, in those moments, I was witnessing a unique case of repentance.... That was the last watch.... Yet our God redeems and saves from death all who were lost and perished.

The lady again asked me with a broken spirit, "After all that I have committed, is there still hope?"

I felt an astonishing shiver within, and my tongue rejoiced, uttering words of hope with such power I had never experienced before. I depicted our good Savior saving a little sheep from the lion's mouth .... About to be devoured. The time of visitation has passed Luke 19:44 .... But blessed is the name of the Lord who saves my soul from death, my eyes from tears, and won't allow my legs to be moved". Ps. 121:1 I said, "The Savior of the right thief is present and capable. He who justifies the ungodly is risen from the dead; all our sins, as great they might be, will vanish if we seek Him without a doubting faith." With such words, I comforted her.

Her face shone with the light of hope.... Tears were running out of her eyes as rivers, yet her face was at ease, and her countenance was transformed like the shining sun. She spoke with a magnificent tone of voice and asked, "I trust every word you told me that the Lord accepts me. Would you then offer me what I was deprived of for 30 years?" I answered, "Certainly." She said, "Place your cross upon me and absolve me." I stood up to pray the absolution, and I could not stop crying....... I left, promising to return the following day to give her the Communion.

I rushed to our father, Bishoy Kamel........ I told him everything regarding what I did and regarding my promise to the lady concerning Communion. He said to me, "Let us pray so that God may keep her alive till tomorrow, and that she may receive Communion and that her soul may be comforted, and she may be in peace."

And so, it was...... I prayed a Liturgy in the early morning and went back with the virtuous lady. She was perplexed about what was happening, and a lot of unanswered questions were on her mind about her neighbor's friend. I thanked Christ profusely, for I found her awake and alert. When I entered her room, she closed her eyes, and with all her might, she cried out, saying, "Blessed is he who comes in the name of the Lord."……. I have never seen a person receiving communion with such joy.

"This is the bread of life. This is the eternal covenant by the blood of Christ. This is the token of Salvation the power of Resurrection and the reserve of Eternal life.

Words cannot express the goodness of Christ and His kindness. When words become deficient, the heart talks and the eyes shed tears. The person then becomes spiritual and acknowledges all that is heavenly.

I will not forget that day for the rest of my life. It was not a day of this world but indeed was a day of heaven on earth. The Lord's rejoicing for His lost sheep is magnificent and ineffable. He calls everyone in heaven and on earth saying, "Rejoice with Me, for I have found My sheep which was lost."

There was Joy in Heaven…….For it was only a matter of hours and that soul went to whom who loved her, redeemed her, and saved her in the last watch of an immensely night. But when the light of Christ's Resurrection has shone, darkness dissipated forever."

I passed by the same street where the sick lady lived at night, and I saw a great multitude of people gathered to offer condolences to her husband. The man held a high rank. I reminded myself that dust was for dust, but the soul was justified from all transgressions. There is no correlation between the works and thoughts of men and the works and thoughts of God. I remembered the words of the Lord; "Let the dead bury their own dead, but you go and preach the Kingdom of God."

39

Perfect Patristic Conduct

During the early days of my priesthood in 1967...... Next to our Church at Sporting resided a good, pious man from a religious family who exhibited great love for Christ. His brother, advanced in age, was a monk belonging to the Paromeos Monastery. That monk developed a ritual, in his old age, of visiting his brother, who resided within the Church's vicinity, annually for several weeks.

That Father had a hunched back due to the effect of the years; his body was weak, and his mobility was slow. However, his face was glaring with the "light of the Grace" as if it were the face of an angel. Every Sunday, his brother brought him to the Church early. And since he, the monk, was not capable of standing, he then would sit down before the Sanctuary facing the Altar. He sat there, without a movement, for hours. His eyes were pointed toward heaven; his lips were uttering words of prayers and hymns with an inaudible sound. His Angelic appearance filled the hearts of many with peace. Numerous people sought his blessings.

The pious life of that Father, the monk, amongst the elders of the Paromeos Monastery, was attested for by them all. As he, since youth, was chaste, simple, caring, and was adorned with meekness and the many years of worship had bestowed him with multiple folds of Grace.

Whenever I got the chance, I would visit that blessed father at his brother's house. What drew my attention was his scrutinizing patristic conduct and his Adamant eagerness for salvation. Every time I visited their house, he acknowledged my presence, came out of his room, and greeted me with a beautiful smile and genuine, heartfelt warmth. And he would sit next to me whilst inquiring about my service. Hence, I sought his prayers and blessings. After a few minutes, he would extend his hand to a set of books and hand me one of them, saying, "Kindly bring us solace by reading the words of this book."

Those books were a collection of the Saints' biographies, Patristic sayings and quotes, the Paradise of the Monks along with the Holy Bible which was an integral part of his life. They were all scribed by hand and covered with leather. It was he, that Father, himself who hand-scribed them.

One of his favorite accounts was the account of Saint Marina[170], who put on the garb of a man and became a monk. The monks didn't know anything about her. They attributed her soft voice to her austere asceticism. She was falsely accused of defiling the virginity of an archon's[171] daughter, and she was expelled from the monastery. When the daughter of the innkeeper (The archon) gave birth to a son, her father brought him to St. Marina, thinking she was the child's father. Saint Marina took care of the child despite being homeless, moving among the surrounding shepherds till the child grew up. She fed him the milk of the faith, the life with God, and the continuous prayers.

The monks asked the Abbot to pardon her, he consented to their request and readmitted her to the monastery. After he had laid heavy penalties and severe rules upon her, which she completely fulfilled with great perseverance. When she departed in peace, they found out that she was a woman, and she was innocent of all false accusations. God has honored her by performing signs and miracles, through her, after her departure.

While I was reading that intriguing spiritual account, that father was listening in profound silence. And his tears kept running down his face profusely from the beginning of the reading till the end. I was marveled. The man was remarkably familiar with that account...... He knew it by heart since he was the one who wrote it. There was nothing new that would have yielded such an effect from him. From where, then, were all that affection and those tears? How come such repetitions would not turn into routine?!

I am sure that the righteous people's hearts, within, are blazing with Godly love. And their longing, within, for what is heavenly always increases and never diminishes. And the fire of the Spirit, within, kindles and does not extinguish.

---

[170] St. Mary known as Marina the Ascetic. The Church commemorates her departure on the 15th day of the blessed month of Mesore.
[171] He was an owner of an Inn who supported the monastery.

As I finish reading, the man delves into a state of deep affection. His intensified grace would touch all those who were present. Afterward, there would no longer be any need for conversation whatsoever. I would then stay silent for several minutes and excuse myself upon seeking his prayers on my behalf.

I have learned tremendously from that genuine monastic behavior. I have learned how "heed" was practiced so that a man wouldn't lose his vitality and sensitivity for the Spirit—and not allow the outer coldness (The love of the world) to seep into his heart. I have learned how the fathers were diligent concerning their salvation. Subsequently, all their relationships with others, their dealings with the people, their meetings, and visits were all for the sake of Christ. I have learned the value of time…. There is no time for wasting, joking, tattling, or any talk that is not edifying. All times are an acceptable times for the work of the spirit.

40

From All Social Classes

The life of Saint Matruna, the martyr, whom the Church commemorates annually on the 10th day of the blessed month of Thoout (September 20th), witnesses for our "Living Church" who honors martyrdom for the sake of Christ regardless of the martyrs' secular positions, prominent names, or of those who possessed high ranks, or those who were wealthy and notable.

That saintly martyr was a poor maid who worked and served a wicked, dominating Jewish lady. She, Saint Matruna, loved her true master, Jesus Christ, and was witnessing for Him. Therefore, from an outward perspective, she was an enslaved servant. However, from an inward perspective, she was free. The Lord had liberated her… "Therefore if the Son makes you free, you shall be free indeed." When her lady of the house failed to divert her away from her faith, as a bondservant, she was obedient to her, but she never compromised neither her faith nor her worship for the One who offered Himself for her and realized such steadfastness and such strength. She resorted to violence. She kept St. Matruna in solitary confinement without food and water, along with severe torture, till she submitted her pure, chaste soul in the hands of Christ.

That ungrateful lady tried to conceal her crime by throwing the saint's body off a building and claiming it was an accident. As she was striving to complete that evil task and hide her crime, she was not hidden from the eyes of God, who uncovers all secrets and knows the intentions of the people. Her feet slipped, and she fell to her instant death.

Our wonderful Church did not neglect to honor such a saintly martyr despite the fact that she, the saint, did not occupy a leading position such as "Head of a Convent," nor did she accomplish significant tasks or conduct projects that commemorated her name. She did not bear children who acquired high ranks in the Church—none of these things. On the contrary, her memoir was fragile, poor, unknown, and almost forgotten by all people. But once she was bestowed with the heavenly crown and was accounted amongst the ranks of the martyrs, she obligated the church to commemorate her life and her name in the Synaxarian. She entered the choir of the martyrs and reserved a place next to St. George, St. Mina, St. Mertcurius, St. Damiana, and Mother Dolagy.

O How wonderful is the Church that adorns the souls by a spiritual measure and honors her saints according to the magnitude of the sacrifices they offered, lovingly, to Christ the King?

Another Account:

The sweet fragrance of that poor bondservant and martyr reminded me of a simple, poor fishmonger. The man carried, above his head, a large basket full of fish as he was roaming the streets of Choubra. [172]District and its poor adjoining regions. It was a known fact that the majority of the mobile fishmongers were rude and resorted to violence in their daily dealings with the buyers. Not to mention their vulgar language and their profanities. Subsequently, most people not only avoided dealing with them, but they feared them. On the contrary, that blessed brother Saad seemed radically different. He was, despite being in that harsh environment, living a Christian life, praying continuously, and enjoying a living relationship with Christ Jesus. When he talked to his customers, he was truthful and not deceitful. He was meek and did not shout. When he sold them something, he was faithful and honest.

The prevailing custom in the dealings amongst sellers and buyers was tiresome haggling, offensive language, and multiple-fold swearing. However, Brother Saad was only speaking to his customers with Christian talk, which was "Yes or No" (One word). That Christian conduct seemed strange when encountered by non-Christians. But as time went by, people attested that Brother Saad spoke only the truth and that everyone entrusted him. For he did not cheat nor overprice his commodity, nor was he greedy for repugnant profit. He also did not curse or swear.

---

[172] A famous Christian district in Cairo.

And as it happened, when he would come to any area, people gathered around him to buy with unparalleled trust. Hence, he was the most successful among all street sellers. He sold all that he had in the least time, joyfully accepted the little profit, and continued to live happily in peace with God and with the people. But he did not stop there at the pleasant dealings with the people, gaining their trust and profiting from his trade. Rather, he often talked about Christ with both Christians and non-Christians similarly—a simple talk derived from love and content life. As the people realized his honesty, they accepted his words, and many were changed as a result of his truthful testimony to Christ and his love of the Commandments.

This reminded me of what Father Mikhail Ibrahim, God repose his soul, informed me. At the time of his secular employment, he had a non-Christian co-worker who was fond of his virtues and his personality. During that time, Mikhail Efendi was the unblemished epitome of the Christian life, as well as a faithful witness for his Christ and his Savior. That friend said to Mikhail Efendi, "Christians don't deserve to have you; I wish you were Muslim." Mikhail Efendi responded, saying, "What traits do you see in me that you like?" The man answered, "You are a righteous man, honest, loyal, loving, meek, and have superb qualities." Mikhail Efendi said to the man, "My brother, all what you see in me I receive for Christ. If I leave Christ, all these virtues will depart from me."

Likewise was brother Saad, simple in his work and his knowledge and poor in appearance. Yet in truth, he had obtained great richness for Christ. It was his joy to attribute all that he had acquired to the "Source of all Virtues" and the "Giver of all Blessings". Hence, his tongue never ceased to witness for Christ.

I have learned that God can work by the "Few" and by the "Many." "Not by might nor by power, but by My Spirit, 'Says the Lord of hosts.'"

Christ does not leave Himself without a witness.

41

Faithfulness in What Is Least

During the early sixties, our church[173] Embraced out-of-state college students. Our Father Bishoy Kamel hedged them with exceptional care concerning their lodging, provisions, and living expenses. Especially those who were truly destitute. He also enrolled many of them in Sunday school service, believing that if he raised them in the "Spirit."... They will be as the little leaven[174]. Once they go back home or after they graduate, they will be, wherever they may go, witnesses for the work of Christ's Grace. The Lord had blessed that ideology, and the fruit of that service was prosperous and abundant. Many of those youth were consecrated and became devoted to the Lord. Many of them still recall, joyfully, those wonderful, blessed days.

Among those young men was a youth who was attending the College of Mechanical Engineering. He was deeply religious, scrutinizing his conduct to a degree that rejoiced God's heart. He was also a disciple of Father (Baba) Sadek[175]. He met with him on a regular basis, seeking his Spiritual guidance and drawing from the abundance of grace that was richly flowing in his teachings and from the "Word of Life" that his blessed mouth was uttering.

However, that brother was tempted in regards to his studies…. Despite his faithfulness in studying and his undisrupted class attendance, he was unsuccessful in passing the end-of-year exams. He failed the fourth year twice

---

[173] St. George's Church of Sporting in Alexandria
[174] Galatians 5:9
[175] See "The Sweet Aroma of Christ…"Part one

and was given one final try by the college. (In these cases, the students get expelled if they do not pass the exam's third try).

That was the exact situation the young man was facing; his entire future was at risk.His whole life was dependent on passing the fourth year of college. If he passed the exam, he would then move on to the fifth year.Subsequently, he will enjoy a bright future as a certified engineer.However, if he did not, he would be expelled from the University.And in that case, his only option was to enroll in any other university, wasting the five[176]. Years spent in the engineering school, and start all over again.Therefore, all the beloved brethren from the Church and colleagues were laminating his situation, praying for him, and encouraging him.

But truth be told, that brother manifested steadfastness and rare courage. His heart was fixed and reliant on God.He was always cheerful and thankful, and he submitted to God with amazing trust.He continued his studying diligently without confusion, despair, complaint, or grumble.That behavior of his provoked the astonishment of all his companions.Because the "Spirit of Confidence and Joy" that he obtained through living in Christ was apparent in all his actions, hence, he became a "Living Example" for the overcoming of trials encountered by those who are walking in the paths of the Lord.

During the examination times, toward the end of the school year, it crossed my mind to visit that brother to reassure and encourage him.... So I went to his residence.He greeted me, as usual, with a happy smiling face and with Christian cordiality.We talked about God's wonderful acts, read the scripture, and recited the psalms.Then, I inquired about the status of his examinations.He then told me how God was glorified by doing wonderful things for him that same day.... He said, "You know Doctor Seroor, the head of the department."I responded, "I know him"………. (At that time, I was a professor in the College of Engineering).... He was a good-hearted man; his knowledge was copious.He educated thousands of engineers.... The man was fearsome, prestigious, and respected by everyone.Not only the students but also the teachers and the professors.He did not, despite his tender heart, tame his uttered words.Often, he would harshly rebuke, and other times, he would raise his voice and shout.So I asked, "Were you tested today in Dr. Seroor's subject?"He answered, "Yes".I asked again, "How did it go?!"He responded, "It was an extremely hard exam."My heart sank when I heard from him those words, and I felt sorry for that poor young brother.So I encouraged

---

[176] Total 5 years, since he had to spend 2 years trying to pass the fourth year.

Faithfulness in What Is Least

him, saying, "I pray to the Lord that you answered much better. And since the exam was extremely hard for everyone, then the professor will take this matter into consideration". The youth agreed, "Truly so." I inquired, asking, "How so?" He said, explaining, "Dr. Seroor was also the head of the testing center; upon entering the examination room, he found out that the students were complaining about the difficulty of the exam. Consequently, he and the rest of the faculty stepped outside for some time to allow the students to exchange information and answers. After a while, he came back in and asked, 'What's up guys, what is going on?' They responded, 'The exam is tough, Doctor.' He told them, 'Figure out a way,'". I exclaimed, saying, "To that extent, he allowed and permitted the students to act." The Youth responded, "And way more than that, the testing room turned into a Circus." So I asked him, "What did you do." He answered me saying, "Tell you the truth, I squeezed my brain and strived to answer the questions to the best of my ability. I did not turn my head either to the right or the left. My conscience won't permit me to take what is not mine". I inquired, asking, "What happened next?" The young man answered me, saying, "The time limit for the exam was three hours. After one hour and twenty minutes, I answered all that I knew. I tried to recall more information, even just one word, but I couldn't. That was all my ability and all that I knew". I urged him, saying, "Go on and continue." He went on telling me, "I felt that my presence in that exam room was useless and that my spirit was getting uncomfortable in such ambiance. So I immediately rose, about an hour and a half into the exam time, and as soon as Dr. Seroor realized that I was about to turn in my answer sheet. He screamed in my face, 'Where are you going?' I told him, 'I am done.' He took my answer sheet and browsed it. When he realized that my answers were incomplete, that no question was fully answered, and that all the responses were not satisfactory for achieving the passing grade, He said with a sharp tone, 'Go back and complete your answers.' I informed him, saying, 'That is all I know, Doctor'. He said, 'This will not get you to pass …. These are extremely insufficient and poor answers'. I said to him, 'There is nothing more in my mind to recall. Otherwise, I would have written it.' He advised me saying, 'Ask your colleagues'. I told him, 'Doctor, I can't do that'. He screamed with a loud voice, 'I am ordering you to cheat.' I said, 'Believe me, Doctor, my conscience won't let me do so.' He cursed as he was saying, 'Kid, where are you from? Who are you?'[177] I answered, 'I am Christian, Sir.' He said, 'To that extent, your conscience won't allow you!!.... All right, kid, because of

---

[177] Indirectly asking him about his religion.

your honesty, you will pass the exam'. He marked my answer sheet and gave me a passing grade. I passed the exam even before it was officially graded by the school system". My body shivered when I heard those words; we glorified the Just God who avenges His elect. We rose .... Praying .... Glorifying .... Praising .... And thanking God.

That brother successfully passed that year.... And the following years. His Honesty became the "Distinctive Mark" of his life throughout the years. Glory be to God, who won't fail those who trust in Him.

Also, another amazing account concerning one's honesty during school examinations was the account of a student who lived by the virtue of honesty since her childhood. She lived by it in the Church, in her home, and in the milieu in which she was raised .... Thus, any sort of dishonesty or deceit caused her great panic. That account occurred in the United States while she was taking one of the final exams. She was in her last year of Med School.

She received the test paper, which was also the answer sheet as well, for it was a multiple-choice format exam[178]. The student has to mark the correct answer. That blessed sister began to answer the questions, hundreds of questions that had to be answered in a brief period of time. Such tests require speed and precision in reading, retrieving information, and answering questions. Thus, they require extreme concentration. She began to, after praying and seeking guidance from God, as well as asking for the prayers of the saints whom she loved. It was her habit to assign every exam to one of the saints, seeking his help[179]. That was her faith, and that was her ritual throughout her school years and during all her exams, hastily and accurately to mark the answers on the first page, then the second, and so on and so forth .... The exam had more than two hundred questions.

Upon answering more than three-fourths of the questions, she glimpsed her colleague who was sitting next to her. She noticed the answers marked on her colleagues' papers. She, spontaneity, compared both their answers. And what a surprise... The answer to the first question was different, and so was the second, the third, and so were all the questions on the first page. All her answers were different than her colleagues' answers. How could that be!! Could she have answered incorrectly? Her colleague is diligent and meticulous ...... What then, O Lord? What shall I do? At that point, she was facing a vicious trail.

---

[178] This format was never used in the Egyptian school system at that time. Abouna Loka presented the reader with a brief description.
[179] To pray to God on her behalf.

A thought entered into her mind, saying, "Quickly fix your answers and change them according to the answers of your colleague".

The response came from within, "This is cheating… I can't do this". Another thought tempted her, saying, "If you don't do this, you will fail the exam." Those thoughts lasted for several minutes, leading to her bewilderment and confusion. However, she came to herself. She crossed herself by the sign of the Cross, saying from within, "Enough with this matter."

Immediately, her eyes ceased peeking. She became adamantly determined to continue with all honesty, depending only on God. She rejected those thoughts, saying to herself, "It is good for me to die as an honest person rather than to live as a cheater. I will answer, by God's Grace, according to my ability and my knowledge without resorting to such a shameful thing even if I fail the exam".

She recovered her strength and concentration and finished the test, overcoming the evil thoughts and the counsel of the Wicked. Abiding by her God's Commandment, "Faithfulness in what is least," and seeking her Christ. The One who had compassion for her.

Outside the exam room, she encountered her colleague. After greeting her, she asked her anxiously, "How was the exam?" Her colleague answered her saying, "Everything was alright".

She asked her, "What was your answer to the first question?" She answered, "I picked choice (A)". The Blessed sister responded, "No, It is the third choice (C)". Her colleague protested saying, "How could it be so, and the first question was about (so and so)?" The blessed sister shouted saying, "What subject you were evaluated on?" She answered, "Physiology".

What a surprise…. The blessed sister was being tested in another subject. Both were being tested on two different subjects at the same time. The blessed sister came to herself and cried out with thanksgiving to God, for He had saved her from such trial. If she had obeyed the evil thought and cheated, she would have definitely failed the exam. Thus, as she held on to her honesty, she saved herself from the "Snare of the fowlers." The Lord had prospered her way. She successfully passed the exam as she continued glorifying God, who had done wonderful things for her.

42

Impossible with Men

We may fall into despair upon facing some hardships during this life as Satan gets hold of the soul and tightens his grip. At this time, man resorts to "Human Solutions," or he recklessly makes unwise decisions that may bring him misery for the rest of his life. The only way to salvation is by holding on to the Lord Christ and keeping His commandments. So that man can reach a happy end, even if people despise him. Thus, he will not lose his heavenly portion and the inheritance, that of the saints, in Christ's kingdom.

It is an absolute certainty that nothing is impossible with Christ our God, for the things which are impossible with men are possible with God[180]. And He can, according to His will, bring forth from the eater something to eat and out of the strong something sweet[181]. It just takes faith and trust in Him, He who can save to the uttermost[182].

In October of 1977, two weeks before my travel to the USA, one of my daughters, she was a Sunday school servant, approached me requesting that I visit a family related to her. I declined her request due to lack of time since the unplanned travel caused me great confusion as well as many accumulated issues that needed my attention before traveling. In addition to matters pertaining to the service. She persisted, saying, "Just for 10 minutes at any time." I asked, "What is the urgent need for this visit?" She surprised me. It was an old problem

---

[180] Luke 18:27
[181] Judges 14:14
[182] Our Lord and Savior and king of us all Jesus Christ. Hebrews 7:25

between a husband and a wife that ended with a divorce thirteen years ago. Since then, the wife has been living at her father's house along with her son and daughter.

I said, "My daughter, where have you been all these years? What can I do in a brief period of time to fix such an intractable problem? It is too late." She responded, "But I have faith that the Lord may intervene!" I was ashamed by her words, so I allocated a specific time on a Wednesday evening and went to visit that family. They were all present.

I was greeted by the head of the household, an elderly merchant from Upper Egypt. He welcomed me with reproach for not visiting them prior. I apologized, saying that I did not know of them, nor was I informed of their address.

We read the Holy Bible spoke the Word of life and talked about the acts of God in His saints.... Everyone was highly affected and responsive to the Word of God.

When we were done talking, the man said to me, "The time has passed. Will you eat a piece of bread[183]?with us?" I answered, "Yes, we can eat an Agape meal together." I cannot describe the magnitude of happiness which the man had manifested whilst in disbelief....... The mother and her daughter immediately began preparing a fasting meal, Foul Medames[184]. – Olives and hastily prepared the table. The man said to me, "Kindly bless." I responded, "Very well. But before I eat, I shall have a word with you." The man said, "Please say it." I told him, "The scripture says, 'A time for every purpose under heaven[185] .... Behold, now is the accepted time; behold, now is the day of salvation[186]" He responded, asking me, "What do you mean?" I answered, "It is time for God's work." He inquired, "What is God's work?" I said, "The heavenly peace." He asked again, "My father, what are you talking about?" I explained, "Satan succeeded in his works all these years. Hatred, fights, idle talks, resisting love, shattering a family, and destroying the Sacraments. Now it is time for God's work. Christ, may His name be glorified with one word that can demolish what Satan had built in many years. Because the Son of God came to eradicate the works of the devil." The man realized that I was hinting about the issue of his daughter concerning her divorce from her husband thirteen years ago. He answered me with a sorry but firm tone, saying, "My

---

[183] Piece of bread is synonym to and interchangeable with a "Meal."
[184] Fava beans cooked in a special vessel. It is a traditional national Egyptian cuisine.
[185] Eccl. 3:2
[186] 2 Corinthians 6:2

father, this matter ended a long time ago. There is no use for such talk... Let go of this issue, and kindly eat with us." I said, "I won't eat if you don't give me a word." He responded, "My father, that is not the way to confront issues." I said without thinking, "Just for Jesus' sake." I cannot express how deeply the man was moved upon hearing that phrase.... Or how emotional he became while saying, "My father, why do you utter such words? His sake is a sword on my neck. For His sake, I shall slaughter my son. I am not worthy nor deserve to do anything for His sake." The man wept. The weeping of an elderly man in a household charged the entire ambiance with affection. Tears were shed profusely as if a rushing, mighty wind filled the whole house. We prayed fervently and thanked Christ, He who is controlling our hearts. We ate our food with immense joy and continued our talk about God's acts and Christ's supreme power and authority—the Almighty God who is capable of all things.

I left that blessed house fully affected and impressed. How that is, the simple souls comply with the voice of the Spirit without intransigence. And as soon as the desire for goodness embarks within, they follow, surrendering their own will. I marveled at those who cling to their will, fanatical about their opinions, and insist on enmity till the end. I was more saddened by the countless homes that were destroyed and whose children were scattered and by the unprecedented loss of souls, with or without a reason. How many sermons, guidance, and how many reminders of Christ's Gospel and His commandments were rendered? Yet few abided. I regretted, wholeheartedly, the numerous cases pending in the court of Law to demolish the holy Sacrament and to break the matrimonial bond that was established by God. I wondered.... Where is the respect of this Sacrament.......? Where is the acknowledgment of Christ and the Church? Where? Where? I answered my questions thinking that if there is such good faith if there is such tremendous love for Christ who died for us, if there is such trust in God's works.... If there are such people as that blessed family, there will be no problems at all.

The next day, I went to visit my husband. I found him to be a simple man, living alone in a rented apartment that he acquired for himself thirteen years prior. He managed his own life, employed, and paid child support for his children as per the court's ruling. He spent time with them during visitation hours without causing any problems. I met with him to learn about his circumstances. Then, without further ado, I informed him about all that Christ had done the previous day. He was in disbelief whilst saying, "Impossible .... Impossible." I assured him that this is the way God works. We prayed together.... He was deeply moved.... He said to me, "I prayed a lot for my family.... I wept a lot.... I thought that God neglected me.... But now I truly know that the Lord is good, and His mercy endures forever[187]."

I brought him to his father-in-law's house without prior appointment or permission.... Upon entering the home, his children rushed towards him, crying, as did his wife. He bowed down, crying at his father-in-law's feet. The man lifted him while tears were running down his cheeks, saying, "Forgive me, my son, it is my fault." I have never in my life encountered such an emotional situation. Once more, we read the Holy Bible and spoke the Word of life whilst the heavenly consolation was overwhelming us all. We prayed joyfully.

Afterward, they, the husband and wife, asked me in private, "What shall we do now? We are divorced, according to the official legal documents. But how about in the sight of the Church and God?" I said, "Yow were separated from each other due to a reason or another of the disagreement reasons that Satan sows. By which he agitates the souls and the emotions. But the Lord did not allow you to sin. You, as a husband, lived alone by yourself and did not associate with anyone else, either through marriage or through sin. And you also, as a wife, resided in your father's house. Hence, you were protected from the suspicions of sins. You did not seek another husband, nor did you associate yourself with anyone other than him. Therefore, what is this separation's effect on the sacred bond of matrimony? Nothing at all.... For you, according to the Church and the Spiritual, sacred bond, husband and wife. You do not need anything except prayer, repentance, and confession concerning the times of ignorance and lack of love. As for repeating the holy matrimony sacrament for you, this is not feasible according to the Church canons.

I allowed them several days for prayers because of my lack of time. They came back afterward and confessed. I gave them the Holy Eucharist and recited them the absolution. They returned to their home which was abundant most of the time, except during the few times when the wife visited it. Perhaps once a month, since she lived permanently at her father's house along with her children.

I went with them to their house, raised incense, and prayed. I wished them wholeheartedly blessed days. I recommend that they pray a lot, fast, and partake in the Eucharist. Before my travel, I entrusted the divorce case to one of my beloved lawyers, and in turn, he canceled the case...... That unprecedented case caused an astonishing echo amongst the Christian lawyers and Judges.

---

[187] Psalm 106:1

They were glorifying God the almighty. It is genuinely so, "The things which are impossible with men are possible with God."

43

Courage of the Martyrs

In November 1975, precisely on day 16 of the month, which is the feast of the consecration of the great martyr St. George's Church at the city of Lod in Palestine. This coincided also with the consecration of our Church at Sporting in the year 1968 by the hands of the departed Abba Maximus, the Metropolitan of Al Qalyubia. On that day, we were praying for the Divine Liturgy early in the morning in a solemn ceremony. Abba Maximus loved to celebrate this day with us every year.

On that day, Satan put in the heart of one of his assistants to place a bomb on the first floor of the Church. He anchored it underneath one of the wooden chairs and kept that chair in a tilted position so that if someone moved it back to its default position, the bomb would explode. But the merciful God showed mercy on that day. The bomb was discovered miraculously, and the Lord saved His people through the blessing of the Holy Sacrifice and the prayers of the great martyr St. George. That incident was becoming known everywhere.... The perpetrator was arrested afterward, also in a miraculous way, and received his punishment on earth and in heaven.

I recall, on that day, a peculiar feeling emanated from the congregations' hearts. There was no worry, sorrow, or fear. It was something that transcends logic and mind! Even Church attendance doubled after that miracle ...... Thus, we realized that our congregations' faith became reinforced by God, as such incidents restore the faith and strengthen the weak hands.

One of the examples of this type of faith that we witnessed on that day, which is still engraved in my memory, was a particular lady who was living a true repentant life and having a profound fellowship with God. She was a mother of two daughters and a wife of a virtuous man. She was a faithful disciple to Father Bishoy Kamel and spiritually attached to him since he had saved her from a devil's snare during her youth. She felt indebted to him, striving not to forget God's benefit, which was rendered to her by Father Bishoy Kamel.

I saw her, that day immediately after the Liturgy upon knowing about the bomb, crying fervently and shedding tears profusely…… I approached her, inquiring, "What is the matter? Are you Okay? Is everything all right? She responded, as she was trying earnestly to control her tears, "We were about to become martyrs for Christ in a blink of an eye…… What a significant loss!

I marveled enormously and wondered. How was it possible for the heart to reach such elevated love and acquire the insight for all that is heavenly? I said, within, "Is the martyrdom era, for those who love Christ, renewed?! Did the desire to shed blood for Christ revive?!

I realized, with all honesty, that if the desire for God's Kingdom kindled in the heart. Man will favor suffering over pleasure, and the soul will be eager to bear the Cross with joy and contentment. On the contrary, if the heart is devoid of the flame of the faith, it will solicit an exodus even by denouncing the faith. I entreated God wholeheartedly to keep this flame always present in His Church. For He is able to do so because He is the one who said, "I came to send fire on the earth, and how I wish it were already kindled!"

On that same day in the church courtyard, also after the Divine Liturgy, the news reached the Patriarchate's vicar. He, in turn, informed the officials, and they immediately came to the Church. The Church courtyard became packed with police officers, detectives, and investigators…… It was overwhelming.

Behold …. Another lady, as she was coming down the stairs, faced a high-ranked police officer. She shouted, saying, "The gates of Hades shall not prevail against it." The man turned to her and did not comprehend what she was saying. So she began interpreting the verse for him saying that the Church is built on the Rock (The everlasting strength), and her groom is alive. His promise stands forever, and even though Heaven and Earth will pass away. Yet, Christ's promise will never pass away.

I was marveled by such an encounter, for I knew that lady very well. She was extraordinarily meek and of an angelic nature. I never heard her shout or become angry. I did not believe what I saw; how was it possible for such a lady to acquire courage and fearlessness as such? How did the Spirit make her utter testimonial words for Christ which a regular tongue fails to utter?

"If we truly think of Christ as our source of holiness, we shall refrain from anything wicked or impure in thought or act... For the quality of holiness is shown not by what we say but by what we do in life."

— St. Gregory of Nyssa

44

Astounding Faith

When Christ's grace works in man....He, by grace, transcends beyond the limitations of nature and overcomes its characteristics that are embedded within us.It is a known fact that jealousy is a natural instinct of man.Yet, the Book of Proverbs leads the ignorant and rules the blind in the way of wisdom,

"For by means of a harlot a man is reduced to a crust of bread; and an adulteress will prey upon his precious life.Can a man take fire to his bosom and his clothes not be burned?Can one walk on hot coals and his feet not be seared?So is he who goes into his neighbor's wife; whoever touches her shall not be innocent."

"Whoever commits adultery with a woman lacks understanding; he who does so destroys his own soul.Wounds and dishonor he will get, and his reproach will not be wiped away.For jealousy is a husband's fury; therefore he will not spare in the day of vengeance.He will not accept no recompense, nor will he be appeased though you give many gifts[188]."

The man who becomes jealous and enraged when he catches his wife in an act of sin and, due to jealousy, commits a punishable crime.The secular courts extend him mercy, as most likely, he will act irrationally and illogically.

The Church history documents for Saint Paul the Simple, the disciple of Saint Anthony, his unique stance as he was tempted by his wife when caught in adultery.He meekly advised her, but she returned to sin.Thus, he quietly left

---

[188] Proverbs 6:26-32

her and headed to Saint Anthony. He became a monk and lived an unparalleled life of asceticism and plainness.

However, God does not leave Himself without witness, but in every generation, there was someone whose Grace had supported him to transcend beyond the limitations of nature, as we have previously mentioned. I encountered towards the end of the sixties as we were at the Church of the great martyr St. George in Sporting; living a spiritual life was the main and only concern for many of the Church's congregation…We were living in the days of spiritual renaissance that were founded upon prayer, fasting, chastity, love, and the striving to keep the commandants of the Lord Jesus, along with Father Bishoy Kamel, at noon. Our Church at Sporting does not close her doors day or night; she is always open, likened to the nest of the swallow and the home of the sparrow. Everyone who seeks help, shelter, or relief from the hardships of the world flees to her.

A pious man, known to us, entered the church. He was gentle and lowly in heart. A man of peace who was known by his meekness and low voice. He entered while holding his wife's hand. She was in her thirties, as he was probably ten years older than her. The man was not in his usual state of repose. Rather, his face was so swollen and gloomy that the blood was about to burst out of it. Also the woman was not in a better condition as well.… Her countenance raised concerns. Father Bishoy Kamel took the man aside upon seeing him. The man could not withhold his anguish, nor was he able to speak slowly or with a low voice. He shouted, saying, "Have mercy on me, O Lord, have mercy on me, Abouna Bishoy.… Help her.… I don't want her to perish.… Save her from her sin, I saw her with my own wyes. I didn't come here for revenge or to complain… I came so that you lead her to repentance."

The man was crying and almost fell to the ground, but Abouna Bishoy held him as a father held his son while trying not to cry. However, God bestowed Abouna Bishoy, during such incidents, with unique power and courage. Hence, he controlled himself and consoled the man with words of comfort.

I will never forget for the rest of my life the image of Abouna Bishoy in the Church as he turned towards the altar while raising both his arms and shouting with a loud voice saying to the man, "Christ my God shall not charge you with sin, but He shall forgive and absolve you all your sins."

The wonderful approach of that man was the cause that led to his wife's salvation, as Abouna Bishoy hedged her with special care and strengthened her will till she rejected, wholeheartedly, the counsel of the enemy.

How much has repentance changed the souls? How many rebirths? How many sinners were reformed and became, through grace, the epitome of Christ's ability to justify the libertine?

45

Simplicity and Faith

In the mid-sixties, one of the Church servants was attending the "Servants' meeting" regularly. Numerous times, he brought, along with him, his elderly mother.... She was advanced in the days of Grace and a life of simplicity that was scarce to encounter. We, as the youth in the Church, loved to see her and enjoyed her pleasant wishes for us and her profound, simple words. She always proclaimed, saying, "There is a prayer that can match the liturgical prayer." So I asked her with curiosity, "What do you like in the liturgy prayer?" She answered, "Every word.... It is sufficient to hear Abouna say, 'O lover of mankind'... one gets elevated upon hearing it." I reproached myself immediately and said, "Truly, the simple ones precede many of those who claim education, or philosophy, or knowledge."

Our brother, the servant, said that he bought a small cassette player. It was considered a rare item at that time, and when he arrived home, he inserted a cassette for the Divine Liturgy. And while he was sitting down completing some tasks, he turned around...... And behold! His mother was standing, as if in the Church, while in a state of prayer. He laughed within and said to her, "My Mother, this is just a recording." She interrupted him, saying, "Be quiet, my son. This is the Liturgy Prayer." He responded, "Yes, my mother. But we are not in the Church. There is no Priest nor a Sacrifice." Yet, she rejected such talk and insisted to remain standing. In vain, he tried to make her sit down.... Thus, he no longer did such a thing again. Because every time she hears the sound of the liturgy prayer, she stands in reverence and won't sit down at all.

Although it had been almost thirty-five years since the occurrence of that account, I remember it whenever I saw lots of people use the cassette player to hear the Divine Liturgy prayers, whether at home, in cars, or perhaps in public places. I marvel at the lack of listening or attention …… So, one perceives them as preoccupied with whatever they are doing as they get used to hearing the prayers. Thus, the prayers lost its significance and effect. It became, for them, the music that is played at the public shops that no one listens to. It became just background music for the crowds of people and the various noises and sounds.

Yet, I don't deny that some people still get consoled by hearing the prayers and reap a real benefit. The matter depends on the person's willingness and eagerness.

I know certain loved ones who have gone abroad to Saudi Arabia, where there is no Church or Liturgy…. And they have brought with them some tape cassettes that recorded the Divine Liturgy…… On Sundays and Fridays, the man, who was religious, pious, and occupied an elevated literary position, and his wife, a virtuous lady who loved Christ, would start the cassette player in one of the house rooms. They would stand in reverence until the conclusion of the prayers as if they were inside the Church. They were comforted by prayers and tears of spiritual longing…. For them, that was the simplest compensation in the land of alienation, expressing the extent of the longing with which their hearts were burning towards the Church.

46

The Christian Epitome

The world is in dire need, nowadays, for the Christian epitome. The world becomes in need, as a destitute poor person, for all that is spiritual and all that is virtuous and pure. The disease of sin stormed the world and almost destroyed it. Even the nations' presidents who seemed pillars and considered role models by the people, their thrones were shaken, and they fell into the worst sins of fraud, lies, and fornication. Hence, the mouthpiece of the general public says, "If the master of the house beats the tambourine, then the trait of the household is the abundance of filth and sins[189]." Subsequently, the world deteriorated by the lust. Ideals and values only exist in history books and the memoirs of good men who departed from this world. If a person is found, in such ambiance, who testifies for Christ by his perfect reputation, hence, he becomes very precious in the sight of God and the sight of men.

However, we are not unfair to our days (Time). But we are saying that the scarcity of the "Living Christian Epitome," even amongst those who work by religion or those who regularly attend the Churches, became a common phenomenon within all circles. Speeches and books are copious, and life according to Christ is scarce. Nevertheless, the Lord did not leave Himself without witness[190]. Even if it is scarce, it is present, living and witnessing the ungodliness of the world and the storms of lust. And even if it is scarce, it is honest and steadfast against this torrential current.

---

[189] The people follow the morals of their kings and presidents and imitate their conducts.
[190] Acts 14:17

One of the examples of the amazing honesty and circumspect was what I observed in one of the College of Science's professors. He was a man well-spoken of for his knowledge within all circles. He was known for his extreme politeness and his kind attitude. A top-notch Christian personality. His tongue never uttered a vulgar expression. Nobody knew him other than being serious, meek, pleasant, longsuffering...... No one ever saw him angry or raising his voice .... He was, amongst everyone, a sweet fragrance .... And his life was like a water stream running quietly, irrigating and quenching thirst. Everyone benefited through him.

That pious life brought life to many people; it drew estranged souls. He was advising his students, by wisdom and simplicity, to seek a better life. His conduct was the greatest witness to his sayings. He was supported by his honest words.

In the early seventies, a young man in his twenties approached me. He was residing close to the Church, yet he was far away from her at the same time. Many servants toiled for his sake, and in vain, they tried to bring him back from his road of perdition. Abouna Bishoy visited him numerous times, but the young man was dodging. He was promising and not fulfilling. Finally, he was avoiding Abouna Bishoy...... In such cases, Abouna resorts to prayer, which is very effective.

The young man approached me as I concluded the youth meeting and started to receive confessions, and sat beside me and said, "I want to repent." How happy I was just to see that young man return and perceive his sincere intention to repent and change his life! He said, "I quit smoking several days ago, and I abandoned bad companions with sincere intention and firm determination. Please help me in the way of my repentance.... Teach me how to read the Bible, and teach me how to pray."

Upon hearing a sincere confession accompanied by copious tears and reciting the absolution, and as I was highly affected, I asked him out of curiosity, "What prompted you to start a life with Christ ...... Did you hear an inspiring sermon?" He answered, "No." "Did you go to one of the monasteries or meet one of the Fathers?" He answered, "No." "Have you heard of anyone getting sick, or have you lost a loved one?" He said, "No." I asked, "What then?" He responded, "Since the beginning of the school year and Doctor (....) Is our professor and teacher. He has captivated me, as well as others, with his elevated manners. Thus, we all honored the man and respected him. Several days ago, during the lecture, the professor asked one of the students to pay attention. That specific student was extreme in his behavior, tremendously violent, and substantially fanatic. Everyone takes heed and does not deal with him or even get close to him. The professor was talking to him with the utmost gentleness and in a polite manner. We were stunned by an erupted volcano by that impolite student; he showered the professor with insults and profanities. He attacked Christianity and converted the issue, stupidly and without reason, into religious friction.[191]…… An astonishing situation that electrified the atmosphere of the class. Yet the professor remained quiet; his facial continence did not change; he was not troubled by the profanities, nor did he comment with a single word. The entire class was triggered, shouts from here and there; Muslim students opposed that student and almost engaged in a physical altercation…. At that moment, I saw the professor hold the microphone and, with serious firmness, restored serenity for the class. Then he said, addressing the impolite student, 'My son, I am sorry if I disturbed you when I asked you to pay attention during the lecture …… But believe me, I am concerned about your best interest. But as for me, being a father, I have to tolerate my children even during times of wrath. What ties me to you is the bond that is between a father and his children more than the bond that is between a lecturer and students. I have the right, as a professor, to discipline you for this conduct. I can do this and more, but my duty as a father is to endure you and forgive you. I would rather be a father more than a professor…. Please do not comment on this matter.'

To everyone's surprise, we saw that student rush toward the professor, trying to kiss his feet and say, 'Forgive me, professor. I am at fault, and you do not deserve anything bad.' The professor raised him whilst embracing him, saying, 'You all are my children, and I love you all.' The entire class applauded…. The professor continued the lecture upon, leaving a deep impression on us. At that moment, I said to myself, 'This is the best life that I ought to live; this is the life in Christ. Any other is not called or considered a life.…... From that moment, I decided to live by Christ; I decided to repent and confess. For I witnessed the power of the Christian life and how it overcomes the wickedness of the evil people.'"

I said to him, "My son. Likewise, the righteous martyrs, witnesses to Christianity, were drawn by their patience for pain and by their forgiveness, even those who tortured them and hurt them. They converted the heathens into believing in Christ. How powerful is the life of witnessing to Christ, and how great is its impact?"

---

[191] Friction between Christians and Muslims began to prevail in society during that time.

That righteous man lived whilst being honored by his generation, those who are from the Church and those who are from the outside….He finished his good race by living the Christian perfection. His home was truly a Holy Church. He and his wife were pious. They did not have children…... When he fell asleep in the Lord, and while we were at his house, one of his closest friends, who was linked to him by spiritual tie and Christian friendship, informed me the departed, may God repose his soul, was commissioned to Cairo to tutor the students of the "Graduate Studies." Numerous times, he would travel to Cairo but wouldn't find the students available due to their busy schedules or not being able to attend for one reason or another. He would then return to Alexandria. He adamantly refused to receive a salary for those times…. The head of HR insisted that he logs those times, telling him, "You traveled, squandered your time, and spent money. You have the right to be compensated. It is not your fault that the students did not attend the class." He adamantly refused, saying, "I did not get to teach the subject. I did not make the proper effort that is sufficient to receive my wage." The head of HR and his colleagues marveled at such wonderful honesty and circumspect conscience by which that pious man lived.

All his brethren and colleagues mentioned him as the epitome of perfection and unique ethics. And if they praised him, he said, "I am a weak person. I strive for perfection but have not achieved it yet."

Many of his students were influenced by his life. They were striving to live such an attractive life that emanated the sweet fragrance of Christ.

47

Do Not Let the Sun Go Down on Your Wrath

The departed Hegumen Matthias Raphael accompanied me throughout a trip to Upper Egypt concerning things that pertained to the Church in the year 1972. On the way to our return, we visited the village of "Deir El-Naghamish[192"]....... It is a village that all its inhabitants are relatives as well as it is the hometown of Pope Yousab, the second[193] And his relatives, priests, and monks. The ambiance of the village suggests extreme simplicity, love, and Christian living that resembles a virgin's freshness, which was not tainted by the world. Without science or philosophy, they practiced the Christian virtues, for they were received by the younger generations through their fathers without hindrance.

As we tread a small trail that ends with a family house in which our father, Matthias Raphael, may the Lord repose his soul, was raised. He began to tell me about his relatives and his grandfather Peter the priest and his uncles...... One of the funny accounts that I recall was that two of his cousins, at that time they, were in their fifties and considered pillars of the family while in the field[194], outside the village, and at noon on one of the days, they had a heated argument resulting from a misunderstanding. They yelled angrily. One left the other and returned to the village, they were alone in the field, and no one

---

[192] Souhag, Egypt
[193] Pope # 115. (1946-1956 AD)
[194] They were farmers.

was present with them, as if the situation ended by that argument and as if nothing had taken place. The issue concerning the argument was insignificant.

An hour later, after that incident, the man who left his cousin and returned to the village went to his cousin's house and called out, saying, "Peace.... Is (So–and–So)[195] Here? One of the house's occupants responded to him, "No, Uncle (....)...... (So-and-So) still at the field. Please come in." He said, "No. Thank you." He left, then returned after ten or fifteen minutes and asked again, "Still, (So-and-So) did not return yet?!" He was told, "No. He hasn't returned yet. Please come in.... What is going on?" He looked up toward heaven and said, "It is okay.... I shall return once more."

That situation was repeated four or five times within the hour.... Till all the household wondered and asked, "What is the matter? ..... It is not your habit to do this." The man was distraught, and whenever he did not find his cousin, he returned. He looks up towards heaven and seems anxious. As it got late and his cousin didn't return, he hurried towards the road outside the village that led to the field. The sun was about to go down.... And the man was running, despite being an elderly person. On the way, he encountered his cousin returning.... He met him and fell on his neck, kissing him, asking for forgiveness....... Yet his cousin says to him, "My brother.... I transgressed against you.... And you come to me!" The man responded, "No. It is my fault.... I raised my voice.... Forgive me.... I was afraid that the sun would go down. I have made you sad.... And the Lord commanded: 'Do not let the sun go down on your wrath.'"

As the account became known, everyone realized that the man was worried lest the sun go down while feeling that he saddened his brother.... To this extent, they were living the scripture, by the spirit and by the text together, in extreme simplicity and scrutiny that was mind-boggling.

Upon hearing about that incident, I felt sorry within about what I witnessed and listened to every day—concerning bickering, quarrels, hatred, and schism. Even harm. How can a Christian person live in enmity despite being the disciple of Love?! How could he hate a human being? Or be angry at someone? Rather the worst, how could he continue in enmity, not for days but years? I realized that we had lost the Christin life entirely.

---

[195] Concealing the name of the man as per the narrator.

When those two individuals exercised love…. Everyone knew that they were disciples of the Lord in accordance with his commandment, "By this all will know that you are My disciples, if you have love for one another[196]."

One of these examples that witnesses to Christ is more effective than hundreds of sermons and thousands of books. Because there is no greater testimony than the "Testimony of Life", and there is nothing more powerful in life than keeping Christ's commandments.

O Lord, grant your children the grace of peace that is founded upon true love. And keep them from hatred, schism, and anything that opposes and is against You—O Eternal Divine love.

---

[196] John 13:35

48

The Holy Baptism

On one of the given Sundays of the year 1967, toward the end of the liturgy, while we were dismissing the congregation, a poor lady carrying a little child approached Abouna Bishoy Kamel and asked him to baptize her child. For he was sick, and she was afraid, he may die unbaptized.

That day, Abouna Bishoy was carrying the Holy Sacraments and was on his way to give Communion to a sick, hospitalized person. He turned to me and said to the lady, "Abouna Loka can baptize him." ...... I looked at the child; he was almost dead. He appeared pale and bluish, his eyes were closed and swollen, and he was breathing with extreme difficulty. Truth be told, I was afraid and terrified to baptize such a child. If his breathing were as difficult as it was, what would happen if he were fully submerged in the baptismal font? I imagined that he would die in my hands.... I said to Abouna Bishoy, "I can't; the child will not tolerate it, and I am afraid."

At this moment, a young deacon who was present and heard our conversation exclaimed, "Would anyone die by baptism?!" Abouna Bishoy turned toward the deacon and then toward me and said, "Baptize the child according to the faith of this young deacon if you are afraid."

He then left and headed to the hospital to give the Communion to the sick person. I entered the Baptismal chamber compelled...... While I was praying upon the child, every now and then, I looked at him. Was he still alive? I wondered.

I completed the baptismal prayers. While within, I was praying that God may strengthen my faith and cast fear away from me.

After renouncing Satan and confessing Christ, I anointed the child with the Hagielaion oil and finished reciting the written prayers. I took him from his mother's hands and very carefully let him down into the Baptismal font, saying, "I baptize you (....) in the name of the Father, and of the Son, and of the Holy Spirit." I submerged him hastily into the Holy water, then brought him up. Was he still alive? Was he breathing?

Thanks be to God; the child took a deep breath and then continued breathing normally. I sealed him with the Holy Myron, put on him the baptismal cloth, and tightened the girdle. After the procession, I gave the commandment to the mother and dismissed her in peace, saying, "Next Liturgy, he may receive Communion if he is still alive."

Upon his return, Abouna Bishoy asked me, "Did you baptize the Child?" I answered, "Yes. This was my first encounter with such a situation; please absolve me, for I was scared that the child might die in my hands by not tolerating the submersion into the water of the baptism."

Abouna Bishoy assured me saying that we, the Priests, should have a deep potent, and powerful faith in the Godly Sacraments.... Isn't it not, the Baptism, Resurrection? For we die and bury by Baptism. And just as Christ rose from the dead, we rose as well for the new life.

Then, he told me of what had taken place in the early days of his service. He was baptizing a girl belonging to a wealthy family. During the prayers that preceded baptism, a poor woman carrying a little child approached him and said, "May I baptize my son." Abouna answered, "You may," and continued the prayers for the two children. When the poor woman removed her son's clothing, his body was full of boils. The wealthy mother grumbled and told Abouna, "It is not possible for my daughter to be baptized with this child lest this disease affects her." Abouna tried to convince her that the Holy Sacraments have Divine power.... She was not convinced and insisted that her daughter go into the Baptismal font first.

Abouna did not wish to complicate the situation due to lack of time, for it happened shortly before the start of the Liturgy, and it was not the time for a debate. He baptized the girl first, then the poor boy, regretting within himself the weakness of the Faith concerning the Sacraments. The following week, the poor woman came to the Church with her child, who was fully healed, whilst the wealthy mother complained that her daughter's health was not all

The Holy Baptism

that well. Abouna showed her the poor child and said to her, "Because of the lack of our Faith, we don't receive many blessings." He led her to repentance …....Her Faith was strengthened, and she glorified God by informing many people of this account.

I was affected by hearing those words. And I waited to see the boy that I had baptized, wondering what might have happened to him. I did not recall that I asked his mother for their address. Nor did I know her name. I inquired from Abouna Bishoy, but he did not know her as well.

Several weeks passed, and on a Sunday after the Liturgy, I saw the poor lady in front of me. I quickly went to her and asked, "How is your child?" She pointed with her finger……I looked.…... and there was the child crawling on the floor of the Church; his face was shining bright and full of health. I held him between my arms and kissed him joyfully.

The dead person has changed, for he acquired a new, powerful life.

49

The Perpetual Prayer

Always ought to pray[197]……. Pray without losing heart[198]……. These verses were the pivot of life in the account of the Russian Pilgrim[199]… He spent his entire life in that amazing trial. As his life becomes entirely prayer and his prayer entirely life…. No separation between the life and the prayer…. "I give myself to prayer[200]"……. The Pilgrim was supported, in his endeavor, by the teachings and sayings of the great saints of the wilderness who devoted their lives to prayers. And they had documented their "Living Sayings" in the Book of Philokalia. It is one of the spiritual books that Abouna Bishoy Kamel translated part of it.

We, likewise, in our lives and our endeavors in the world, may not be deprived of such enjoyment if we acquired this yearning and became faithful in training for the life of prayer. This is not impossible; what is needed is faithfulness, patience, and practice. Abouna Bishoy used to assign his children, during confession, a practice for perpetual prayers, such as: "The Jesus Prayer," As he strived to make them love to utter the precious name abundantly and call out the name of salvation that belongs to our Lord Jesus Christ…. Or the prayer "Save me, O God!"……. He named it the "Rescue Psalm[201]"……. He called these prayers the "Sagittal Prayers." …….. That is, it is a brief short prayer, but effective as a sharp fast arrow.

---

[197] Luke 18:1
[198] 1 Thessalonians 5:17
[199] The Way of a Pilgrim.
[200] Psalm 109:4
[201] Psalm 69

Many from all walks of life were trained as they realized that the name of the Lord Jesus is truly a "Strong tower; the righteous run to it and are safe[202]."

One of the memorable moments...... I recall that Abouna Bishoy and I were riding in his car on our way for visitations around the Church's vicinity. Suddenly, he said to me, "Come, I will show you a beautiful sight." I asked, "Where?" He stopped his car, pointed towards one of the buildings, and said, "Look at the doorman....... (So-and-So) do you know him? I said, "Yes, I do." He said, "Do you see what he is doing?" When I focused on the look, I saw the doorman sitting in front of the building and bowing his head downwards. I said to Abouna, "What is he doing? He told me, "He is praying.... He just learned the Agpya prayer, and he prays all day and night. He sits in front of the building praying. He is not occupied with anything except prayer and lifting his heart towards God." We sat in the car while talking about the efficacy of prayer and its blessings. Therefore, regardless of man's line of work, it cannot distract him from prayer once his heart is attached to it.

In that meantime, a loud voice of one of the lady tenants was heard, calling the doorman to fulfill her request. I saw him immediately respond to her. And with all meekness and serenity, he inserted the Agpya in his pocket and looked towards the direction of the voice. The lady descended the basket from above. He picked up the money, which was inside the basket, and went to buy her what she requested...... Abouna Bishoy informed me that all the tenants of the building, as well as all the neighbors, love that man tremendously due to his politeness, obedience, swift service, and honesty. However, they did not know that the source of attraction was the life of perpetual prayer and the connection to Christ, which that simple man was living with all truthfulness and sincerity.

I remembered a colleague, he was my childhood friend, who was a college professor. The life of prayer took hold of all his emotions and all of his heart's feelings. Hence, he meditated in the Law of the Lord day and night.

While he was performing his job, he would yearn for prayer. So, as soon as the chalkboard gets filled with the lesson, which he was tutoring the students, he refuses to have it cleared by one of the students. He insists on doing it himself. Thus, he turns towards the chalkboard, lifts the eraser, and begins to erase the board systematically from top to bottom in parallel lines with the utmost calmness. The students thought that it was due to the extreme discipline and cleanness which that brother processed. But in actuality, he was seizing the

---

[202] Proverbs 18:10

opportunity to acquire several minutes of deep prayer by which he exits the work circle, the classroom walls, the collage buildings, and even the boundaries of the visible physical world to enter into the elevated atmospheres of the Spirit…… Those who have experienced the power of prayer know that it lifts and elevates the mind and the heart towards God. The heart and the mind are ruptured instantly to heaven. If the spirit of man is willing, then time is irrelevant and unneeded. It is the willingness to fly high in spirituality, for the fire of the spirit is kindled and won't extinguish.

I encountered, throughout my life, another example of prayer without hindrance…. When prayer is prayed perpetually, it becomes as natural as all life necessities. It becomes like breathing for the body. It occurs automatically and spontaneously without force or effort and acting or imitation.

I know a lady in Christ who lived the Christian life in simplicity and depth simultaneously. I frequented his house, as I am closely related to her…. I would see her in the kitchen, where she was spending prolonged hours serving her family in all love, humility, and sacrifice, wearing an apron on top of her clothes, and in its pocket, there was an Agpya book. Whenever she gets a chance, during kitchen work, even for several minutes, she takes out her Agpya book and lifts her head with a prayer…. Even if she just recited only one Psalm……. She did that all the days…. I joyfully would tell her, "The food is delicious because it is cooked with Psalms." She, with all humbleness and shyness, responds, "What Psalms!!! And what prayers!!!! And where is the time that we spend with the Lord?!!!…… I am embarrassed to be occupied with these things[203]."

In reality, there was nothing that diverted her from prayers, readings, and a calm life. For she, according to what is apparent, was like Martha who performed multiple services. Yet she obtained Mary's heart, the worshipper, the quiet one who chose the good portion that won't be taken away from her.

And among the things that all those who knew her attested were that the life of faithful prayer imprinted on her a unique form of meekness. It manifested in the calmness of her low-pitched voice. I never witnessed her being angry, but in the calmness of the Angels, she lived the days of Heaven on earth. As the life of prayer adorned her with the adornment of the Holy Spirit, the meek and calm that is precious before God. Until she entered into the Glory, she crossed over like the crossing of the calm breeze.

---

[203] Kitchen and housework.

50

A Physician Lives the Life of Prayer

The physicians who deal with the human body once it weakens and gets stormed with diseases are the most capable people to realize the truth about the human being's nature. Concerning the infirmity of the flesh and the fact that it is evanescent.

And those physicians whom I have known, I perpetually brought their attention to matters that were extremely dangerous. So that God shall be glorified by them and through them.

The first matter that needs no proof is…. The body in which we live is extremely feeble. Therefore, there is no room, then, for boasting, arrogance, reliance on oneself, knowledge, or experience that leads a person to the abyss of pride….Seeing the body, as it really is, of the sick people is exactly like a man seeing his own self and acknowledging the despicableness magnitude of our nature and its weakness. This is the path of humility in the physician's life.

I have read about a doctor, whose knowledge surpassed the people of his time, that was one of the pioneers in the treatment of cancer. However, he dealt with the patients like a transcendent god …... He uttered brief phrases and minimal words as if his heart became like a stone that was void of emotions and without appreciation for pain and suffering.

An unexpected incident occurred in the life of that doctor…... He was diagnosed with cancer…. He experienced pain as he started a series of treatments…. The same road that he saw other people tread …... But this time, it was felt and perceived by all standards and aspects…. Luckily for him, the treatment was positively effective, and he was cured of his illness…….But in truth, he was cured of a far more dangerous disease, which is pride.He returned to his work and his sick patients a new man.Merciful, compassionate, and tremendously pitiful.Patients became, for him, as his own flesh.

As such, we have been directing the attention of our beloved toward this fact since the initiation of their professional lives…Thus, many had grown exponentially, not in terms of the success they had achieved in the medical field but according to the development of their spiritual comprehension and realization of that fact[204] And living by its guidelines.

There was another matter that we alerted the minds for, and that was…. Man's capabilities are limited no matter how great they are, and that "Unless the Lord builds the house, they labor in vain who built it."[205]Therefore, man always ought to remember that God is the only one who knows the reason behind a man's illness since he[206] Is the workmanship of His hands[207]And He formed him in the womb before he was born.

A successful physician always acknowledges that the hand of God is the one that extends and grants healing for both the soul and the flesh… Christ is the physician of souls and bodies…. Thus, if the Lord willed and used weak vessels[208] so that He might be glorified…. Then, we ought to give glory to God when He makes our ways successful, and we thank Him if He used us for His glory.

Many beloved people lived and adhered to the Lord, glorifying Him in every day, in every hour.They felt the sincerity of God's faithful promises, and they were amazed by the many things that had happened in their lives.

One of the living examples that testified for Christ's grace and the work of the Holy Spirit was one of our loved ones.He was a renowned physician and adhered to the Lord since his early youth.He frequented our father, Mina, the hermit, in Ancient Egypt, confessing to him and seeking guidance through his paternal advice.When Pope Kirollos sat on the throne of St. Mark the Evangelist, that brother had already graduated from the school of medicine for several years.He became the physician for the Pope during his stay in

---

[204] The body is weak and feeble.

[205] Psalm 127:1
[206] Man.
[207] God.
[208] Human beings

A Physician Lives the Life of Prayer

Alexandria and at St. Mina's monastery. The Pope was fond of him, loved him, and encouraged him in his spiritual path since that brother devoted his life to live as a holy celibate while being in the world[209]. His spiritual life was manifesting vividly and had a good testimony for all the believers and from others as well.

Once his virtues, knowledge, and God's work in his life were revealed. He, then, became one of the most famous doctors and the busiest of them.... He was constantly long-suffering and patient, jovially and copiously praying. He would never place his hand on a prescription pad to prescribe medicine before lifting his heart in a short prayer first. Patients thought that he was squeezing his brain and concentrating on prescribing the proper medicine; on the contrary, he was seeking grace, entreating God's help, and glorifying Him for His love and His mercy.

God bestowed that brother with an astonishing heart that was full of love, deep in humility, and generous in giving. His field of work became a field for serving Christ. Plenty of poor people found in him the tender love of Christ. As he was treating, dispensing medicine, and offering aid in secret.

He practiced the "Sacrificial Service" thousands of times with all sorts of people without discrimination or favoritism. When he was treating one of his patients and realized that his condition was critical, he would not leave him. But he devoted his time, prolonged hours, sitting next to his bed.... And if necessary, he would go, personally, in haste, whether at midnight or dawn, to the only open pharmacy located at "Mehatet El-Ramal," which had medicines available during those times. Then, he eagerly returned to follow up with the case[210] staying awake all that time without a personal request from anyone nor was he concerned about any consideration.... In vain anyone tried to reward him for such work.... He did not get paid any wages for those tasks from anyone whoever he might be.... Even the medicines that he was purchasing in such cases, which were very expensive, he didn't get their price from anyone.

His behavior was wonderful in the sight of the people, for he was not like the rest of the physicians who just performed a duty. But rather, he was commissioned by God to do mercy with all men. Thus, the people loved him tremendously, for they saw in him a depiction of a rare form of love which he received from the One who gave Himself for our sake.

---

[209] In the secular world.
[210] The sick and bed-ridden Patient.

51

The Lord Shall Give You the Desires of Your Heart

Among the loved ones who were contemporary to the beginning of the Church of Saint George at Sporting, a religious family who became attached to the Church, which was displaced from El-Mansoura[211] A long time ago. Then that family bonded with our father Bishoy Kamel with a robust spiritual bond…. The head of the family was a committed and disciplined man, living by the fear of God, and he had a "Living History" with Christ as well as a good fellowship. He had a virtuous wife in the truest sense of the word, for she raised her children in the fear of God. Hence, they all grew servants and deacons, loving God and adhering to His commandments….This is something desirable for the soul to encounter …. That is to find such a joyful spiritual ambiance. If the soul grows in such an environment, it will find support—a powerful support against the evil torrents that are in the world.

The eldest son graduated from the university and occupied an excellent position. As he reached the age of marriage, God blessed him with a religious girl from a Christ-loving family. He became attached to her, and his parents rejoiced. For he was the First Fruits of joy and also as a token for the eternal joy.

The young wife was blessed by God with a magnificent heart, childish simplicity, and pure innocence that was free from the impurities of the world. She was confessing to me as she left her hometown, her father of confession,

---
[211] A Governorate in Lower Egypt.

got married and lived in Alexandria. I found in her a depiction of the pure heart and simplicity of life. I always prayed for her to grow in Grace and the knowledge of our Lord Jesus Christ.

She once approached me asking, "Is every request we ask of God, He grants?" I answered her, "We are accustomed to placing our requests before God, trusting in His benevolence, and that He chooses what is good for our life and beneficial for our eternity, and he gives us according to the riches of His exalted grace and according to our heart that is directed towards Him because it is written, 'The Lord shall give you the desires of your heart.'" She responded, "But I ask of God with all trust and faith. However, it is a strange request!" I asked, "What is it that you requested?" She said, "I ask the Lord to give me twin girls…. I will be delighted…. They shall grow together, and I shall care for them, dress them both in the same identical clothes, and give them the same hairdo… This is my wish and my request of God." I was astonished by that statement, and I dismissed it as naïve childish dreams. How could such things be considered a request?

But I was reconsidering my thoughts saying, "Is it my concern? She is asking the One who accepts the prayer and commands, 'Ask, and it will be given to you[212]'…… So, what do I have to do with evaluating the prayer or its acceptance? Let her be. He who knows the hearts of the humans is the One who gives liberally and without reproach."

Therefore, I told her that regardless of what we ask for, He hears. However, answering the prayer only pertains to Him alone…… She came back after several months and informed me that she was pregnant, and she was still persistent concerning her request to God through the intercessions of the Holy Saint Mary and the prayers of the great martyr Saint George. I continued praying for her while marveling at her faith.

She came to me one day and was very emotional, saying, "Would you believe this? I entered the Church today, and I approached the Icon of Saint George to light a candle. And Behold, the candle had two wicks. I almost flew with joy. It was as if God was talking to me in a voice clearer than any other voice…. Wouldn't this be considered a sign from God?" Truth be told, there was no answer in my mind or my mouth, but I would say to her that God is omnipotent. She came to me on another day with signs of joy appearing more vividly on her continuance, and her faith was exceedingly firm. She said to me, "Once again, after lunch, I reached for a banana …… I peeled it, and

---

[212] Matthew 7:7

Behold, it was twin bananas in one." At that time, there were no devices that revealed the babies' gender in the womb of their mothers ...... The gender of the baby stays unknown until birth.

She completed her days in peace, and upon delivery, she gave birth to twin girls. She was exceedingly happy, not only because of the two girls but because God had granted her request and answered her prayer.

I marveled within, at such firm faith and simple hearts capable of receiving from God in such an inexpressible way. She raised them according to what she promised before God. They grew in the bosom of the Holy Church like two flowers planted by the rivers of the Spirit.

Thus Far, the Lord has helped Us.

PART 4

52

Let Me Die the Death of the Righteous

The children of God are apparent according to the saying of St. John the Beloved in his epistle, and they are distinguished from the children of the world, who are also labeled; "The children of the devil." It is the same saying that the Lord Jesus told the Jewish people: "You are of your father the devil." He also said concerning him, "He is a liar and the father of it."

What distinguishes God's children while they are living on earth emerges vividly at the moments of their departure from this world. This becomes a cause and a method of comfort for the believers, for they witness with their own eyes the genuineness of the faith manifested in a way that eradicates any doubt. This reminds us constantly of the saying in the Book: "Let me die the death of the righteous, and let my end be like theirs!"

The Lord has allowed me to personally meet many of those blessed people whose departure from this fugacious world became a blessing to many, a motivation for those who were far from repentance, and a hope for those who were walking the road of Salvation.

The theme repeated in numerous ways was the gift of insight bestowed upon those righteous before their departure. They saw Heavenly affairs and Godly visions that could not be expressed. One of those was a pious rural man who feared God, lived by His commandments, and was benevolent and kind to everyone. As the head of the family, he was a peacemaker who gave himself to many prayers. He set the perfect example to the rest of his family. They saw in him the Christian perfection in terms of behavior, keeping the commandments of Christ, the love for fasting and prayers, and the sanctification of the soul and the senses. He truly was a righteous example, a sweet living Gospel to everyone. He was the Priest of the family; many had sought his good advice in all aspects of their lives. He was a blessed man and a source of blessings to many others.

The man fell ill in his last days…....yet his prayers did not cease day and night. The thanksgiving he offered to Christ was astonishing. He would say to those around him, "Pray…....pray." He Would plead with them to read the Scripture for him, especially the Psalms. And when they read the Psalms, he would request, saying, "Repeat again." Psalms were his comfort in his sickness and his old age.

When the time of his departure from this world approached, all his family, which exceeded a hundred persons, including loved ones and friends, were gathered in the house. It was a huge house built according to the old style. They all felt the anticipated loss once he departed.

The man would ask those around his bed, "Pray for me the Psalms of the Sext hour." For the time was close to Noon. As they were praying the Psalms, they were deeply affected and troubled, so he would open his eyes and pray the Psalms along with them. As it was his last moment, he crossed himself with the sign of the cross. While being fully alert, he shut his eyes and departed. Everyone began to weep; some ladies, their daughters, and relatives cried and wailed uncontrollably.

The man opened his eyes and said, "Why are all these screams? I asked you to pray the Psalms….my children; you have disturbed me…. I went to heaven and can still hear the heavenly praises." Immediately, one of those present got a paper pad and a pen and said to him, "Please, Grandpa, tell me what you heard so I can document it." The man responded, "My son, these are words that cannot be written. Can the language of heaven be written on earth? No, my son…....." The man closed his eyes and opened them in heaven for Eternity.

How wonderful is the departure of the righteous!!!…. Truly, "Precious in the sight of the Lord is the death of His saints."

53

Only Let Your Conduct Be Worthy of the Gospel of Christ

Another example of the rare spirits I had known to be living a life of humility likened to Christ, a virtuous man occupying an eminent position. He was an expert engineer. Yet, as per the testimonials of all who had collaborated with him, no one had ever seen him angry. This was contrary to all leading positions that required firmness, usually led to punishment, and a strong personality that ought to be feared by the subordinates.

The elevated position did not affect the personality (Attitude) of that pious man.... He was meek and calm and maintained a pleasant, soft tone. Surprisingly, everyone honored him for his humility. His pleasant words were very influential among all of them. None of his subordinates wished to disobey his commands. Hence, the work flowed in a spirit rarely found in other secular organizations.

The man acquired his placidity from his fellowship with his Savior, who said, "Learn from Me, for I am gentle and lowly in heart." Therefore, he gave himself to many prayers, which he spent many hours on. In addition, it was joyful for his Spirit to read the Bible with a simplicity void of philosophical modulation. For him, the Holy Book's contents were for life and never concepts to load the mind with or enhance intelligence.

The Gospel was for the life and only the life.... He told me that the most wonderful verse he was attached to and relied on all his life was what was written in the Epistle to the Philippians: "Only let your conduct be worthy of the Gospel of Christ."He had read it early on in life during his first year in engineering school.He felt that this verse embraces the whole life, so he held on to it……memorizing its words unlike any other words……and repeating its words not in the same manner the tongue repeats the words.He was uttering this verse amply to his children and his family, advising them to live by it.

The man's mingling with people was minimal; he did not have many friends for fear of wasting time.He was a calm person, and he strived to continue being that way.His friends, whom he had chosen, were like himself in seriousness, simplicity, and humility.When they gathered together, they depicted the saying of the Psalm, "Behold, how good and how pleasant it is for brethren to dwell together."

Often, they invited me to join them, as they had met in one of their homes. I was happy to be in their midst, to read the Bible with them, or to pray together.

I felt that I was being relieved from troubles, for my Soul had found solace among those beloved ones.

One day, in the early morning, I was awakened by a phone call. The man's wife was screaming, "Help me……My husband……."My Spirit was troubled…. I am not sure how I wore my garments, how I ran on the streets, or how I reached their house.

His wife opened the door……. She was in a state of astonishment.She said, "Come and see."

I entered his room…. He was asleep…. His face was bright…. His hands were on his chest, holding the Holy Bible.I reached with my arms and took the Bible out of his hands.It was open at the Epistle of Philippians…. My eyes fell upon the verse, "Only let your conduct be worthy of the Gospel of Christ." Its letters appeared as if they were glowing….

It is the verse of life…. The just man lived by it, lifting him to the heavens. He departed, clinging to this verse until he entered the Kingdom of Heaven. Blessed is he.

54

Meekness of the Lambs and Bravery of the Martyrs

We were comforted by the chronicles of the pious saints and the commemoration of the righteous chosen ones during a house visit to one of my beloved brethren, a benevolent man who lived according to the Christian life and faith. He said, "I think that regardless of any extent of revelations concerning the lives of God's children, they won't measure up to what we have experienced during my father's life; may God repose his soul."

Many relatives of that blessed brother were present that evening; they were eyewitnesses to what he was about to reveal concerning his father.

I said, "May we all obtain solace by hearing about the lives of the righteous."

He, while trying to hold back his tears, despite the fact that it had been more than twenty years since his father's departure, continued saying.

"My father was in his early forties, very healthy, and never gotten sick. He was more pleasant, caring, and compassionate toward needy people than anyone in our family. They considered him naïve, for according to their view, he was squandering his money on those in need. He was kindhearted and a merciful person who could neither afford to see nor hear violence or quarrels…. if he happened to be looking out of the balcony and witnessed some people in an altercation, he would rush back inside, for he couldn't stand hearing vulgar expressions, words of insults, or even loud voices."

"He was studious in attending the liturgies and praying the Agpya...... Ecclesiastical teaching and homilies were scarce in his days, particularly in the town where he resided. However, he did not need such teachings because living a Christian life and acquiring virtues were far more important to him."

"My mother, present that evening, was naïve and knew nothing about life except what only pertains to her home and children. She never had to leave the house except to attend the Church."

"My father was wealthy; he owned land and properties and had plenty of money. He managed all his business affairs smoothly while sparing my mother the burden of any responsibility. He provided for all her necessities so that she could enjoy a carefree life. Their life was like a beautiful hymn; we have never heard of any problems between them or seen them engage in a dispute or even disagree."

During this talk, his mother quietly cried, tears running down her angelic face. So, I said, "We are commemorating a person who is in heaven (the port of peace) and relishing eternal joy above all earthly pleasures. So why cry? Please lift your thoughts to where Christ is so the enemy (Satan) won't trouble us."

The blessed brother continued his talk. I interrupted, asking, "When your Dad departed, how old were you?" He answered, "Sixteen." I responded, "Then you were aware of what was happening around you." He said, "Certainly." I said, "Please continue."

"One morning, my father had breakfast with us. Afterward, we left for school, and he stayed home with my mother.... She asked him, "Aren't you leaving for work today?" He answered her, "No, I am off today." He then asked her to come to his office and said with a pleasant smile: "I would like to brief you about some of my documents."

He proceeded to inform her about all his possessions, including land, properties, and money in the banks. She got worried and asked, "Why all this? I don't want to know anything at all." He calmly answered; "You must know.... I spared you this burden for all these years, but today, you must know everything to continue with the responsibility."

She broke down in tears. My Father calmed her down by patting her back and saying, "Why are you acting as such? God, who manages all the creation, will manage your life and look after you.... I completed my days on earth and will be with Christ today."

My mother collapsed, saying, "That is not possible.... This is nonsense.... You are in your prime years and healthy. If you feel sick, we should call the family doctor." My father responded, "Believe me, my dear, I am, as you said, young and healthy, but this is the will of God." My Mom said, "Please, enough with this silly talk; if you want me to share the responsibility with you, I will."

My father concurred and proceeded to inform her about all his business affairs. He then made several phone calls, and my mother left for her room. Afterward, my father left the office, went into the bathroom, showered, put on new clothes, lay on his bed, and read the Psalms from the Agpya. My mother found him asleep on his bed.... he submitted his soul into Christ's hands. She began wailing in disbelief.

Moments later, my Aunt showed up. At that time, she lived in a town about an hour and a half away from our house. She stated, "My brother was not human; he was an Angel."

My father called her earlier, saying, "I am traveling now, and I want you to come right away because my wife is upset, and I would like you to be with her, please." My Aunt responded, "What bothers her about your travel?" He answered, "I don't know." She said, "There must be something else." He told her, "When you arrive, you will know."

The neighbors gathered in our house as soon they heard about my father's sudden departure.

Then, a person from the funeral home arrived, informing us that my father (Arch engineer Paul) had contacted them two hours earlier regarding a death in the family and asking for the setup of a marquee. That person, a Muslim, when he heard the details of my father's death, he proclaimed saying, "Truly, your worship is true. You had saints and still have saints; I have seen with my eyes and heard with my ears."

When my mother and my aunt entered my father's office to inquire about his documents, they found a letter written by him on top of his desk. It was his own obituary. He prepared everything because he knew that my mother, at this moment, would not know what to do, and she did not have any brothers who would help her.

We believe God had bestowed my mother with a spirit of discernment through my father's prayers. She was prestigious among the farmers who worked at her farms. She didn't experience any of the difficulties often encountered in her situation. Thanks be to God; we trust that my Father's Spirit is living with us, praying and interceding on our behalf.

We then prayed and felt within us that our brethren who departed and went up to the paradise of joy are the greatest support for us here on earth.

55

Whom I Have in Heaven
Psalm 73

Regarding the Visions and the Heavenly Revelations that are perceived by the righteous in the event of their departure, which serve as final consolation prior to the removal of their Earthen body…for here (on earth) we live by faith which is the substance of things hoped for and the evidence of things not seen, we say, that those Visions are the beginning of the end for the days of faith (life on earth) …. The dense body begins to perish as an opaque cloth, which obstructs the vision, yet upon its disintegration and the loosening of its fabric, vision becomes possible through it. Till it entirely deteriorates, then the vision becomes clear and unhindered. Or as the same as the darkness of dawn that gets interspersed by the rays of the sun upon its rising, dissipating it till light is absolute.

This does not happen only to the righteous…… Despite the difficulty of the removal of the Earthen body, we do not want to remove it but rather wish to acquire the Heavenly body moreover, as this is the nature of the flesh and the consequence of living in a confined body, or at least it is what science labels, "Instinct of survival." This instinct is embedded in our nature. However, the new instinct of the new man and the new creation desires the Heavenly and longs for it with unexpressed emotions, just as the saying of St. Paul, "Having a desire to depart and be with Christ, which is far better." We also may say that these Visions and Heavenly revelations establish within the soul the trust in the Lord and the courage to face death. This is truly marvelous.

I knew a virtuous sister since I began serving in Los Angeles in the late Seventies, 1978…She was a devout wife and a mother of three children who came to Los Angeles in 1978. A year after her arrival, she was diagnosed with Cancer and started the treatment. The road of therapy lasted more than 15 years, through which she fluctuated between weakness and strength, sickness and health, torment, and joy…. However, to all who knew her, she became a beautiful icon of patience, thanksgiving that never ceases, and courage during the days of distress.

I kept visiting her for a month before her departure; doctors declared that treatment wouldn't benefit her anymore; we shared a true Godly love through fellowship in Christ. And as she heard the word of life (Bible), she held on to it with unrivaled courage and unfading hope in Christ.

However, Satan, the enemy of all that is good, does not let go of a chance to plant seeds of doubt, hoping that the soul, during its state of weakness, would be susceptible to his arrows.

NEVER; those who hold on to the Victorious are victorious, and those who abide in the Lord of Resurrection do not die.

This reminded me of what I have read in the book "The Sayings of the Fathers" concerning one of the Fathers on the day of his departure. His brethren surrounded him so they might receive his last blessings. He turned and saw Satan by the window of his cell, so he said to his disciple in a loud voice, "Hand me my cane, for he thinks I am frail and about to die." As soon as his disciple handed him the cane, Satan disappeared. All the assembled brethren witnessed this. They glorified God, who grants His children victory and strength in the hour of their death…. "They are truly VICTORIOUS."

This blessed sister asked me while we were gathered around her, saying, "Tell me the truth which is of Christ; why is it that the children of God suffer and are tempted by diseases and aches while the people of the world rejoice?

She was asking on behalf of her children and all those gathered around her, for they were confused and dubious. She wished that they would hear a word of benefit for themselves. And if they listen to it from the mouth of the Priest, they would be assured of God's wisdom and trust His love. I answered her while aiming my talk to everyone, "I will not answer this question on my own, but I will direct you to the written Godly word that reveals the thoughts of God concerning us… How easy it is for the Bible to answer people's questions so that there is no room for doubt and no room for the devil to deceive.

I requested the Holy Bible and opened it to Psalm "73," which talks about this issue in astounding detail, revealing the last results of God's intents. The Psalmist was confused about how the people of the world lived in prosperity while the children of God were tempted. Hence, he said, "My steps had nearly slipped." …… and "Until I went into the Sanctuary of God." then he realized their end. They were cast down to destruction just as the grass of the soil, while the children of God, whenever they may enter into the glory upon the fair judgment, will be blessed with what eye have not seen, nor ear have heard, nor have entered into the heart of man…… Therefore, the Psalmist concluded his talk by saying, "I was like a beast before You, and I was so foolish and ignorant."Confessing that God's judgments are unreachable and His ways past finding out! Hence, he exclaimed, "Whom have I in heaven but You?And there is none upon earth that I desire besides You."

We read the Psalm in serenity and then again, word by word. Its words consoled us, and as much as the Grace furnished that evening, we received and accepted as support and nourishment for our lives.

After two or three weeks, the blessed sister reached her final stages, as per the opinion of the doctors. They said it was a matter of days and she would leave this world.As an ongoing custom, they sent phycologists to prepare her emotionally to accept death.But by Christian kindness, confidence, and courage, she informed them, "I am not afraid of death for I know where I am going… Thank you for your kindness, but please do not revisit me; perhaps someone other than me needs you.As for me, I will not die in days, as the doctors said. For my life is in the hands of my Christ, and He is the one who revives and is the one who permits death."

And so, it was not three days.God had extended her time three weeks…… afterward; she delivered her soul into the hands of the Lord in wonderful peace and heavenly calmness.I went to her home, read the Bible, and received comfort from the words of the Eternal Life.Two days later, it was the funeral.… her three sons stood around the casket upon the conclusion of the prayers.I was surprised that they recited Psalm 73 overtly in front of all present in the Church.They memorized it, for she made them recite it numerous times daily.

56

Prayer Is Better than Life

The generation before ours had the tradition of sleeping early and waking up in the middle of the night or early morning for prayers and praises.

Since ancient times, night has been allocated for worship. Its serenity helps the soul in prayers and praises.

Christians are considered new creations chosen for praise and thanksgiving because of the grace of Jesus Christ. Prayers in the early morning, as the darkness dissipates, reflect the dissipation of the darkness of death as the Lord has shone upon us, eliminating the sting of death by His Resurrection. It is a joyful time of resurrection, light, and life.

What a joyful hour that the Christian person experiences daily, biased toward the true light, putting on the armor of God, and fighting darkness...... And darkness doesn't comprehend him.

What helped the previous generation of believers acquire such piety was their inability to stay up late at night, for there was no electricity, hence no television, and no venues for parties that ended late at night.

There were none of the things, as nowadays, that consumed the time and diverted the mind and the heart away from life and the spirit of prayer. None of the things that distorted the thoughts by sins of lust, lecherousness, and debauchery....... Where is the Spirit of Prayer from all these, then?!

Here are some examples of the pious people who lived by prayers and spent the nights offering gratitude.

In the late sixties of the last Century, precisely 1968, I got acquainted with a family from a city called Mahala (in Lower Egypt) and resided in a county called Elibrahemia (In Alexandria). An elderly man living along with his wife in a small apartment...... Their children were married and lived in various places according to God's plan for their lives. The man was pure and simple, living in humility as he aged gracefully. He and his wife depicted the saying, "They were both righteous before God, walking in all the commandments and ordinances of the Lord blameless." When I visited them, I witnessed a superb icon simultaneously portraying the advancement in days and grace.

The man had gotten weak, and his health deteriorated. Yet he continued with his prayer ritual. He was always praying and enjoying fellowship with Christ, whom he loved, and the support of the saints hedged him.

The man would start his day by reading from the Old and the New Testament, then reading the newspaper, especially the obituaries section, which he labeled "The Synaxarion of this day." He then proceeds to eat breakfast, run some errands for the house, and then yields to rest. In the afternoon, he recites the Psalms, and at sunset, he prays and eats supper before going to bed around 8 PM. His neighbors cherished his company, for they considered him a blessed man. They kept in touch with him through visitation; however, once they knew that he slept early, they limited their visitation time to 8 pm or, at maximum, 9 pm.

The man would wake up around midnight...... wash his face and hands, as per the Tradition of the Fathers, and then stand up for prayers, reciting the midnight Psalms and some doxologies and hymns he had memorized during his youth. He received this prayer ritual from his uncle, known for living a pure, pious, celibate life. This uncle kept himself holy spiritually and physically.

The man's pious wife would join him in prayers most of the time, but sometimes, overpowered by fatigue, she would pray while resting in bed. As the man advanced in age, he continued to rise as usual at midnight. His wife said to him sympathetically, "My brother.[213] You cannot do this anymore; why don't you pray while lying on your bed? God will not hold this against you." She kept telling him these words whenever she found him slow in his motion. However, he always assured her that prayers heal the ailing body and console the heart

---

[213] It is very common in Egypt for the husband to call his wife "My sister", and for the wife to call her husband "My brother" when they advance in age.

It is customary for Egyptian newspapers to mention the names of the departed people daily as requested by their families. They reserve several pages for such tradition.

and spirit. "For if my body is fragile.... prayer would support and strengthen it, the Lord Jesus said, 'The Spirit indeed is willing, but the flesh is weak.'"

One night, he lost his balance and fell while getting off his bed. His wife, disturbed, helped him to his feet, refuting, "I told you, my brother, that you are not capable......do you want to die?" The man answered as he was leaning on her for support, "My sister, I prefer ending my life while prostrating to my Savior, knowing that I don't deserve it. I die while praying is better than I die laying on my bed."

The man, pushing himself, washed his hands and face. He stood up, lifting his hands despite severe weakness, and prayed. Then he prostrated to the floor while saying, "Holy God......" His prostration was prolonged.... the wife was following up with the prayers while on her bed.... She fell asleep, maybe for several minutes, then woke up and saw him still prostrating. She wanted to call him but feared that this might interrupt his prayers. She waited a bit longer...... Maybe he fell asleep! She talked to him.... He didn't respond.... she got out of bed.... drew near to wake him up……...!

His body was in a state of worship, yet his soul was among the true worshippers who worship God in spirit and truth. God is seeking such worshippers. The good woman was stunned that his request was granted at such speed. Truly, Prayer is better than life.

57

In the Name of Jesus

In the summer of 1968, I was visiting the home of one of my beloveds, Samir El Wazzan. He belonged to a prominent family from the Governorate of Aswan, with whom (The family) I had a wonderful benevolent relationship in Christ. We were gathered at their home, located on Ulbokha Street in the county of Choubra, being comforted by reading the Scriptures and meditating on the lives of the saints and by our "one accord" prayers. Present along with me, at that meeting, a good young lad who was a friend of that family.

While we were assembled, one of the brethren said, "My grandmother is inside, and she wishes to be amongst us. Would there be an objection?" I answered, "Of course not; why should she be inside alone?" The brother elaborated, saying, "She is embarrassed, as she is timid by nature." I said, "There are no strangers here; I am a priest; Brother Akram (the young lad) is known to the family and all of you…. So why the embarrassment?"

The brother went and brought her…. She was so advanced in age…. Over eighty. She was swaddled by her black clothes, as per the tradition of her culture, and only a part of her face was visible. She greeted me with extreme shyness. I said to her, "Please join us." …. She went to the room's corner and sat on the floor. So, I said, "Mother, it is not fitting for you to sit on the floor." And I made room for her beside me on the sofa…. Her grandsons tried convincing her to sit beside me, but they couldn't. She kept saying, "Shame on you boys, how could I sit alongside the Priest? It is an honor I don't deserve." I marveled at the genuine humility of a lady as old as my grandmother. So, I said to them, "Let her be."

We resumed our talk from the Bible as she was listening silently. Then I wanted her to be at ease, so I asked her, "Tell me, mother, have you lived in Upper Egypt alone?" She answered, "No, we were a big family, old and young, living in one house. The family house…" I said, "So you were living with your Mother-in-law." She said, "Yes." Then I added, "And with your sisters-in-law in the same house?" She answered, "Yes." I smiled, saying, "So, have you ever quarreled with each other?!" The Lady was shocked; "Shame! Quarrel?!…. how could that be? We used to pray the doxologies together while working and operating the grindstone."

Some of the youth asked me, "What do these sayings mean?" I explained the grindstone to them and how the women knew the Tasbeha by heart. And while they were doing the housework, they kept praising and praying…. They were living an authentic, genuine Christian life.

As we stood up to pray, the lady asked one of her grandchildren, "Would it be possible for Abouna to pray over my head? I said since I heard her, "With gladness." She said, "But you will take…!" I inquired, "Take what?" She said, "Money." I responded, "Mother, prayers are without money…. Moreover, we are in an era where the priest receives a salary." She said, "If you don't accept, you will not pray for me." I said, "Believe me, I am not in need." She said, "Who said you are in need? Take it and do as you wish. Don't you know people who are in need? I answered, "Alright, I accept it from you as a blessing."

She placed her hand into a small bag and handed me her offerings. My friend Akram (the young lad), who had a sense of humor, said to her, "Do you just give for the sake of giving? …. Grandma! Are you giving away your money? Give me as well." She answered him, "Say 'In the name of Jesus.'" He said laughingly, "In the name of Jesus."

The lady reached into the bag, and without counting the money, she placed it into his hands. All who were present joyfully laughed. I prayed over her head as she wished, and then we all prayed the Vespers Psalms. When we were about to leave, the young lad said to her, "Thank you, grandma…." attempting to give her back the money. She responded very firmly, saying, "What! My son? You asked in the name of Jesus, and I gave you. It is impossible for what I gave in the name of Jesus to be taken back."

This brother tried to give her back the money, but she left for her room.

It was a lesson for all who were present regarding the simplicity of the Christian life, humility, the life of prayers, and the life of giving and offering in the name of Jesus.

"We recognize a tree by its fruit… we ought to be able to recognize a Christian by his action. Being a Christian is more than making sound professions of faith; it should reveal itself in practical and visible ways."

– St. Ignatius of Antioch, Epistle to the Ephesians

58

The Sermon on the Mount

It was an "Annual tradition" for the Christian students attending the School of Engineering at the University of Alexandria to conduct a ceremony at the Church of St. George at Sporting (the vicinity name). They invited the teachers and the professors. The ceremony was interspersed with contests and simple, humorous acts in which both the professors and the students participated, spending some time in the spirit of joy and fun.

Afterward, our father, Bishoy Kamel, or any other father (Priest) present, would give a spiritual sermon to strengthen the bonds of love and aid in acquiring a better life.

1966 I was invited to the ceremony with many other teachers and professors. Next to me sat one of those professors, Dr. George. I had minimal knowledge of him since he worked at a different branch. When we met (at work), we only acknowledged each other. He was a calm and quiet man by nature, not social, and his friends were very few.

During the ceremony, Dr. George's name was announced to take part in a contest. The man stood up, his face turned red and went up to the stage. One of the students asked a series of questions, and he answered.

Question: What is the number of the Bible Books? The man replied, "I do not know any numbers except the 'Absolute Zero.'"

Everybody burst into laughter.

Another student asked him a question from the Old Testament. The man responded, "My son, this question is impossible to answer."

A third question followed, yet the man did not know the answer.

Another student played a piece from the Church hymns. Dr. George was then asked about it. With a sense of humor, the doctor took out one Egyptian pound ($1) from his pocket, gave it to the one who played the melody, and said, "May God bless you, my son."

All those present laughed and applauded…. yet wondering how a professor didn't know this or that question.

At that point, Dr. George took the microphone and said to the audience, "Believe me, truly, I do not know the answers to these questions. And this is my fault. To tell you the truth, I know nothing except the Sermon on the Mount," which is recorded in the Gospel according to St. Matthew chapters 5, 6, and 7. I read these every day, and I try to live according to its commandments to the best of my ability."

The hall burst into applause. The doctor then got off the stage and returned to his seat beside mine. My respect for the man increased. For he, as much as he was able, strived to keep the commandants of Christ and tried to live by them. I greeted him and said, "Truly, indeed, Christianity is a way of life that manifests in the behavior. It would be my pleasure to get to know you better." Almost a year later, I was ordained priest. Hence, I got the opportunity to know him closely…. I visited him at his home…. Tremendous humility and meekness…. Simplicity in life….and true love was anchored in that placid family.

When we recalled what was said in the ceremony, I found him truly a forgiving, tolerant Christian man; in situations of injustice, he didn't grumble. If he were compelled, he would go the second mile. The other cheek, he would give willingly with joy following the commandments of his Master. The words of the Sermon on the Mount were engraved and inscribed in his heart, mind, and actions, whether at work, home or in all his dealings with all the people.

I truly realized that Christianity is neither memorization nor information for a person to load into his brain to enhance intelligence. But the mystery of the Christian life is within the love of Christ and in keeping his commandments—not by the words of the tongue but by the works and the truth.

59

The Feast of Nayrouz

On the night of the Nayrouz Feast of September ten, 1976, our Church at Sporting was highly crowded, for we (the Church Priests) have channeled the emphasis of our congregation toward celebrating this feast, not only because it was a National holiday for the Copts but because it was the beginning of the calendar that originated from the ancient Egyptian calendar. But even more so on the basis that the Copts were the ones who chose the year 283 AD, the year in which Diocletian (The greatest persecutor of Christians) ascended to the throne of Rome. This confirms the pride of the Copts in the martyrdom for Christ. Our Church has offered her best of virtuous and pious souls to Christ. Each of them had a distinctive love for Him.

The biographies and the accounts of the martyrs may appear similar, and their testimonials may seem repetitive. But in reality, each of those martyrs is different and possesses a unique sweet aroma. We were assuring our congregation that our Coptic Church truly is the mother of all martyrs and that every Coptic person is biologically related to one or more martyrs. If one is to go back in time, he will find, within his family, more than one martyr.

The martyr's blood certainly circulates through every Coptic person's veins.

It was the habit of Abouna Bishoy Kamel, during the Nayrouz, to gather as many of the martyrs' Icons as possible and initiate a Church procession right after the prayer of "Efnoti Nai Nan." He raised lots of incense to the icons as he walked, almost leaping because of the spiritual joy that flowed out of his heart. The congregation would receive that spiritual joy and rejoice inexpressibly.

During the vespers, as the praises rose toward heaven, stones and bricks were thrown at the Church. Satan was fed up with this ever-renewing spirits of the martyrs who defeated him. So, he used his followers and helpers, just as it was in the days of Stephen, filling the hearts of some of them with hatred and anger. They gathered at the tram station before the Church and started stoking the building with bricks. The bricks hit some Church windows, and the shards spread like fire.

Suddenly, one of the ladies screamed as a stone hit and smashed her reading glasses; her eyes and face bled profusely. Church personnel and some youth ran toward the tram station, but the brick-throwers fled. I came down from the Church (from the upper floor) hastily.... I contacted the officials.... they came to the Church immediately, apologizing for such shameful acts.

Abouna Bishoy Kamel ran toward "Linda," the injured lady, trying to contain the bleeding from her eye and her face. Surprisingly, despite the pain, the lady kept uttering words of thanksgiving, saying, "Thanks be to God Abouna, Anjaiel (Abouna's Bishoy wife) was sitting next to me, and thanks be to God she was not hit by the stone. Thank God that none of the young girls were also hit by it. I am an old woman; my eye is not that important. This is the blessing of Nayrouz.... I am Joyful."

All who were present were astonished by that spirit and those words. Abouna Bishoy rushed her, driving his car, to the ophthalmologist.... Dr. Maher Mikhael was one of our beloveds. The doctor lifted the bandages that were placed on the eye.... It was still bleeding, and glass fragments were scattered within. He informed Abouna, "I can't do anything right now." He gave her a painkiller and another pill to help stop the bleeding, saying, "She can come tomorrow to reexamine the eye."

Abouna Bishoy and the lady returned to the Church.... We were still with the officials who sympathized with us, mainly because of the lady's injury.

Abouna Bishoy adored that lady because of her kind heart and unblemished love for Christ. So, he always said, "Linda will be tossed into Heaven. As soon as they see her, the Angels will let her in without uttering a word."

The lady insisted on staying up with us the night of Nayrouz, during which we would recite the Psalms and the Praises and conclude with the Nayrouz Liturgy. We tried to dissuade her from staying and advised her to rest at home. In vain were all our attempts to convince her. She stayed up praying the Psalms and the Praises until morning.... Then she received Communion and left for her home.

Abouna Bishoy and I accompanied her to Dr. Maher's office in the evening. He lifted the bandage from her eye, and what an astonishing surprise for all of us! The eye was fully intact—there were no traces of a scratch, a cut, a glass fragment, or anything else.

We glorified Christ and leaped with praises. Her injured eye became as flawless as her other eye. The doctor assessed its vision……..It was perfect.

Glory be to You, O Lord. Blessed are You. For Your Glory is manifested in all Your Saints.

Intercede all you saintly martyrs on our behalf and brace our faith until the last breath.

60

Not by "Measure" God Gives the Spirit

On a Sunday evening about eight years ago, I went out for visitation near the Church where I serve, called "Torrance" ......A mountainous area that is adjacent to the ocean. Such places are much quieter, and their streets are not lit at night so that they may keep the rural calm. The Family of Dr. Magdy lived in this neighborhood: he, his wife, and their two children. It was a home that I was visiting for the first time. I got to meet and to know them....Dr. Magdy was from Alexandria; he had known Abouna Bishoy Kamel since his days of serving at the Church of St. Mary located in Moharram Beck. The wife, named Magda, was a pleasant and peaceful lady, and humility was apparent in her countenance.

We gathered and read the Bible....... Their knowledge of it was minimal due to many years of traveling between Canada and the United States, and most of the time, there was no Church nearby. Besides, it was also due to the busyness, rush of life, and social obligations.

Anyway, we read and talked about comprehending the Bible and living joyfully according to its words. We read that Ezekiel the Prophet indeed ate the Divine Word, which was in his mouth like honey in sweetness. I informed them that we study the Bible during Vespers every Saturday. They accepted with joy and started attending as much as their time permitted.

Our sister Magda was like a thirsty soil deprived of water, but once water was available, she rushed with all sincerity and seriousness to drink for it (That is the Fountain of Life) .... The life of prayers that she discovered in the Psalms became her daily source of happiness and joy. In the Eucharist, she found the green pastures and the still water (Ps. 23). In the Liturgies and the Mystical Communion, she found satiation, joy, and comfort. A great door (of knowledge) was opened for her by the Holy Bible. She started reading it with such an astonishingly illuminated mind, with awareness and an unparalleled accurate understanding. Then she aimed toward the spiritual books, seeking them diligently, reading and learning.... her spirituality multiplied.

She heard that there was a seminary school, so one day, she came to me inquiring, "What is the Seminary?" I answered her, "It is a college for spiritual and ecclesiastical studies." She asked, "Is it possible for me to attend this college?" I said, "It is very possible." She joined the Seminary with a serious attitude. And as a student, she was devout in her attendance.... Whenever she acquired some spiritual knowledge, she shared it with her husband in any way and whenever possible.

Her husband was extremely happy for her and always said, "Magda, who had no knowledge of anything, had become full of blessings and virtues. By the Grace of God, she can teach many others." In reality, what she had gained and learned in such little time was tremendous, and it gave the impression that she had spent many years acquiring such knowledge.

And then all of a sudden.... She felt the symptoms.... Then the labs and tests.... Then the discovery of bladder cancer.... Then the operations and the exhausting treatments.... And the weariness and the cruel pain.... A vicious spiral that took them by surprise. But in all that, their lives in Christ were getting brighter, and Grace had imprinted the features of saints on her face. She never ceased to offer Thanksgivings day and night. Her endurance, non-complaining, and non-grumbling attitude astonished everyone around her.

A pious lady living in a faraway area showed unparalleled care for Magda. She left her home for extended periods to stay by her side, especially during her hospitalization. They spent all the time in prayers and Holy readings; even their silence was for Christ's sake and glory. That blessed, pious lady witnessed and declared, "In my life, I have neither seen such ugliness of disease nor have I ever seen such endurance."

Magda was always smiling, not talking much, and no one had ever heard a rebuke from her till the last breath of her life...... Her relationship with Christ was mysterious and astounding. The Grace had led her to a deep knowledge of Christ in an extraordinarily short time. She believed all the mysteries hidden from her on earth would be revealed in heaven.

I visited her, and every time I did, I discovered wonders…… Truly, "Wonderful is the Lord in His saints." And wonderful are His dealings with the chosen souls…. Who can comprehend them?

One day before her departure, I was with her at the hospital. She said to me, "Take care of Tassoni ……." That Tassoni had a complicated family issue…. Her husband had a stubborn mentality and sharp attitude…In vain were all the attempts of many people who tried to change his ways in life. I told her, "You know everything, personal characters are different…. Can one's character change?!" She answered, "Yes, it can." I inquired, asking, "How?" She said after closing her eyes for several seconds, "THE GRACE……. THE GRACE." I thought to myself, for I was deeply touched, saying, "She certainly knew the path…. The Grace is capable of everything." I told her while smiling, "I promise to take care of this, so what are you offering me? She answered with such a magnificent seriousness as her face shone with Grace, "I promise to pray for you there in Heaven." I said, "We have an agreement." I prayed for her and left.

I feel that she is supporting me with her prayers there as she promised, and I am confident that all the chosen souls have favor with Christ. And what a favor….

61

January 11th

Our Father (Abouna) Bishoy Kamel, may God repose his soul, taught at El-Ramel High School upon graduating from the faculty of science in 1951. At that time, his age was about the same as most of his students. Hence, he became friends with them, and they appreciated him tremendously and respected him for his copious knowledge, decency, and manners.

Abouna Bishoy had acquired a distinguished, wise personality despite his young age.

Later, his students always boasted that they were among all he had taught. They saw in his unique, rare behavior the role model and the epitome of the perfect life that ought to be lived. The Christian students were incredibly joyful with the portion they received.

Among the pupils of Abouna Bishoy were two brothers, now they are professors at the college of medicine, whose father, Dr. Maurice Mikhaeel, may God repose his soul, was a good Christian man who loved Abouna Bishoy with such love that was pure and scarce. Once every while, we would visit the home of Dr. Maurice, seeking comfort through the Word of God and by praying. On one of those visits, toward the end of December, all the family was gathered. Women and men, relatives and loved ones. Among those who were present was the brother of Dr. Maurice. A sailor that spent most days of the year traveling at sea between the countries of the world…. He was a quiet man…In his Fifties…He has been living alone since he was unmarried.

The man was sitting in silence and was sullen, So Abouna Bishoy, who knew him well, asked, "What is the matter?" The man responded, "Thanks be to God, Abouna."

One of Dr. Maurice's daughters said, "Let me tell you, my holy fathers, what the matter with my Uncle is." I jestly responded, "My daughter, the man, lives alone with God and has no problems." She said, "My Uncle has this belief, I don't know its source, that he will die on January 11th…every year toward the end of December, he becomes distressed, silent, and may suffer from sickness…But once January 11th passes……. He regains his health and is eager to enjoy life. He becomes normal in all and every aspect."

Abouna Bishoy asked her, "Did your Uncle complain to you about this? He then said, "We live for Christ.… No one lives for himself, and no one dies for himself. For if we live, we live to the Lord; and if we die, we die to the Lord. Therefore, whether we live or die, we are the Lord's." Abouna redirected the talk from a personal issue to an issue that concerns everyone regarding our lives and our journey on earth, which only lasts a few days, despite how long we might live. And that Christ commanded us to watch, pray, and be vigilant so that one can preserve himself in faith, holiness, and love and be prepared in accordance with the saying of St. John the Apostle; "And now, little children, abide in Him, that when He appears, we may have confidence and not be ashamed before Him at His coming."

We concluded our visit, we prayed, and we left. When we got into the car, I asked Abouna Bishoy, for I marveled at what I had heard, "How truthful are 'these sayings' or 'this feeling' or, as they said, 'this belief'?" Abouna replied, "There are many secrets that no one knows…" I responded, "This means what we heard is true." He said, "Believe me, the secrets of the soul with Christ are above our thoughts and comprehension ……. Spending prolonged time in the wilderness or at sea leads the soul into meditation. The soul then finds none other than Christ present.… only then can man discover the truth about himself, void of any frills (void of any self-righteousness or justifications), and enter with Christ into a sincere, truthful, loving relationship. Hence, secrets are revealed to him." I said, "Then you believed what we heard." He said, "I didn't deny it.…What if the man has a personal relationship with God…? Why this should be a concern to anybody? Why the curiosity of the people?

Our conversation ended as we continued with the visits and the service.… Time went by, and I forgot about that matter.

January 11th

I revisited the house of Dr. Maurice.... I inquired about the Uncle, and they said, "He is fine; January 11th passed already."

After many years, I can't recall the count, Dr. Maurice's daughter came to me crying. I asked, "What is the matter?" She answered, "My Uncle passed away." I asked, "When?" She replied, "January 11th."

I recalled that day, that visit, and those words of Abouna Bishoy.... I marveled as I remembered the words in my mind.... How astonishing are the secrets of the human soul when it finds Christ and abides in Him? Only then does it discover the unknown.

62

Angelic Glimmer

In early August of the year 1989, we began, by the Grace of Christ, building the Church in the name of the great martyr Philopateer Markorious and Saint Abba Abram, the bishop of Fayyoum, at the city of Torrance in California. Previously, we had no place for praying.... We used to pray one Liturgy every two weeks on Saturday at a Greek Church.... There was a Protestant Church for sale. However, the Copts did not purchase it. A Pakistani businessman bought it to convert it into an Islamic Center. As we realized the necessity of acquiring a temporary place for prayers, we leased that Church from the Pakistani man. That took place on the day of the feast of the Lady Virgin on the 22nd of August 1989... We began praying the Saturday Vespers and Sunday Liturgy in that place.... (It was the will of the Lord that we purchased this Church after several months).

The Lease agreement only permitted us to use the Church for three hours on Saturday evening and three hours on Sunday morning. Yet, we were also praying twice weekly on Wednesdays and Fridays and certain occasions like Christmas and the Feast of the Theophany.... we were able to do so because the Pakistani businessman rented a house, which was adjacent to the Church, to an American man whom he also hired as a property manager. He, the manager, rented some of the rooms and offices for us, which allowed us to pray at other times when needed. We thanked God for He had eased our situation.

The brethren who cared for the Church were blessed, loving, and zealous despite their minimal knowledge of the ecclesiastical economy regarding Rituals, Spiritual Life, Sacraments, or Hymns. But they were eager to learn and had enormous potential, which encouraged us tremendously.

Initially, we organized a class for the adults to learn hymns.... tutoring the adults was an extremely challenging task...... They came exhausted after work to my house, where we conducted all our meetings; we were not allowed to gather in the Church after the Liturgies, once or twice weekly. My son Arsani had spent a great deal of effort with them so that they could just learn the short hymns and the Liturgy responses. On the contrary, when he tutored the little children, those who grew up in the Church, they learned all the hymns, even the annual ones.

Among those who attended the adult hymns class, a unique person in his seriousness and contentious attendance.... A pleasant, calm person.... angelic in character.... very meek.... his tone of voice was more of a whisper than an audible sound.... his features and countenance put all who knew him at ease.

He eagerly asked questions, especially after hearing the Gospel interpretation of vespers and the Liturgy, to satisfy his desire for Spiritual knowledge. He received the Biblical Word with such joy that he lived by it.

In late October 1989, Pope Shenouda visited Los Angeles for the second time.... The first time was in 1977. The second visit took place after the events of 1981 and his confinement in the Monastery for more than three years.... Hence, his coming to Los Angeles was a cause of joy for all his congregation. It was a Feast.... The Churches that he visited became overcrowded.

His Holiness prayed on Sunday, October 30th, at the Church of St. Mark the Apostle, and since we didn't have a Church.... we and our congregation prayed at the Church of St. Mark as well. It was a joyous day; his Hollins prayed, sermonized, elevated some fathers to the rank of Hegumen, ordained deacons, and baptized children.... That day, I saw that brother standing before me like an Angel.... I introduced him to His Holiness, among others....... He asked me about his name.... And he ordained him "Chanter". During his ordination, I saw the tears of humbleness and unworthiness running down his face, which turned slightly reddish due to his shyness and the prestige of the event...... It was his first time meeting the Pope.

He continued attending the Bible study meeting, which we conducted in our house for the youth, who were few. Yet he was glad to be among them while he was an adult in his thirties, working as an engineer, married, and a father of a six-year-old daughter. Once the meetings were concluded and everyone left, he would ask permission to stay longer. We were happy to have him in our midst.

On January 18th of 1990, at 7 PM, we were at the Church to celebrate the Feast of the Theophany...... Lakkan, Matins, and the Liturgy. Everything was primitive. Few people came and prayed with us from the start. When we prayed at the Lakkan, only a few were present. I realized it was a weekday, neither Saturday nor Sunday; people were at work that day and expected to go to work the next day.... They haven't adapted to the Church Rituals yet. We prayed the Matins....However, the number of people hasn't increased much since the Liturgy began. The deacons were only four....... We had no issues regarding the congregation's responses and hymns, for Arsani has been leading the prayers since he was ten years old at the Church of St. Mark in Los Angeles, where we served in 1977. But who was to pray for the Altar responses during the Liturgy?(Well, in such circumstances, the priority was praying and obtaining the Grace through the Baptism of our Savior. It was a beginning.... a tiny seed that shall grow by the Grace of Christ.)

I instructed one of the deacons to enter and serve at the altar, and then I told that brother (who was serving as a chanter), "Serve at the altar."He softly apologized, saying, "I don't know how."I responded to him and said, "We will pray together; knowledge is insignificant."He said, "I never entered into the Altar."I assured him, "That is OK." …….. He tried to apologize again, so I told him, "As you can tell, we are few and have no choice. What matters is that we pray, offer the sacrifice, and lift our hearts to God. Mastering the hymns is not as important as praying in Spirit and with the humble heart that God shall not despise."

We offered the Lamb, recited the thanksgiving prayer, and offered incense. Then the deacons began reading the Epistles…. He came to me during the readings and said, "How can I serve in the Holy Altar while I know nothing? This is beyond me, for I am unworthy."I said, "Believe me, none of us are worthy of approaching the Altar, but we do so because of Christ's grace. We approach not because of worthiness but because of the need."He said, "Allow me then to confess my sins and my unworthiness…."

He then spoke into my ears with rare words of humility and humbleness. I was embarrassed and pitied myself, for I realized that many simple people violently took the Kingdom by force and without blemish, as the saying of Abba Anthony.

Arsani recited the long hymns up to the Gospel. It was past 10 PM. I said a short sermon in about ten minutes, and we started the Liturgy of the Faithful. I prayed the Liturgy hastily, contrary to my practice, and indicated to

Arsani not to recite prolonged hymns throughout the Liturgy prayers. I don't know why. Or why did I feel such an impulse?

During the Communion, I realized that the men and women who approached to receive communion were so few that they could have been counted by hand. I gave the Body of Christ to the Deacons once, twice….and up to seven times……We dismissed the Angel of the Sacrifice……. dismissed the congregation…. and offered our thanksgiving to the Lord Christ for his inexpressible Grace……. Then, everyone headed home.

That brother was the only one from his family who was present……His wife was exhausted after work…. His little daughter fell asleep……His mother feared sickness because the weather was frigid…. Hence, he attended the Liturgy of the Feast by himself.He drove back to his house. It was midnight, and he woke them up and gave each one the "Eulogia."His wife asked if she would prepare food for him, and he answered, "Okay."And rested on his bed till the food was ready.She left for a few minutes, and when she returned to him, he was gone to Heaven…. He didn't taste the earthly food…. He had already eaten the Heavenly bread till satiation…. What an astonishment…. He zapped like an angel from his first serving of the Church Altar to his eternal serving.

O Lord my God, what is this incredible measure?Is this how the Chosen Ones depart?

A few days later, his wife, a pious young lady whom I had known since my serving days at the Church of St. Mark, came to me saying, "Three days before his departure, I entered his room…He was writing a letter…. When he saw me, he was troubled…? I inquired…. He said, "Nothing."Today, I found this letter in the pocket of his suit."She handed me the paper, an incomplete letter written to the Holy Virgin Saint Mary.

Here, I am precisely recording the letter.

"In the name of the Father, the Son, and the Holy Spirit, one God, Amen. Los Angeles on January 15th, 1990.

The Mother of Humanity – The kind Mother – The chaste, pure Lady – Aaron's Censor – The Bush that Moses saw – Noah's Ark – The Pure Turtle Dove – The Mother of Light – Eve of the New Testament – Carrier of the ember of the Divinity – Salvation of the Churches – The Ark of Covenant…

To you, my Lady, I write this letter asking and entreating my Master Lord and Savior, your son, the Lord of Lords, and the King of kings, Jesus Christ, for I have waited for so long.I have waited since 1968.I have been sick for more than twenty years.I have been waiting for your healing touch.

My sufferings were prolonged while I still hoped that you would grant me power, strength, and healing…. Plenty are my illnesses…. Plenty are my pains…. To whom shall I go…? You have my cure.

You have granted many thousands and millions the grace of healing from incurable diseases… And just as you did with those, ask your Son to have mercy with me. And thank Him also for all His bounties and His Grace.

I want to thank Him not only for the apparent Grace but also for the Grace within us that no one can acknowledge. I can acknowledge it only through your intersession Mother of the Light…. Intercede…. Save my soul…. O God…."He stopped here and didn't continue.

I was surprised as I read this letter, which he wrote three days before his departure. He asked the Holy Virgin to thank Christ for his hidden Grace, which he acknowledged and lived by …… This is the mystery of Christ and the works of His Grace.

I folded the paper and kept it in my pocket in a small notebook until this day…. While browsing this notebook, I found this letter. So, I wrote these words, hoping they would offer consolation to anyone who reads them.

63

Just Believe

The El-Barnashawi Family.a family that lived in El-Fayuoom City during the time of Saint Abba Abram. In the Sixties (Past Century), part of the family resided near the vicinity of our Church in Sporting.I used to visit them and hear from their elders about the amazing wonders they had seen and experienced with St. Abba Abram.They were in their youth during his time.It was about 50+ years after the departure of Abba Abram (1914) when I met this family. The whole family was affected by the life of Abba Abram, and their conduct depicted it.

We can affirm that Christian virtues, qualities, and amiable behaviors embellished the generation. In general, that generation (Christians and non-Christians) was conservative and lived by the fear of God. In particular, concerning the children of God, that generation brought forth numerous righteous and pious people.

One of the members of that family, Dr. Tadros El-Barnashawi, was in his late fifties.His uncles had mesmerized his heart and mind by informing him about their astounding encounters with Abba Abram.Those encounters testified to the truthfulness of life with God, the grace of asceticism and Chasity, and the life of prayers demonstrated by this Saint (Abba Abram). Not to mention his humbleness, his love for poor people, and the voluntary life of the poverty he willingly chose to live.

Dr. Tadros's wife was truly a saintly lady. She lived in serenity and by the fear of God.... I felt a great blessing when I visited that family, seeing it as the perfect model of what a Christian family ought to be. A mother who acquires such virtues is capable, by the Grace of Christ, of preparing her children to grow into blossomed trees in God's imperishable vineyard.

I had never heard of that pious lady being angry or troubled…. Through her meekness, she was able to absorb all the pains of life and transform them into prayers. Prayer was her way…., and prayer was her life.

It was the habit of that pious lady to ask me to pray the "Unction of the Sick" from time to time, especially if one of her family members was sick or if she was passing through unpleasant life circumstances that came unfavorably as an opposing wind.

When she requested that I pray for them the Unction of the sick…. I gave them a 7 AM appointment. On the appointment day, I prayed the Unction at another house before them. Due to circumstances beyond my control, I knocked on their door half an hour late. They greeted me, as usual, with their love, which I cherished and was joyful by its manifestation in them…. I sat down to prepare the Censor and the wicks for the Unction, during which we were talking by spiritual words…… The entire ambiance brought forth, in the soul, the aroma of Christ…. I was not in a rush…. We prayed for the "Unction of the Sick," then I anointed them with the "Holy Oil."

As I sprinkled the house with water, I noticed Dr. Tadros showed signs of distraction, looking at his watch and hastening his movement. Then I glimpsed in the room, where I was sprinkling with water, a travel bag at the door.

I realized then that they must be traveling…. I asked, "Are you traveling soon?" And before the man could answer, the lady intervened and said, "By the Grace of Christ Abouna, we will travel; my sister in Cairo is sick. We will go and visit her, for she will undergo surgery; please remember her in the Liturgies." I said, yet not fully comprehending, "Does this mean you are traveling today?" The Lady said, "If the Lord permits us, we will travel now." I asked, "Are you traveling by train?" She said with a charming smile, "Yes…" I asked, "What time?" She answered, "8:30". I looked at my watch, it was 8:30…. I apologized, saying, "It is my sin that I delayed you so that you missed the train." …. The man said, "Of course, we missed the train, but what can we do!" Then he directed the talk to his wife; "I asked to postpone the Unction." She said, "No worries, by the Grace of Christ we shall travel." The man said while appearing troubled; "What does that supposed to mean?"

At that moment, I realized what was happening earlier behind me as I was praying, which I couldn't fully understand then. I turned my head during prayers as I heard a murmur. I saw the man pointing at his watch to his wife, but she placed her finger on her mouth, indicating to him not to talk but to keep silent and continue the prayer.

I apologized for my tardiness and said it would have been helpful if they had alerted me so that I could have prayed faster or postponed the Unction until they returned from Cairo.

My apologies and remorse sincerely touched them, so they said, "It is not your fault you didn't know anything." As we were in this situation, the lady said, "May I burden you, Abouna, by a silly request? I said, "I am at your service." She asked, "Do you have a car?" I answered, "Yes." She said, "So that we don't waste time waiting for a Taxi, would you please, if it is not too much trouble, give us a lift to the train station?" I answered, "Gladly." The man said, "Why should we go to the train station, and we already missed the train? This is a strange thing that you are requesting." She told her husband, "Just believe, we were delayed because we were praying. Prayer is capable of everything…. They moved mountains with prayers…. They healed diseases through prayers…. They quenched fires by prayers…. Aren't we always talking about Abba Abram?"

I said, "Let us not waste time…." We went down the stairway quickly…. I got into the car… and drove as fast as possible toward the train station. I told myself, "This lady's faith and humility can perform miracles."

We arrived five minutes later at the station. Their house, located at Elebrahemia, was not far from it. As we rushed toward the entrance, one of the staff asked us, "What time is your train? I answered, "8:30". He responded, "It is late 20 minutes." Then he pointed toward its direction, and behold, it was just arriving. I was amazed. I glorified God, worshiping Him within me. I looked at this pious lady; her face was shining bright… She looked at her husband and said, "Just Believe."

64

Examples of Loyalty

The more our world drowns in vices, sins, corruption, and degradation, and as darkness swells, the more the need for light becomes exceedingly urgent. Also, the world's need for contemporary saints is illuminated by the light of Christ.... However, they are rare, and as scarce as they become, the more precious they get in the eyes of God and men.

(Precious stones are valued solely for their rarity and lack of circulation amongst the people.)

The Christian Virtues are usually expressed as jewels and precious pearls, for they are everlasting, unaffected by time, continually sparkle on earth and in heaven, and remain as such forever. They are - the Christian Virtues- derived from Christ Himself and are for Him. He is the purpose and the means for acquiring such virtues.

One of the most valuable Christian virtues is.... Loyalty.... The glorious history of the Church documented astonishing countless accounts. For instance.... Pope Zacharias, the 64th Pope among the Patriarchs of our Church, was persecuted by El-Hakem BeAmr Allah, who cast him twice to the lions. Yet they didn't harm him by the power of God, for he was chaste and meek. History states that this Patriarch had an Ethiopian disciple, as per the tradition of the Patriarchs of that era, who was at his service night and day. He was highly loyal to him. When the ruler decreed that the Pope be cast to the lions, this disciple clung to the edge of his lord's (The pope) garment. What an astonishing act that was above and beyond rational understanding...... Because of his loyalty, the Lord had delivered him from the mouth of the lions. The same lions that became domesticated around the pope licked the feet of this loyal disciple. We can concur that this type of loyalty was similar to Elisha's devotion to his master, Elijah.

(It is a Spiritual loyalty that elevates the disciple to partake and receive blessings as his mentor and reach the same level of his spiritual stature. They both- mentor and disciple- share in Christ: Prayers, Fasting, Sanctification, and Cross bearing).

(Indeed, these are Spiritual matters and values that are unlike those of the people in the world and the social fidelity that exists in this fleeting world. So often, loyalty founded on personal gains and interests turns into hostility, for the world is changing. And all its values are founded on the dust of the flesh, which will inevitably perish). However, therefore, if the virtue is founded on the Spirit of Christ, it is destined for eternal everlasting.

Another historical account concerns a Christian leader in the Church who also held a ministry post in the secular state. When the potentate visited him at his home, he saw a sick, tired old lady. He inquired about her; the Coptic Minister answered, "She is my wife, Sir." Later, the Potentate, out of pity, gifted the minister three beautiful young ladies, asking him to marry any of them.

History says the minister returned the gift to the potentate, thanking him and saying, "Sir. My wife, in my sight, is the most beautiful woman in the entire world. I am happy with her and know none other than her."

(That was a profound spiritual devotion and loyalty that stemmed from the works of the Holy Spirit in the Sacrament of Holy matrimony. The Sacrament of the Eternal Unity… One body and one soul. This was not a social or human devotion.)

(That Coptic minister demonstrated that such loyalty did not concern the flesh, its needs, its adornment, or its desires. For all, it is from dust to dust.)

Why should we limit the accounts to past historical times when our Church is alive forever…? I have witnessed dozens of accounts that depicted such Spiritual loyalty.

- I was visiting one of my beloveds from Alexandria, a successful teacher who was recognized for his knowledge and dedication. His wife, in her forties, was diagnosed with rheumatoid arthritis. The disease hindered her mobility and deformed her extremities. Her hands and feet were bent and twisted. Her fingers and knuckles were swollen. It was a painful sight to look at. As I was visiting him, he was sitting next to her and, with great tenderness, was kissing her hands and saying, "She is my dear wife and the blessing of my life, which I am not worthy to receive."

- His neighbors, relatives, and loved ones witnessed how he served her without grouchiness while honoring and cherishing her.... Incredible.... He continued to care for her for years and years. When the Lord eased her sufferings, people couldn't believe the magnitude of his sadness and the tears that this faithful, loyal man shed. He manifested by his actions and conduct that the Christian marriage exalted above the flesh and carnality as high as heavens exalted above the earth.

- Another example of devotion is a young lady whose husband used to work at one of the "cotton pressing" factories. She knew suffering when a terrible accident occurred to her husband. One of the factory machines fell on him, pulverizing his back and paralyzing him from the waist down to the lower extremities. He became disabled for life... Unable to control anything. That faithful young lady, who was truly religious and pious, continued to care for him. In vain were all the efforts of the people who tried to influence her to change her mind and heart. Telling her not to squander the rest of her life caring for her disabled husband. They said to her that she was entitled to a divorce and this and that....... However, her faithfulness was far greater than to be affected by people's talk. She kept saying that we, in our Church through the Sacrament of the Holy Matrimony, are not bound by flesh only, but we become one soul and one spirit as well. Flesh will perish into dust. She continued as faithful, loyal, and devoted to her husband. The Lord granted her strength and peace. Hence, she was a source of comfort to her husband. She continually encouraged him to live a life of prayers and thanksgiving.

- I have known a priest whose wife suffered from a mental disorder.... She behaved hysterically and manically even at home....... Medicine was ineffective.... That honored priest strived tremendously, caring for his wife with unparalleled devotion.... Most of the time, she was not in sound sanity. He served her- as a slave, served his master, and took care of all her needs with patience and loyalty for 15 years. No one from his congregation or his loved ones knew the magnitude of what he offered in secret. He was a man who kept his secrets sealed, for God entrusted him. He told me, "Believe me, my father, I am this unprofitable servant who hasn't done his duty.... God loved me and chose me to serve, yet I feel that I am lacking in my care toward my wife."

- This is an absolutely wonderful...The Spirit of God, who works within us, desires that we strive for good works to receive joy.

- If we are glorifying such true Spiritual accounts and refraining from negatives such as betrayal, rejection of virtues or selfishness and self-love, the frantic pursuit of one's self-interest, casting away morals and principles, treading on all that is valuable for the purpose of having all what is satisfying to the soul even if it is against God's commandments. Because we see all this around us nowadays, which is an unfortunate indicator of the "Regression of the Spirit."

- Since contrasting is essential to acknowledge the meaningful essence of things, I, therefore, give the following account to promote the virtue of loyalty in the eyes of whoever is seeking it.

- A wealthy man with privilege and honor among the people of his village of the diocese of Abu-Teig in Upper Egypt. His wife had gotten sick with a disease that immobilized her for numerous years. They didn't have lineage (Children). He and his family wished he would have a son to inherit his wealth and bear his name. They, his family, and he were anticipating the death of the sick wife. Hence, he could remarry and have children. But since his wife's sickness was prolonged and she didn't die...... Some individuals advised him to seek the Metropolitan of Abu-Teig, his Holiness the departed Abba Markos, asking for permission to remarry. When he met with Abba Markos, he was known to him; he asked him, "Is your wife alive?"The man affirmed and said to Abba Markos, "She has been faltering between life and death for years."Abba Markos said to him, " Megadess, be patient. Life and Death are in the hands of God. It is better to wait."The man responded, "Sayedna... You are familiar with life in the villages; I have no one to help me with cooking, laundry, and housework. If a woman comes into my house, people will gossip. I am exhausted and can't bear this situation any longer."

The Metropolitan feared that the man would behave foolishly, which could harm the people of the village, such as joining another Denomination.... etc.

So, he asked him again, " Megadess, do you wish to marry so that you get help or to have children?The man responded, "No, only for the help."Abba Markos said to him with authority, "Fine, go ahead and marry ...... But even if you marry ten women, you have no lineage."

Unfortunately, the man went ahead and got married; his first wife died a few months later.His second wife was young and never married.Yet she didn't bear any children; they sought many doctors and did all the tests.They both were perfectly normal.

In vain was all the man's efforts. He died without lineage, as prophesized by Abba Markos.

That behavior had an impact on many people.It was a lesson for anyone who dared to neglect morals, betray trust, follow his desires, and seek glory.

i. The 6th Fatimid Caliph. His birth name was Abu Ali Mansur. He ruled under the Title "El-Hakem BeAmr Allah," which means "The ruler by the authority of God" Or "The enforcer of God's order."

ii. The disciple was loyal to the point of death.He was cast to the lions as well.

iii. Arab rulers owned concubines.

iv. Megadess: A bestowed title upon visiting the Holy Land.

65

Account of a True Repentance

During the Sixties and the past century, Egypt faced a wave of lewd fashion for women's and girls' apparel. The People of Egypt compete to follow and imitate everything that is European, sometimes without discerning between what is useful and what is harmful or what is proper and what is improper. Most of the girls and women in Egypt began wearing short, revealing clothes. That became a phenomenon that troubled many of the spiritual fathers. In Vain were many of the warnings and the advice… As if they were gone with the wind. Many girls stopped coming to the Church to avoid the looks of displeasure and condemnation or hearing words of conviction. It was also the behavior of many of the female servants and the priests that further pushed them away from the Church.

On the contrary, Abouna Bishoy Kamel, guided by the Spirit of wisdom and discernment, was unique in his behavior as a wise winner of souls. He had compassion for people without compromising and was steadfast, with all his might, in faithful teachings. He led everyone to it by the spirit of meekness, humbleness, and genuine love. He had delivered many souls by saving them from the snares of the devils.

One Sunday during the Holy Liturgy, a young lady in her thirties came to the Church while dressed improperly. Many of the attendees that day were offended by such attire. Some gave her a look of disgust, while others commented with unpleasant demeaning words.

It was the habit of Abouna Bishoy after he concluded the liturgy prayers and dismissed the congregation to stand by the Church door, greeting the people and inquiring about their living status. He greeted everyone with a pleasant smile while uttering, discreetly, in their ears, words of comfort and encouragement. That lady was among the crowd. Abouna Bishoy greeted her. It was his first time meeting her, and he said with an encouraging smile, "Where do you reside?" She gave him the address…. He memorized it immediately.

Abouna Bishoy visited them in the evening of that same day…. a home he was visiting for the first time…. He read from the Bible…. He uttered a few simple words of Grace, yet they were according to the truth of God that permeated the heart, which enabled the soul to discover and know Christ. The whole family was transformed as if their eyes were opened (Luke 24). Grace visited them, hence becoming in a state of continuous joy and spiritual growth.

After some days, not many, that lady insisted on burning those improper clothes…… Abouna tried to convince her otherwise. She refused by saying, "I don't like anyone to wear them."

As usual, Abouna Bishoy never uttered a word concerning peoples' attire. He aimed to reach the soul's essence, thus healing it and bringing it back to Christ. Then and only then, the outlook became adjusted since it is the visible expression of the inside.

The approach: "First cleanse the inside of the cup…That the outside may clean…" was the one utilized by Abouna Bishoy, for he was entrusted by Christ, through His love, His tenderness, and His care, to save the souls.

66

Alive Conscience

How wonderful are God's commandments when they, truly and certainly, are acknowledged by the people, realizing its victorious power over sin and overall what is in the world?Christian humility is the epitome of all the virtues amongst our saintly Father, mainly if it is acquired and practiced by leaders and pillars of the Church.Hence, they ornament the teachings of our Good Savior.

In the mid-fifties of the past century, precisely during the period in which the Patriarch's throne was vacant post the departure of Pope Yousab the 2nd, the departed Abba Athanasius was visiting Alexandria. He was the Metropolitan of Beni Suef Governorate and the Patriarch's surrogate then.He was a man recognized- by everyone – for his life of asceticism, adherence to the truth, and seriousness of talk and action.Everyone respected and feared him, including the Metropolitans and the Bishops of the Church.

The man, in his good advanced age, suffered from Diabetes and other numerous diseases that made him tense, easily annoyed by loquaciousness, and unable to bear arguments.One day, as he was leaving his cell in the Cathedral of Alexandria, he was intercepted by some people asking to receive his blessings. Among them was a "Shoe polisher," a poor kid who was present most of the day in the courtyard of the Patriarchate on the premise of someone requesting his services.He approached the Metropolitan and said, "Sayedna, shall I polish your shoes?"As he rushed to leave, the Metropolitan answered, "No, My son."The kid asked more than once with persistence as the man tried to push him out of his way. The Metropolitan got annoyed, and in frustration, he raised his staff to the boy's face and said firmly, "Get out of my face."

That scene occurred frequently as the mendicants and the destitute persistently asked. Numerous times, the Church fathers escaped them or pushed them away. The people also rebuked them harshly and with unpleasant expressions.

Abba Athanasius and his accompanying people left, heading to their destination.

He returned in the afternoon……. It was a day of fasting…. The Cathedral Vicar and the servants prepared a simple meal in the evening. Abba Athanasius was about to break his fast, which was close to 6 PM. He sat at the table, and before blessing the food, he said to the Vicar, "Bring to me the young boy the 'Shoe polisher.'" The Vicar responded, "Sayedna, no one is present now in the Courtyard of the Patriarchate…. They all leave in the afternoon…. And that boy, we don't know where he is…. Please bless the food and eat… Tomorrow, we shall bring him…. Besides, those boys and those mendicants are used to such treatment. Some people rebuke them while others curse them due to their annoying persistence."

The vicar's efforts to persuade Abba Athanasius were in vain. He insisted, "I won't eat if someone is angry at me." The Vicar asked, "Does anyone know where the boy lives?" One of the servants answered, "I know him; he resides in an area known as 'Khait El-Enaab.'"

The boy came. Abba Athanasius insisted on being forgiven by the boy by having him say, "God forgives you." He took money out of his pocket, gave it to the boy, and said, "My son, I am an ailing man. I can't bear the stress. Don't do this again." Afterward, he blessed the food and ate with all those who were present with him.

All the contemporary people who witnessed that incident learned how the conscience could be alive and dynamic and how humility ought to be, even toward the least significant people.

That incident rebukes the person who finds excuses for his actions and who treats people with lesser status in Un-Christian conduct. And don't hold himself accountable.

Watch and contemplate. How the Fathers lived by scrutiny, kept the Law of Christ, and followed the Commandments.

I mentioned that story to El-Megadess Ibrahim Gerges, father of Dr. Issa Gerges, owner of Victoria Hospital in Alexandria, and the secretary of the

Alexandrian Committee, who was one of my dear beloveds. It was joyful for both of us to obtain solace by talking about the lives of the contemporary righteous people. Megadess Ibrahim informed me, "I hosted the departed Abba Athanasius whenever he came to Alexandria. It was customary to spend one day and one night at my house… Once, he was resting in my son's room at school and didn't know of this arrangement. My son dashed into the room to retrieve a book. He was amazed seeing Abba Athanasius, without the Bishopric attire, wearing inferior clothes and lying on the floor. Surprised by the unexpected door opening, Abba Athanasius asked, "Who is it at the door?"

Dr. Issa realized what happened; he retreated immediately and shut the door. His father yelled, "Shouldn't you knock first." Dr. Issa apologized; "I wasn't aware anyone was inside the room."

Megadess Ibrahim apologized to Sayedna. His Holiness was as simple as a child, quick in his forgiveness.

No one was aware of the mysteries of his life and the mysteries of his ascetic life till his departure. He concealed, even from his loved ones, his private life.

It was a sealed Paradise.

67

Examples of Thanks Giving in Illness

The Saintly Scholar Fathers of the Church placed the sick, who give thanks to God without protest and accept the illness of the flesh and its weakness as a blessing from Him without grumble or fear, at the top of the roster of those whom the Lord beatifies. They shall receive the heavenly crowns like those who fight for innocence and purity and like those who submit themselves fully to obedience due to their love for Christ.

I have seen throughout my life rare examples of thanksgiving in illness despite the cruelty of physical suffering.

I had known a pious lady, an unblemished servant of Christ. I was spiritually bound to her family since 1965, as I served occasionally at the Church of the venerable Archangel Michael in Kafar El–Dawar. That blessed sister, her good husband, and two little children set the standard for the "Meek Christian family." Nothing occupied their minds except their life with God, and nothing brought joy to their hearts except their assembly around the prosperous table of the Word (The Bible), satiated by its richness. The Church, with her Sacraments, her Feasts, and her assembly, was the ideal community for their spiritual growth and consolation. Just like the sparrow that found his home, safety, and destination. (Ps.84) and just as they say of the Lord, "A house built on the rock," Christ Himself, when the rain descends, the floods come, and the winds blow on it. It does not fall, for it is found on the rock.

One of the two children, a pious youth due to his religious upbringing during his early twenties, was tested by a highly harsh trial. While he was practicing swimming, he jumped into the water. However, he lost his balance and hit the solid edge of the pool. He was rushed to the hospital unconscious. After extensive medical efforts, he regained consciousness, but his spinal cord was severely injured, resulting in lower body paralysis. Moreover, there were minor injuries to the upper vertebrae that affected the arms. It was a harsh trial by all means.... It shook the hearts of his loved ones. Prayers were raised, and tears were shed.

That young lad became disabled and immobilized, needed a wheelchair and in need of assistance in all essential aspects of his life. It was a demanding task, physically and psychologically, for him and the caregivers.

However, many loved ones testified that the Virtues mother, through her faith and love of Christ, and the father, by his strong faith, had passed that trial with steadfastness and total trust in God. So, their experience became a source of comfort to many.

The hand of our merciful Lord had transformed that trail into bountiful blessings. The good young lad became a cause of support for many people. He studied computer science and used that knowledge and skill to serve, communicate, encourage, and inspire them. He never ceased serving his Good Savior.

Years passed, and the mother was never weary or complaining. But she served in thanksgiving despite her inner inexpressible torment as a mother. No one had ever seen her grumbling or frustrated. She was a symbol of endurance.

The Father was diagnosed with a cardiovascular disease. God was glorified and healed for all the prayers by his loved ones, which were offered for his sake.

Years later.... The mother felt pain and lumps in her chest. She didn't tell anyone. She was only worried about her son, as he was attached to her as a little child. However, after several months, she could not keep the secret. A family doctor was visiting them, and he noticed that her visage appeared ailing. He inquired persistently...... She informed him. The doctor suspected the severity of the disease, so they rushed to the hospital for more tests and X-rays. The cancer had metastasized in the body and reached the bones.

The doctor came to me in panic as I was on a short visit to Egypt. He conveyed all the details concerning the diagnosis. I immediately went to her home.... I was stunned...I found her in a state of heavenly peace. All that concerned her was her son.... She didn't want him to lose his faith in God....

She hoped that he would accept the situation.... As for herself, she said, "I am not worthy so that Christ will give me all these crowns."

Abouna Bishoy always stated that this specific sickness (Cancer) is beneficial as it gives the person a chance to repent, cleanses and purifies the soul, and brings it closer to God as an acceptable Sacrifice.

As that blessed sister talked, I was reminded of the words Abouna Bishoy told me when we were in London in January of 1977. He asked me, "Do you know, Abouna, why Christ gave me this sickness? I asked, "Why?" He answered, "So that I repent, the priest must truly be repentant and continually live a life of repentance to lead others toward repentance."

I have read that the early Church Fathers defined the Bishop as A penitent leading penitents to Heaven.

We were very much consoled when we aimed our thoughts toward heaven, and our faith was boosted. We weren't troubled much regarding illness and the sorrows of the flesh. The Holy Book declares, "All flesh is as grass and all the glory of man as the flower of the grass."

We prayed and submitted all our concerns to Christ, the author of our lives.

How beautiful is the life of submission? How wonderful is the life of Thanksgiving? Especially to those who knew the sorrows of the flesh.

68

Beautiful Icon

I was pretty marveled and unable to inhibit my emotions in front of that young lady, a beautiful icon in her thirties…….A poor person who had compassion for those in need. She had devoted herself to their care, allocating a considerable portion of her affection and her time to the sick ones among them.She visited them, offering them comfort and solace, reading the Scripture with them, and reciting the Psalms to the maximum of her efforts and their ability to bear.She also cared for them financially despite her limited resources.

Was the service of Christ get to be disrupted because of materialistic matters?!Was He, who sent his Apostles without a moneybag, to abandon serving the poor?!Never… She didn't lack anything…….

Christ's ability, mighty arm, and incomprehensible economy supported her.

What really was astonishing was that, as she was serving them with such a fiery heart, she kept entreating Christ to grant her their sickness. O, how often had she wished to sacrifice herself for them!

However, she kept pondering, in her heart, whether that matter was contrary to God's will. She had the desire to share their sickness and carry their yolk. That question continued to kindle her heart with an inexplicable emotion.

She had married a few years earlier and had given birth to a baby boy, who was three years old.

A beloved brother, a gifted surgeon, and a servant of Christ informed me as I was present at Victoria Hospital in Alexandra that the blessed sister was sick.And he had performed mastectomy surgery on her.He discovered that the disease was widely spread, frighteningly endangering her life.

I saw her in the hospital room, and I testified before Christ that I had witnessed the steadfastness of the saints, which was evident in that young lady. Her bright smile, a manifestation of her inner peace, never departed her face. She said, "I asked Christ to give me His peace. And He gave me peace. I have never, throughout my life, had comfort and peace as much as I had in my sleep last night.... When I was placed on the operating table, I felt like being with my beloved Jesus stretched on the Cross. I told Him, 'In Your hands, I commit my spirit.' I am confident that He will do with me according to His goodness and love for me before the foundation of the world."

(There is no other support for the soul during her tribulations but the support of the "Faith in Christ." The soul realizes that Christ, tempted in all points, can sympathize with our weaknesses.)

When I heard from that sister, I was reminded of her desire to share their pains and ails with the sufferers of the saint Abba Agathon, who desired to exchange with a leper. In which he takes the leper's mutilated body and gives him his intact body.... Also, I was reminded of that holy father who always prayed, saying, "Lord, allow me to suffer as my weak, ill brethren."

(This is the test for Christ's love and the teachings of His saintly Apostles; "Who is weak, and I am not weak." "Bear one another's burdens, and so fulfill the law of Christ.")

I left that amazing patient's room and returned to the surgeon, inquiring more about her condition. He advised that the disease had metastasized, and she was not expected to live no more than several weeks...... I traveled and came back to Alexandria after seven months. I asked about her. She was rejoicing with inexpressible joy. God has bestowed heath upon her. She served with a renewed spirit, mind, and intense love, particularly toward those crushed by various diseases.

Serving others shouldn't involve abstract emotions or words of sympathy and lamentation but rather a true and real communion in their sufferings and by the life and hope in Christ, trusting Him who bore our transgressions and eradicated the sting of death for our sake.

69

The Litany of the Travelers

It is not in vain that the Church allocates, within her Rituals, a special prayer specifically for the sake of the travelers. The Church prays this litany every day of the week at matins. Except for Saturdays, we pray the "Litany of the Departed," on Sundays, we recite the "Litany of Oblation." The ritual of the oblation is in accordance with the Old Tradition dating back to the "Apostolic Era." When St. Paul recommended that everyone bring offerings to the church on Sunday of every week. Upon his- St. Paul- arrival, the collected oblations will be sent to the poor people of Jerusalem.

Because travel has been dangerous since ancient times, prayer is necessary so God may straighten the way, whether by sea, rivers, lakes, roads, air (nowadays), or any other means.

In the litany, the Church implores the Lord to accompany the travelers, be with them in their departure and throughout their journey, and be a fellow worker with them in every good deed. And brings them back to their homes safely. Then, the prayer aims to serve a superior purpose: the Eternal life we seek. The priest prays, "As for us, too, O Lord, keep our sojourn in this life without harm, without storm, and undisturbed to the end." We are all traveling to our heavenly home, and this journey is fraught with danger. Therefore, we implore Christ to lead us to a haven of peace.

This is the economy of the inspired Church. How pleasant it is for a man to live by this economy to obtain comfort.

Numerous beloved fathers and brethren had seen the hand of God during their travels. A perfect example is the account documented by St. Paul in his second epistle to the Corinthians. His ship was wrecked, and he spent nights and days clinging to a wooden board. He was despaired even of life, and he had the sentence of death in himself. But God had miraculously saved him so that he should no longer trust himself but rather in God. (In whom we trust that He will still deliver us.)

Thus, the succession of generations had abounded testimonials. The wonderful acts of God were manifested in the lives of the believers, who offered "Offers of Peace" because they were delivered from a guaranteed death.

I remember that, in 1967, I traveled from Alexandria to Cairo for an ecclesiastical service. That was on a Saturday; I prayed at St. Mark Patriarchate in El-Asbakeya on Sunday morning. I went up to the 2nd floor to get the blessings of His Holiness Pope Kirolos the Sixth. He greeted me, as usual, with his fatherly love and pleasant smile. He inquired about myself, the status and conditions of the service, and our Father Bishoy Kamel and our Father Tadros Yacoob.

I asked His Holiness' permission to leave, for I had already decided to travel that Sunday. His Holiness asked me, "Where are you going, my son?" I answered, "I am traveling to Alexandria, Sayedna."

He asked, "When?"

I answered, "Today."

He said, "Today is Sunday, my son...... No one travels on a Sunday.... It is the day of the Lord."

I said, "Absolve me, Sayedna. I have an obligation to attend a wedding this afternoon and other commitments."

He objected, saying, "But on Sundays, we pray the Litany of the Oblations, not the Travelers."

I pleaded, saying, "I am sorry, Sayedna.... I can't change this situation.... This is beyond me.... absolve me and allow me."

He responded, saying, "Don't do as such again."

I said, "Pray for me."

Contrary to the usual, He grasped my head and prayed for me a prolonged prayer. He then dismissed me with pleasant words and a big smile. I kissed his hand and went on my way.

I took a train to Alexandria; during those days, it consisted only of three railroad cars, and my seat was right behind the driver's compartment. The driver was visible to me through the compartment's glass window. The train traveled about 25 kilometers from Cairo, and as it approached a city called Kaha, I saw a terrifying scene...... A cart carrying large containers was stuck

The Litany of the Travelers

on the railroad. A miniature donkey was pulling the cart, and the load was hefty. So, the donkey gave in and fell …. Only God knows what those large containers had in them…. Chemical substances or anything else might have been likewise dangerous.

The train was at full speed; the driver didn't have a chance to slow down or use the brakes as the distance was so close…. I heard the driver scream and saw him attempt to jump out of the train. All the passengers who saw that frightening scene, like me, screamed. I shouted with all my heart, requesting aid from God…. It was the danger of death.

What an amazement…. Realizing what was happening, some farmers pushed the cart with all their might and force… A miracle occurred, and the cart was pushed away when the train passed. It was only several meters to a collision…. It was only seconds between life and death.

I immediately remembered Pope Kirolos's words. I touched my head, which he grasped as he prayed for me…. He knew the danger I was about to encounter…. He interceded on my behalf to save all who were with me and me. That day, I glorified God and thanked Him for his wonderful act.

After several weeks, I was in Cairo…. I met His Holiness Pope Kirolos… He asked me, "Will you travel again on a Sunday?" I answered, "Never." I then told him all that had happened…. I had a feeling that he definitely knew. I said to him, "Your prayer saved me from death." He responded in all humility, "It is the prayers of the saints, my son."

PART 5

70

Practical Faith Overcomes the Enemy

In the early year of 2001, His Holiness Pope Shenouda the Third visited Los Angeles for several days. He frequented the dentist's office multiple times during his visit. I was accompanying him there, as usual. (Thus, I enjoyed the pleasant times I spent in the Pope's company.) The distance from the house to the office was about an hour or more. Thus, we were discussing spiritual topics, which benefited me tremendously, and I counted myself blessed that I spent those enjoyable times with His Holiness. We didn't discuss politics, even ecclesiastical politics. However, the majority of the time, the talk was about faith, about the words of the Bible, about the acts of God, and His wonders in His Saints.

One time, the conversation drew us to the accounts of faith and their documentation by those who witnessed them. And how much they truly confirm the faith, comfort the souls of those who strive to walk the narrow road, and support the weak.

His Holiness told me, "I will inform you about an account that involved me personally when I was still a young man in my late twenties before becoming a monk." I responded, "I am all ears …. What was it, Sayedna?"

He continued, "We had a friend who was fascinated by readings concerning Existentialism and atheistic philosophies …. So he kept reading and reading till he was much immersed. Those readings influenced him to unconsciously surrender his mind to such ideologies. He ended up an atheist and adamantly denied God's existence!

Our friend started to publicly express his thoughts, little by little, among his colleagues.Such manifestation affected them, as some pitied him while others became vehement opponents ... However, the dangerous issue was that not all his friends could return him to true faith.For he slipped into a bottomless pit of soul-suffocating doubts and skepticism .... Finally, word came from family and friends that there was no one except Brother Nazeer Gaied.[214]I was a layman but very active in the religious sector .... Sunday school service, publications, sermons, and teaching at the Seminary. I believed it was my duty to testify to Christ first; then, it was my obligation toward friendship and my desire for the salvation of everyone's soul. Therefore, I felt obligated to help that friend due to all I had heard from his friends and relatives.

The Pope continued his talk, "We met and spent several days refuting those atheistic ideologies.It was as terrifying as raging seas and crashing waves. But by the grace of Christ, it ended by that friend's manifestation of his full conviction and complete faith in the heart and mind.Not only for the existence of God but also for the Christian faith in the mystery of the Holy Trinity, the mystery of Incarnation, redemption, and Salvation through the blood of Christ, and obtaining eternal life by believing in His blessed name .... We thanked God profusely. Our souls were comforted as that matter became known to all relatives and loved ones."

The Pope said, "Only a few weeks had passed, and behold, those same thoughts that I refuted, and proved their corruption ....Those same thoughts began to attack me viciously.Like severe storms, they began rushing toward my mind in quantities a hundred-fold greater than my friend's!I lived the worst days of my life; I was tormented, unable to sleep, did not enjoy food, and unable to rest ....My heart was rejecting all that, but can my mind rest and calm down?The biblical verses are present in my mind, but the torrents are mightier than the mind."

I said with astonishment: "What happened afterward, Sayedna?"His Holiness said: "I remained in that state for days, then the Grace saved me and enlightened my mind .... So, I remembered a miracle that happened to me years ago."I asked: "What is it?"Here, the Pope turned to me and said: "I won't tell you what it is, and I will keep a secret to myself."I politely responded: "No objection."His Holiness resumed his conversation with me, saying .... "That incident (The miracle) had no rational or logical explanation, and there is no force in all of existence that could do this except the hand of the Almighty.

---

[214] His Holiness Pope Shenouda's secular name prior to embracing monasticism.

When I remembered that wondrous miracle, the disturbing thoughts dissipated from me immediately as if they were darkness closing in on my mind. When the light shone, the darkness dissipated without the slightest resistance, and in the blink of an eye, I returned to myself, living by my faith with the greatest strength and trust in the One I believe in. My love for my Savior, my pride in His life-giving Cross, and devoting my life to Him became brighter than the sun within me."

I said …. "Truly so Sayedna … True faith is a personal experience, and true knowledge of the Lord Jesus Christ and tasting of His benevolence, His care, and the power of His Cross. All of these are not information read in books, or sermons heard … Rather, it is a life lived, and experience upon which such life is established."

71

The Faithful Witness

In February of 1970, I was visiting St. Macarius Monastery at the Scetes. (At that time, the construction of the monastery was expanding according to a Divine economy beyond comprehension. Many beloved brethren, the Lord had pierced their hearts and strengthened their wrists to accomplish the work. Thus, the scope of work expanded to the point that, from one month to the next, the features of the monastery were changing. And even from one week to the next, the hand of construction would have already added to that grand edifice which the Lord's hand was establishing.) That day, I met with the Spiritual Father Hegumen Matta El-Meskeen (Mathew the meek.) He was contemplating the inexpressible acts of God and His incredible hand that became tangible through the indescribable blessing. Daily accounts that glorified God and glorious acts that were attributed to the hand of the Almighty, who is glorified in His saints. Yet, what had taken place the day before was beyond imagination.

Abouna Matta said, in the presence of some monastic fathers who were eyewitnesses, "The majority of the laborers, at the Monastery, are from a village called "Al-Zora" in Upper Egypt, most of whose residents are Christians. They are good people who love God and are also very poor ....They labor at the Monastery for two weeks and receive their wages on Friday evening. Then, they return to spend a few days with their families and return to the Monastery on Monday or Tuesday. Due to this, they would impatiently wait till Friday of every other week to receive the blessing (the wages.) Last Friday, today was Monday, was payday. The Monk, appointed to supervise the work, totaled the wages of all the workers (Carpenters, bricklayers .... Etc.,) and found it to be 283 Egyptian pounds."

(The Monk brought a receipt to Abouna Matta on Thursday and said to him, "This sum is required by tomorrow."Abouna Matta responded, "Pray, my father.")

Abouna Matta continued his talk, saying, "Throughout this week, no visitors came to the Monastery. No one rendered vows, tithes, or gifts. There was no money in the Monastery at all, nor was there anyone who could lend us ... I gathered the fathers and asked them to pray .... The laborers are poor and must receive their wages ... They prayed throughout Thursday and till Friday evening, but nothing changed. The workers were in a state of anticipation. I asked the fathers saying, 'Prepare, for them, a delicious meal and rice pudding with added sugar. Try to find an excuse to keep them several days until the times of refreshing come from the presence of the Lord.' Indeed, the fathers succeeded in convincing them, and they stayed till Saturday. However, Saturday passed, and nothing changed."

At the dawn of Sunday, a certain loved one from the city of Tanta knocked on the monastery's gate. They brought along with them a physician named Farouk Markos, who was visiting the Monastery for the first time. They attended the Liturgy and partook in the Holy Mysteries. After the Liturgy, Dr. Farouk Markos asked to meet Abouna Matta.

Abouna Matta continued saying, "When they informed me, I asked, 'What does he want? I am tired and can't meet with anyone.'" However, he adamantly insisted on seeing me. He said, 'I won't leave till I see him.' Due to his persistence, I went out to meet him. He humbly greeted me and said: 'I came unexpectedly with my friends, and I decided to offer a blessing for the Monastery. So, I brought all the money that was there at my clinic. It is a modest offering, and I am embarrassed to offer it.'"

Abouna Matta received it from his hands, thanked God, and prayed for a good reward for him. He then gave the money to one of the fathers, whom he counted and, behold, found it to be exactly 283 pounds. No more and no less! He was astonished ... It was unbelievable! Abouna Matta gathered the

The Faithful witness

fathers, and they prayed and glorified God as they felt the hand of God truly working with them without any shred of doubt.

When Dr. Farouk Markos encountered that act of God, the Monastery became for him the holy place that his soul desired, and the fathers of the Monastery became his own and his loved ones, and Abouna Matta became his Spiritual father and teacher.Since then, Dr. Farouk began a new phase in experiencing life with Christ, bearing witness to Christ, loving Christ, and serving Christ.

One of my loved ones, the departed Dr. Zaki Faheem, began, a few years prior, serving Christ as a deacon and ministering to the poor.His only source of comfort was service.His household was living for Christ.Christ is life.The life in Christ included all material things such as eating, drinking, and communicating.Nothing except Christ.He and he alone is all in all.

The home of Dr. Zaki was my heart's resting place on my way from Alexandria to Cairo and vice versa.I felt God's presence in his house and among his wife and children.By the joy they manifested, their love for the word of God, and their prayers.

Dr. Zaki was accustomed to waking up at four O'clock in the morning daily for praises and prayer.And whenever he had an opportunity, he came to Alexandria to confess and to pray the vespers and the Liturgy.I rejoiced greatly whenever I encountered his fiery spirit by the love of Christ, his humility that mimicked a little boy, and the generosity of the grace in his love and his care for his patients and the Lord's brethren[215] in Kafr al-Zayat and the surrounding villages.Dr. Zaki Faheem bonded, by Christ's love, with Dr. Zaki Markos.Thus, they lived by one Spirit and with an indescribable love.

At that time, the year of 1970, I met Dr. Farouk Markos.He told me the account of his visit to the monastery of St. Macarius for the first time.Some of his beloved friends, one of whom was a robust servant of Christ seeking the salvation of the souls, informed him that they intended to visit, at dawn, the Monastery to pray the midnight praises and the Divine Liturgy.He said to them: "Why the Monastery?There are Churches everywhere."They said to him: "Come and see.You will feel that you are living in heaven."He said: "If you succeed in waking me up, I will go with you."

---

[215] The poor and destitute.

(It was customary for Dr. Farouk to exert a great effort throughout the day, and once he delivers himself to sleep, he delves into a deep sleep. He does not hear any noise, even the sound of the alarm.)

That day, there was no one home, so he placed the phone next to him so that he might hear it if one of his friends called him. Out of extra caution, he put an alarm clock in a large metal pan[216]. So that once it goes off, its sound becomes stronger. He set the alarm for 4 AM, then prayed to God, saying: "If St. Macarius wants me to go, he will wake me up at the exact time."

Dr. Farouk told me, "I woke up five minutes to four without using all the measures." I asked: "How?" He responded: "By a miraculous way." I inquired: "How so?" He said: "Suddenly, I found myself sleeping on the floor. The bed broke, the mattress fell to the floor, as I was lying on top of it! I checked the time, and it was five minutes to four." I responded: "That is truly amazing." He continued: "I lifted my eyes toward heaven and said to St. Macarius, 'Wasn't there any way other than this!' Yet, I was joyful with an inexpressible joy. I hastily arose, and we all went to the Monastery. It happened that on the evening of that day, before leaving my clinic, I collected all the money there. And I was astonished to learn that it was the exact amount needed, for which the monastic fathers were asking the Lord! Since that day, I have realized that spiritual life is not an illusion but a tangible reality. Abouna Matta became my father of confession, my counselor, and my instructor."

Dr. Farouk visited the Monastery whenever the Lord permitted him and whenever he allocated spare time from his busy schedule. He was seeking the advice of his spiritual father in all issues he encountered in his life, heeds the word of counsel and following it with all his heart without hesitation, knowing and assured that commandants of Christ are the absolute power, and they are the gate of heaven.

He faced many harassments and persecutions, but the Lord was his support and his strength. Rather, it was by the love, within, that he overcame hatred. He had a colleague at work, a non-Christian physician, who submitted numerous complaints against him, all of which were slander and false allegations. The hospital board investigated many of those false accusations, and every time, the Lord delivered him victorious over evil. Furthermore, his superiors greatly respected him for the sake of God's grace, which was apparent in him, and because of his honesty toward his God. Hence, he was promoted to become the

---

[216] Utilizing the echo sound.

director of the hospital. However, he was a unique type of director, unknown to the world, and it wouldn't have been possible for the world to know him.

Dr. Farouk used to greet everyone he knew with a holy Christian kiss, with a pure and simple heart like a child. Therefore, all the workers, nurses, and those beneath him rejoiced in him. As they perceived in him marvels humility, love, and tenderness toward the weak, the poor, and the oppressed. He rarely sat in his office; if he did, it was for a short time to seek God's help, for he considered himself a servant of Christ, even at his place of employment. He considered the Lord Christ to be the actual director, and He is the one who works in him and by him. Any sort of troubles of work or responsibilities, he ultimately laid their burden on the altar whenever he prayed and partook of the Holy mysteries. He always felt that the burden of the responsibility lies on Christ alone.

Life was not devoid of hardships, for all who desired to live godly in Christ Jesus would suffer persecution[217]. He returned to work after a vacation spent out of town to discover that the Ministry had appointed another director, and he, the new director, had already taken over the position after he stormed into Dr. Farouk's office, which was locked and did not wait to receive it from him. The new director was less competent and less knowledgeable. Yet, Dr. Farouk, because of his obedience to his spiritual father who leads him on the road to eternal life, went to the hospital and congratulated the new director, wished him success, and manifested his submission with astonishing humility. (He led all the hospital staff to this peaceful and humble approach. Everyone was affected by this fantastic spirit, which he lived by without hypocrisy.) The Lord has done great things for him …. After two years, he returned to his position and was honored by everyone. He was well spoken of by God and men, and he was blessed in his path.

LOVE …. BLESS …. DO GOOD …. PRAY ….These positive actions, which Christ God commanded us to utilize in the face of enmity, cursing, and hatred, are a guarantee of success for the life of the spirit. Hear the command again: "Love your enemies, bless those who curse you, do good to those who hate you, and pray for those who spitefully use and persecute you[218]." This is how man manifests his sonship of the heavenly Father, who is good toward the unthankful. Thus, He makes the sun rise on the righteous and the wicked[219].

---

[217] II Timothy 3:12
[218] Matthew 5:44
[219] Matthew 5:45

All these actions were Dr. Farouk's method.No one could be hostile to him because: "He who is in you is greater than he who is in the world."[220]

Without any prior warning, hostility filled the heart of the owner of one of the shops below Dr. Farouk's clinic, so he obliterated and concealed the visibility of the clinic and removed the street sign that belonged to Dr. Farouk on the pretext that his shop was being repaired and remodeled.He began to spread false rumors against Dr. Farouk; he insulted his patients, slandering his reputation and belittling his punctuality and competence.Dr. Farouk met all that with his usual smile.He did not rebuke the man nor say a word to him.He allowed him to do whatever he desired.On the contrary, He prayed copiously for him so that the Lord may grant him grace and keep the evil spirit away from him.Furthermore, in his coming in and going out, he kept greeting the man, and embracing him saying:"I lose all things, but I am not losing love … You are my neighbor and my beloved."The Lord has transformed that man's heart, and he has started to serve Dr. Farouk with all strength and sincerity.

The Prayer of Faith:

Dr. Farouk was known for his prayer of faith.He loved prayer and trusted in its ability even if the matter was deemed impossible …. Everything is possible with God[221].He never lost hope in anyone or anything, even in the most violent and evil people.Even in the hopeless cases of medicine, he gave them hope.He often prayed with the sick person, leading him to a life of prayer and fellowship with God. He frequently told the patient the words of the Lord Jesus: "Your faith has made you well[222]."As such was his faith, and as such was the way he preached the "Life of Faith" and the "Prayer of Faith.

I was once with the departed H. G. Anba Youannis, Bishop of Gharbia.As we were contemplating the acts of God and the ability of faith to accomplish the impossible, he said:"One of my beloved people's minds, a religious man who fears God and believes that the prayer is powerful and effective, was occupied with concerns for his elderly mother, who was residing in Alexandria, and wanted to check on her because she was ill.It was past midnight, and he could not access a long-distance phone line, only domestic.It was too late to go to

---

[220] I John 4:4
[221] Luke 18:27
[222] Mark 10:52

one of his loved ones or send one of his students[223] So he prayed with faith, picked up the phone, and called Alexandria.Surprisingly, his mother answered the call, and he was reassured about her.His family was extremely astonished."

H. G. Anba Youannis, Bishop of Gharbia said:"I knew about this when he came to confess saying:'Absolve me, my father, for I have cheated the phone company.I have placed a call unlawfully.I do not have access to long-distance service.'"

I found out later that this blessed son was Dr. Farouk Markos.

Dr. Farouk Markos was fed the milk of faith by his saintly, pious mother, who raised him on a life of faith and prayer.One of the most amazing things I heard was the account of his mother when he approached her during the final year of his Med School, seeking her prayer for him.He was about to take a verbal exam, and he was terrified that he would be tested by a fanatical professor against Christianity.He was worried that the professor would flunk him.Thus, he strongly requested that his mother prays concerning that issue, and he was all confident that her prayer would be answered by God.

His mother said, "Very well, my son, let us pray together."She prayed and sought the face of God, entreating and saying:"My Lord Jesus Christ, let Your son Farouk be tested before this fanatic professor."When she was done praying, Farouk became upset and said:"Mother, I asked you to pray so that I do not fall under the hand of this professor, and you pray for the opposite."The wise and pious mother responded:"My son, if you take the exam before someone else and pass ….You will be proud and attribute success to yourself, which is not beneficial to your salvation.But if you take the exam before this professor and pass, you will attribute the credit to God.The one who is the rightful creditor."

Indeed, he was tested before the same professor.Indeed God was glorified, in his life, when he passed and attributed all the glory to Him, He who delivers from trials and saves his servants who rely on Him.

I was deeply moved when I read some of the letters Dr. Farouk penned to his children while they were in the land of immigration, whether in Germany or America. They reveal the depth of his soul and his genuine bond with Christ. They are suitable as a roadmap for an "in Christ" relationship between the father and his sons. The Lord our God is all in all within the realm of the family.

I am documenting some of them here; perhaps they will illuminate the way for many parents to raise their children in Christ by the Spirit.

---

[223] To use their long-distance phone line or physically send someone to Alexandria.

Excerpts from his letters to his elder son in the USA.

- I am very joyful of you because the news that reached me, concerning you, is pleasant.And I am, truly, proud of you because you have a testimony from the people and from the loved ones that you were able to witness for the Lord.Despite, in the beginning, I was worried about you regarding the new world, and I said within: "My son … will perish in this world, especially by its materialism, money, and dollars."But you have proven that you are a great man, living in the world, but the world doesn't live in you or within you.You labor in the world, but the world does not exploit you to live for it or its servitude.Therefore, I thank God for this. The Lord is with you ….

- I hope you and your brethren care for your spiritual, mental, and physical lives. God be with you, perfect your journey, and open, for you, the closed doors to live a perfect life in all joy because joy is the core foundation of the whole life, regardless of how many possessions you own or any other means for a sensual life. If your life lacks joy, then such a life is not worth anything.

- Obtaining joy comes from the giver of joy, Christ Himself.Cling to Him and adhere to Him to reach the perfect joy Christ bestows upon everyone who adheres to Him and abides in Him ….I am confident that you are truly His children, despite my fear for you in the land of alienation.But God was glorified in you.Your tidings are always pleasant, carrying the sweet fragrance of Christ.And the sweat fragrance of Christ, which is in you, makes us very happy.

- I am confident I delivered you to Jesus, your true father.He won't do anything to you except for the salvation of your soul, even if you were at the end of the world.For God does all good work … And all things work together for good to those who are called according to His purpose[224].I advise you to surrender everything in your life to God so that you do

---

[224] Romans 8:28

The Faithful Witness

not get led into conflicts or the mazes of the world. Until God answers all the questions that come your way, regulates your life, and guides you.

- I want you to know that everything in this world is dust and is not worthy of all these conflicts and mazes that people delve into ...But the real precious value is within you, which is your faith in the Lord and His promises of eternal life. No matter any greatness or luxury you encounter in this world, all is fleeting dust. "The world is passing away, and the lust of it[225]." But your souls are the precious and pure jewels you shall present before God as an offering and oblation to God ....I hope you comfort each other with spiritual things, encourage one another, and significantly support one another. May the Lord perfect the path for you and make us hear all good things concerning you .... Pray for us, for God will listen to you because you are pure .... Pray for the whole world .... Pray for Christianity so that it grows and blossoms .... Pray for the holy Gospel so that God may spread it, as the joyful glad tiding of the Kingdom among people, and invades, by it, the sealed hearts. And opens, by it, the heart of the whole world.

- My beloved son .... I genuinely feel that God is always with you because you are rooted in love. And love is deeply rooted in you, "He who abides in love abides in God[226]." Because the magnificent sacrifices for people and your offerings for others mean, a lot ... For you did not inform me, but I have heard from others about your tremendous sacrificial love .... Even your blood you donated to people. These sacrifices are the mystery and the reason behind God's support of you and the cause for your success in the land of alienation. The secret behind your entire behavior is "Giving" and the "Sacrifice" you truly received from the Gospel, the one Christ pointed out for you, and you learned from the monks you encountered. You also could extract it from the inner thoughts and present it as "Behavior" throughout your practical life ... Truly indeed: "For what will it profit a man if he gains the whole world and loses his own soul?[227]"The greatest loss for the soul occurs if you become self-centered and selfish, caring solely for your own benefit and aiming to gain the

---
[225] I john 2:17
[226] I john 4:16
227 Mark 8:36

whole world if possible. Such selfish gain of the world, for one's own sake, is precisely man's loss of his own soul ... This loss will not only be for the heavenly Kingdom but for the earth as well. (Meaning that man will lose his soul here and there also)

- Take heed of this, my son, because the present time is against faith, and the world is against the Gospel. The current fascination with the things of this world is against God's promises and the things pertaining to the coming age. Fearing for your earthly future is against your spiritual life and eternal future. For the kingdom of darkness does not cease nor refrain from resisting the Kingdom of Light and the Children of the light. If man acknowledged that he was present in the Kingdom of Light and insisted on firmly standing in its realm, the Kingdom of Darkness would continue pushing him outside the Circle of Light. Sometimes with intimidation and sometimes with inducement. Sometimes, it points out, to him, the importance of positions, money, and all other earthly lusts and enhances his desire for them. Sometimes, it fills his heart with the fear of needing, poverty, illness, and a gloomy future if he did not seek after earthly ambitions. Sometimes it throws at him, a left strike, and sometimes a right strike ... The most important thing is how it can make him leave the realm of light and enter the realm of darkness.

- The only thing that can keep you in the realm of Light is that you love and lay down yourself for the sake of God and the people. He who loves and sacrifices his soul out of love fears nothing and desires nothing. He shall conquer and defeat the kingdom of darkness, which captivates the people with intimidation, inducement, fear, and lust!

- Surely, you know that the sign of spiritual life is perpetual growth in the realm of light. If your growth ceases, know that you are in danger. Take heed lest you enter the kingdom of darkness of this world, and darkness overshadows you. Know this: where material things, earthly things, positions, tempting offers of food, drink, appliances, and all other pleasures abound ... Grace will also abound for the children of God and will appear vividly in their lives.

The Faithful Witness

- I hope, through God, that you grow in spirit and advance in knowledge and grace. I become delighted when I hear of your spiritual growth and progress, your sacrifices, and your giving more than my happiness of your worldly success. One biblical action by you ignites me with joy by the Spirit, especially when I hear such spiritual news concerning you.

- Rest assured that you are on the path, and also trust that the mystery behind your joy and happiness and the secret for the world opening up before you begin by loving everyone. One of my colleague physicians at the hospital once asked me: "Why do you love us so much, Dr. Farouk? And despite our many harassments toward you. Yet you love us." I answered him by saying: "I am actually selfish …. I love you for my own benefit." He responded: "How could that be? You love us more than yourself." I replied, "When I love you, I love you for my sake and not yours! Because the reality is that my love for you lets me into the realm of light, rejoices my heart, makes me happy, and fills me with peace. On the contrary, if I didn't love you or even if I became estranged and indifferent towards you, darkness would enter me. It will cast out joy from me. He who loves enters the realm of light and joy. You ask me, 'Why don't we ever encounter you sad? For you have always been smiling for over ten years. We harass you, yet we find you always happy and smiling. No situation can bother you.'" I asked him: "Do you want to know the secret?" The secret is …… Love."

- It doesn't matter if you attended the Church night and day; this would not grant you the solidity to bear the Cross and sacrifice yourself. But when you read the Bible, for it shall be like the sailor's navigation that guides him in all the seas of the world, it shall direct you to the places of almsgiving and sacrifice for others, where there is no chance for inner deception which mislead man little by little. And tricks him into believing that people are cheating you out of your rights.

- This reveals to us that the "Ego" opposes almsgiving and sacrifice; it becomes a stumbling block before spiritual advancement. Hence, a man stands still in place. The fear is that if man stops, this will lead to a severe decline in spiritual life. For I view spiritual life as not only the means by which we reach the Kingdom of Heaven at the end of our journey on earth but also the Kingdom of Heaven in the present, with you and within you in power. Try giving up your rights (Of course you tried), and then talk to me about the joy that will enter into the depths of your heart. "The Kingdom of Heaven …. Love, joy, and peace."

- Trust and believe that your good tidings concerning your spirituality shake me powerfully from within. Because no matter how much you strive in this world and for the sake of this world, in the end, all things will add up to ZERO. Even if you acquired millions of dollars, land, and properties … All of it is worth a handful of dust. I prefer that you live, bare minimum, day by day, being happy, living according to the Gospel, and having pupils living according to the Gospel and not by sermons preached at pulpits, but by daily - living behavior. To me, this is worth a doctorate in all branches of science. The world can give you everything except joy and peace, for they are the gifts of the Kingdom. Thus, our joy is in the hands of others. Therefore, the Lord Jesus Christ deliberately intended to tell you, "You shall love your neighbor as yourself[228]." And the neighbor, here, is any person, whoever he may be, for he who loves enters the realm of light and life. He who loves his brother walks in the light. We have passed from death to life because we love the brethren.

- Love is giving and sacrificing for others. My advice to you is to take heed from this world lest it swallows you up … God willing, you shall succeed in the world, but be careful as you strive lest your heart dries up, and the spirit of darkness that of this world enters into it and gets it to harden. Thus, you experience the spirit of darkness, the love of money, prestige, and elevated positions, which control the human entity.

- Believe me, it is so easy for a person's heart to become hardened and arrogant because this is Satan's program. Therefore, you must show him, Satan, that you are willing to sacrifice your flesh and soul for the sake of our Lord Jesus Christ.

- I hope you take care of your friends and loved ones and do not deprive anyone of the Gospel written on your heart, which you shall manifest

---

[228] Matthew 22:39

through your conduct. This is an essential point at the core of the Spiritual life, for it is the foundation of the building. The rest are the walls, which are the virtues upon which the living Gospel is established. I hope that you continue in your love for everyone. Beware of hatred against any person, whoever he may be. Be persistent at all times on genuine love. Love that is not by words of tongue or by dealings. Rather, through love that is by spirit and truth, which the Spirit of God directs you towards.

Other Excerpts from his letters to his Children in the USA.

- My beloved children ....My heart is always with you as you strive for this great endeavor, and for sure, I know that you will labor greatly in your life. Thus, may the Lord bestow you success and grant, for you, all your purposes for the glory of His Name. I am confident that all things work together for the good to those who love God[229]. I have taught you that your true father, Jesus, is present with you in all things and all places. And I feel He will support you because He is your true father. Thus, your faithfulness and trustworthiness towards Him will increase your enlightenment to open the locked doors and discover what is behind those doors.

- My perpetual advice to you is to give and to sacrifice, for this is the way of joy. Therefore, take heed lest you miss this advice and this commandment because the spiritual ambiance in America is icy, selfish, and dangerous. Indeed, it reflects humane behaviors, but it lacks the heart that is giving, loving, and sacrificial.

- If you trust that prayer is essential, then love is everything needed for sacrificial offering. Ritual and ecclesiastical prayers, alone, will not let you accomplish anything. However, the sacrifice will lead to the joy that the Bible commands.

---

[229] Romans 8:28

- My beloved son …. I know that you are in a situation that pushes you to overthink, but I wish that you think less and, instead, engage your faith. Have confidence and trust in one crucial fact: God can work all things through you—only if you surrender your entire life to Him!

- Be faithful in your work, study, and love for all people so that you permit light and joy to enter your heart. Thus, life becomes very pleasant …. As long as the soul is happy and the body is healthy. Also, your soul shall be free from any anxiety or depression …. I wish that your heart has room for all people, for as much as your heart is spacious, the more you shall be happy and the healthier your body and soul shall be.

- Believe me, there is no other way for joy except almsgiving …. Almsgiving without anything in return, even with the enemies. This is my advice for you forever, which means that the cross of sacrifice is the only way to resurrection and joy. Even if you attended Church night and day and observed all the rituals, there will be no elevation from one spiritual level to a higher spiritual level or from joy to more abundant joy except by almsgiving and sacrifice. You shall sacrifice everything, and when you reach ZERO and lose all things of God's sake … God shall compensate you for everything at once!

- But know this: the world and the present time are against the virtue of love. Also, know that trials and tribulations sometimes surprise the soul with darkness, so be always prepared for them. Of course, America, concerning temptations, is mighty, and it eradicates any spirituality if the person surrenders to the norms and values of the people and their behavior. Take heed not to believe people, as most of the people in America are led to the spirit of the world, and they don't know the Spirit of God, for they are dead spiritually … It is true, according to the flesh, that they live a comfortable life, but they are spiritually dead, and the Spirit of God is not in them nor the true joy. If you searched their souls, even the souls of the scientists, you would find some that have a mental illness. Some of them get rid of worrying and sadness, which compresses the soul, by committing suicide. You will discover that, after reaching the zenith of science, art, and wealth, they terminate their lives. All these people do not have the Spirit of God in them.

- Therefore, you must utilize, from America, the tremendous, illuminated things[230], which are all civilization, science, and urbanization. As for bad habits, neglect them. I hope you realize that once the Cross disappears from your life, it will be terrifying and dangerous for your salvation. Thus, you must be crucified to the world from within and from the outside. And you shall bear the Cross, from which the joy of the Resurrection perpetually proceeds. Hence, you proclaim to all people the joy of eternal life.

- I was exceedingly glad for the magazine, which you have sent me, citing the monk who served, with love, amid the HIV patients, who himself became infected with HIV.I was glad because there were still souls that denied themselves and bore the Cross every day, to follow Christ till death, the death of the Cross, to the point that I wished to come to you so that I can sever the crucified Christ in the image of the sick and the sufferers, and to bear the Cross to death.For such thing exceedingly rejoices Christ's heart.I talk to you spiritually and not as a physical father.I always live by spiritual emotions, and I am confident you are living by the same emotions.Therefore, I love you with spiritual love, and I am happy for you because you have become a source of light in America. And I feel you all have all the traits and the exemplary virtues I always hoped to possess when I was your age.Thankfully, you received them early on because you encountered perfect role models in the monasteries of Wady El Natron, and you truly knew Christ, felt the effect of His Gospel, and smelled His sweet fragrance in America.Which were also seen and smelled by your American friends; therefore, I glorify God for the sacrifice and love of "Ehab," the faithfulness and purity of "Marcos," and the observation of "Wessam" for the commandments of the Gospel and his powerful fellowship with Christ. (This beloved son received a doctorate in engineering from Germany and worked in the USA in his specialization.)

- I thank my God for His gifts to you.Be confident that the people who rally around you in America do not need any assistance, but they saw in you the light of the Gospel that illuminated, for us, the way and eternity."Ehab" received unique fatherhood from God manifested by

---

[230] Good and profitable habits.

love spread to everyone.May God make you a pillar for your brethren, your family, and for the entire humanity!As for "Wessam, "he received peculiar discipleship for Christ ... You have a special status with Christ, and God is glorified in your work and conduct.Each of you has a flavor, and I glorify God for all I hear about you.As for "Marcos," my joy of him is great because you, O Marcos, by your perfect faithfulness and Christian conduct, rejoice in Christ's heart.I implore God that you evangelize Christ, and that by your sacrifice and your love manifest, to the people, the love of Christ…I thank God for His love for you and His support of you.

- Your love for each other ought to be perfect and robust so that neither the world nor Satan can pull you away or overcome you.If you unite spiritually by the perfect bond of love, you shall be mighty.And I don't mean that you should be physically united because being far or close pertains not only to the flesh but also to the hearts but to being united spiritually and heartedly.Every one of you must acknowledge the needs of his brother and fulfill all his spiritual and physical necessities.Let every one of you prefer his brother over himself.The closeness of the bodies and hearts is good, but when the hearts are close, and the bodies are afar…Such dimension has no importance… I, for example, am physically far away from you, but my heart is with you.Between me and you are contents and oceans, but I am very close to you, and my heart is with you.I do not know when I will see you, for I may depart from this world and not see you. (This was a prophecy uttered by the mouth of the pious Dr. Farouk, for indeed, he departed before he saw his children)At that time, there will be no dimensions or oceans; rather, I shall be with you forever.

- Your reading of the Gospel should be consistent, and your study should be firm.Your reading should not be "Hit-and-run" so that the word pierces your heart as a sword.Thus, it refutes you and reveals to you the hidden sins.Consequently, you shall measure yourself, your conduct, and your behavior according to the commandment.The word of God will enter your heart and judge you!How much more would your spiritual growth be if you started today by reading the Bible with a conscious reading?Through your negative daily dealings with the world and the spiritual power of the Bible, you will be built up more and more, and you will become spiritually great people. And you will obtain the joy no one will ever take from you.

- "So now, brethren, I command you to God and to the word of His grace, which can build you up and give you an inheritance among all those who are sanctified." Acts 20:34. This is my command to you …

- Your earthly success will remain worthless until the heavenly light, which glorifies God, emerges from it. My wish and commandment to you is the perpetual connection with heaven and God regardless of any reasons or their importance. Also, despite the lack of time, you should prioritize God and spiritual matters in your lives. You must always examine your lives in the light of the Bible, the commandments, the Pauline epistles, the Catholic Epistles, the sermons, and the spiritual books written by the holy Fathers, for they are powerful and beneficial.

- Go into your rooms, shut your doors behind you, and pray for your Father, who is in the secret place. Stay put, listen, and learn from Him the behavior and the life so that you be comforted and joyful, and your joy may remain whole.

72

Friendship in Christ

The Synaxarion of the 13th day of the blessed month of Paone, the Church commemorates the departure of St. John the 2^{nd,} bishop of Jerusalem. He departed in the year 419 AD. The life of this saint is profoundly touching, and it opens the door of great hope in Christ Jesus. At the beginning of his life, he was an ascetic hermit, abundant in mercy, and had a good report and many virtues that qualified him to be the ordained bishop of Jerusalem. He had a life-long friend, in the Spirit and in the koinonia of the hermit life, who was also chosen to be the bishop of Cyprus. That was Father Epiphanius.

So it happened that upon Father John becoming a bishop, he slipped into fleeting glory, luxurious life, and authority similar to the kings and the princes of the world. He acquired wealth and began making feasts and preparing tables for people of prestige and close friends. The vessels for the table were made of silver and gold, despite the people's poverty during that time. When his spiritual friend, St. Epiphanius of Cyprus, heard that, he couldn't believe anything because he was aware of the magnitude of the ascetic and merciful life they both observed at the monastery.

When such news increased, he traveled to Jerusalem, indicating that he was visiting the holy places but indenting to confirm what he had heard. So when he visited Father John and was honored by banquets, he saw the silver vessels …. History tells us that his heart was hurt by what he encountered!

Then he went to one of the nearby monasteries to spend some time ….From there; he sent messengers to Father John asking to borrow those silver vessels to honor some of his visitors. Father John delivered all the vessels to Father Epiphanius. When he received the silver vessels, he sold them all and gave the money to the poor. He did not keep any of it at all. When Abba[231] John asked for the vessels, Father Epiphanius responded: "Allow me several days." And when he repeated his request, he received the same response as the first time. Thus …. Abba John began to have doubts concerning the silver vessels.

And so it happened that they met at the Church of the Holy Sepulcher … Abba John grabbed the collar of his friend Abba Epiphanius while saying to him: "I will not let you go unless I recover the silver vessels which you borrowed from me." Abba Epiphanius began to awaken his conscience and preach to him with the word of the Spirit. Abba John became blind! But his inner insight was opened, and he wept with the tears of repentance and regret, entreating Abba Epiphanius to pray for him. St. Epiphanius prayed for his sake, and one of his eyes was healed. He told him, "Behold, the Lord Christ has left one of your eyes blind as a reminder for you."

History says: Abba John, from that time forward, diligently walked in the path of charity and tenderness for the poor and needy. He returned to his first status, complementing it with fasting, prayers, and acts of love and mercy for all destitute, to the point that they did not find even one "Dirham" with him at the time of his departure.

This magnificent account reminded me of two young lads who were colleagues at one of the universities in Alexandria. Their spirits were attuned by genuine Biblical love, as they fasted and prayed a lot. They served the Lord a modest service, yet with all faithfulness and joy. They continued steadfastly attending the youth assembly at the Church of St. George of Sporting … Always confessing and partaking in the Divine Mysteries.

When they completed their studies, they were separated due to work circumstances. They met with each other whenever they had the opportunity to do so. Perhaps once a year. Thus, as they delved into practical life and became excessively preoccupied with its requirements, their meetings occurred at distant intervals. Then, one traveled abroad to one of the countries during the early days of immigration around 1960 AD. He integrated into the new milieu, hoping to succeed in that foreign country. There was no Church or Christian Egyptians … That was towards the end of the sixties era of the past century. There were many obstacles: Language, foreignness, and lack of a Church…. Etc. And so it was, under all these pressures, and over the years, he became lukewarm gradually until he ended up with an unacceptable life. He adhered to a female

---
[231] Father.

colleague, became a couple, and his life was a continuous descent into sins .... Fasting was weakened, for there was no motivator until it became absent from daily living. Prayers became lukewarm until it ended up just a brief recitation of "Our Father..." with a wandering mind and coldness that struck the heart.

This brother spent many years—up to 12 years —in such a situation, constantly declining from bad to worse.

After there were no tidings of this brother for years, even if he called, he always said briefly that he was fine without offering any details, and his spiritual brother heard rumors concerning his conduct and his life in the foreign land. He did not believe it! All he knows about his friend is the accumulation of the days of boyhood and youth. Long years in which they enjoyed fellowship with Christ to the fullest extent of a human being's ability ... For Christ is the entire life, the occupier of mind and thought .... The focus of talking and of silence ... He is the aim and the means, of such aim, at the same time ... They did not know anything except Jesus Christ and Him crucified .... By Him and in Him is all the life ....Though Him they knew every man and made wise in everything. How can the paths slip like this? How can sin become acceptable as a method of life? Where are the funds for prayers, fasting, serving the poor, and endurance for the sake of Jesus?

Shall all those funds perish? .... God forbid ... that spiritual brother continued to seek information about his friend from every source through friends and relatives in the United States so that they might reach him or help him.

Then, Behold, the grace started to act. Isn't he my brother in Christ and the partner of my endeavor? How can I forsake him like this? These were sacred thoughts that motivated him to serve and sacrifice and an intense love toward a soul about to perish with hunger in the far country.

As the effect of the grace increased ... He acted with courage ... He took a sabbatical leave from his job ... Obtained a passport and a visa ... Left behind his wife and two sons ... And traveled without delay. On his travel day, he contacted a relative residing in a different state. His relative received him, and he called his lifelong friend from there. His friend was surprised by the phone call! And he inquired: "Where are you?" His Spiritual brother responded: "I am very close to you." Old spiritual emotions were stirred up, and a ray shone inside the dark catacombs, so he cried out, saying: "How close to me are you?" He answered: "I am in New York." To which the brother who had gone astray exclaimed: "No way, I can't believe it ... In New York ... I shall come to you tomorrow."The Spiritual brother responded: "No, I will come and stay with you.I got the plane ticket, and I shall see you, by the grace of Christ, in two days."

And so it was …. He traveled to him … And his friend received him with an inexpressible spiritual embrace …. Copious tears were shed and shed …. He brought him to his home, which he had already prepared as it ought to be … House of prayers.He got rid, irrevocably, of all the past in a moment as if the past and everything that occurred in it did not belong to him.

The sun shone, and the light dissipated the darkness … They rejoiced by prolonged prayers and by reciting the midnight psalms, for his friend had brought him a Holy Bible, a Psalmody, a Synaxarion, and unique vintage spiritual books which they had previously enjoyed reading together.

The spiritual brother noticed that his friend did not go to work for a day, two days, three days, and then the whole week.So he asked him:"Why aren't you going to your work?He answered:"My brother, I quit my Job the day you arrived.Because my place of work is all offenses, by which I was greatly affected.Thus, I wished to cut my ties with all the pasts!"His friend asked:"But shall you remain as such, without a job?"His friend answered: "No ….I trust that Christ will provide me with a better job."(That Occurred within that same week.So he rejoiced by God's economy)

The Spiritual brother wondered, "Isn't there a Church close to you here?"The host answered:"Truly, I haven't thought about this matter for years, but there is a Church about two hours or more away."His friend said: "Would you accompany me there?"

They both went to the Church on Saturday and met with the priest who served that Church there.He had heard from many people about that brother. In vain was anyone's efforts who tried to bring him to the Church.That brother requested to sit with Abouna…. The meeting was prolonged for two hours and beyond.His weeping was almost heard from afar… He was cleansed by copious tears in genuine repentance.In the morning, he partook in the mysteries.

The spiritual brother remained with his friend for several weeks, whose days were like heaven on earth. They were satiated by true fellowship with God and comforted with joy, consolation, praise, and prayers.

As they talked, the spiritual brother told his friend:"I counsel you to go to Egypt to seek a life partner.A religious, pious woman who can help you with the hardships and estrangement here."However, he was astonished by his friend's response:"I have vowed to live the rest of my days in Christ, and instead of the sins which I have slipped into, I shall live striving to control my soul, my flesh, and my spirit."So he said to him: "But such an endeavor is difficult for you, and perhaps you become weak and retreat backward." He assured him, saying: "I don't trust myself, but I trust in the saving grace of Christ that aids the weak."

They pledged to pray for one another and keep in constant contact. The spiritual brother returned to Egypt, glorifying God for His Act and benevolence. After he returned, he continued to receive weekly letters from his friend, which were full of joy and spiritual comfort.

Whenever the priest visited that repentant brother, from time to time, he would find him rejoicing in the Spirit and continuing to pray without ceasing or lukewarmness.Moreover, he sold his house and rented a small apartment.He sent large sums of money to his lifelong friend to distribute among the service they shared, of the poor families and the sick who were unknown to anyone.

The repentant brother remained faithful to his commitment to prayer and acts of kindness.His life was so happy that everyone who encountered him found him rejoicing.

On one unexpected day, while he was on his way to work, his car was rammed by a large truck.It hit him in the rear, causing his head to hit the vehicle's windshield.When the paramedics arrived and removed him from his wrecked car …. He had already departed.

God has fulfilled for him the vow that he pledged.He lived pure, ascetic, and repentant.He departed in a state of prayer, for he enjoyed listening to the Divine Liturgy in his car while on his way to work.The car's cassette player continued to broadcast the Liturgy, for the accident did not destroy it.The paramedics inquired about the language of the transmitted Liturgy. One of them, a Lebanese man, responded: "This is a Holy Liturgy prayed in Arabic language."It was a Liturgy prayed by the departed Anba Benyamin (Benjamin), the Metropolitan of Menufia Governorate.He was praying the part that says: "You have come to the slaughter as a lamb, even to the Cross. You have manifested the greatness of Your care for me.You have slain my sin in Your tomb[232]. The Lebanese paramedic removed the cassette from the cassette player and kept it until he handed it to the Priest and the other personal belongings they had retrieved.

The Priest heard about the accident, and he allocated days, him and some servants, to perform all necessary for that pious man. They found a will in

---

[232] St. Gregory Liturgy.

which it was written that upon his death, his body should be buried in Egypt, in the burial place named after Prince Twadros in Alexandria, next to his mother. His body arrived on the feast day of St. Mina the Wonderworker …. He was mourned by the servants, the fellow youth, and all the relatives.

They were contemplating the wonderful acts of God through His servants and the fact that Christ, truly indeed, is the Savior of the world. And that the gate of hope is wide open as the opening of Jesus' arms on the Cross.

73

How Beautiful Forgiveness Is!

One of the magazines presented an article concerning an account that transpired at one of the monasteries belonging to the Russian Orthodox Church. It discussed a dispute between two monks of that monastery, one of whom was a priest and the other a deacon. The disagreement between them elevated to the point of estrangement so that while the priest was performing the procession of incense, he avoided approaching the deacon so as not to render him a blessing! (To this extent, the dispute has raged between them ... In vain were the monks' efforts to reconcile them.)

It was said the priest became afflicted with a progressive, incurable illness that forced him to be bedridden. His condition worsened. Moreover, he was on the verge of death. The fathers (Monks) exerted tremendous effort to convince the deacon to visit him while on his deathbed. But he showed such cruelty that no one expected. On the contrary, the laid-up priest begged all his visitors to bring the deacon to him.

The priest pushed himself, tried to draw near the deacon, and attempted to offer him a Metania[233]. saying: "Forgive me, my brother." ….. The deacon was filled with anger and said with cruelty: "I am not forgiving you neither on earth nor in heaven!

The account states: As the deacon turned away his face and uttered these harsh words, he fell to the ground. The father tried to help him, but he died at that exact moment. To their surprise, they found out that the sick, bedridden priest was standing on his feet, full of health, as if any illness had ever afflicted

---

[233] Prostration.

him! When they inquired of him about it, he said to them that he was seeing the Angels turning their face away from him while lying on his sickbed. Therefore, he was urgently seeking to reconcile with his brother. Lest he is deprived of the heavenly portion, he also said: "I saw the Angel drawing his sword and striking this brother, the deacon, as he was uttering the expressions of unforgiveness, so he hit him and knocked him down. And when I became, at that same moment, in extreme fear …. The Angel extended his hand to me and raised me!"

This profound account carries a genuine meaning for forgiveness and its ability to heal man, not only according to the flesh but according to what is mightier and more beneficial. This account also terrified the person of cruelty, hatred, unforgiveness, and stubborn refusal of Christ's precious commandment. One of the fathers said, "God's mercy is specious before the murderers, adulterers, and thieves. But it is shut before the spiteful."

I have encountered both types copiously throughout my life. And I was comforted by those who inclined toward the work of the Grace, and for the commandants of Christ our Savior… Yet my heart was filled with sadness and pity for those who held on to enmity and trampled Christ's commandment by their feet. I met hundreds of those who stubbornly were falsely opinionated ….Thus, numerous homes were destroyed ….They regretted it ….But it was too late.

On the contrary, the forces of evil or hatred couldn't overcome souls who possessed the virtue of forgiveness. They overcame evil by goodness.

"For what will it profit a man if he gains the whole world, and loses his own soul[234]?"

"Moreover, if your brother sins against you, go and tell him his fault between you and him alone. If he hears you, you have gained your brother[235]."

The matter is simply summed by "Gain" and "Loss." It is known that gain or profit makes a person happy while forfeiting and losing bring sadness to the person. If you gained the entire world and neglected the salvation of your soul, then there is no valid comparison between what you have gained and what you have lost. For the Lord decreed that gaining the soul and its salvation is more precious and exceedingly valuable than gaining the whole world … Thus if the world, and all the things in it, is compared to the soul … The soul transcends above it … Why? Because the world is passing with all the things in it … But the soul, which Christ acquired by His blood, is truly more precious than the world.

---

[234] Mark 8:36
[235] Matthew 18:15

Therefore, concerning the issue of "Reconciliation" and the Christian pardon and forgiveness, the aim ought to be gaining my soul and gaining the soul of my brother ... For if I rendered all the world and all that I possessed to gain my brother, then I am a winner and profiteer. But if I lose my brother and hoard the treasures of the world, establish my prideful ego, and prove that I am self-righteous ... Then I have lost all things ... Because the loss of my brother, whom Christ died for his sake, cannot be compensated by anything of this fleeting world.

I know a person in Christ who tasted the grace of forgiveness, enjoyed it and applied it in his practical life with relatives and strangers. He was forgiving without a measure and seeking reconciliation and peace at his own expense. And he was reaping the fruit of joy and purity of the heart.

He approached me one day, as he regularly confessed, crying with a frown. He sat next to me crying; he was in his late fifties. I calmed him down with a few words and inquired about what was bothering him to that extent! For I am aware that all his affairs were perfect and peaceful. He said: "A disagreement transpired between me and one of my friends." I inquired: "What happened, my beloved?" He said: "There are monetary matters between us, and while discussing them ... We disagreed." I responded: "This is a simple issue. Monetary matters are easy. The more a person abandons greed and loves giving rather than receiving according to the Lord's commandment, then there is no problem." He said: "Truly I know this, and I acted to the best of my ability as such." I asked: "What then?" He replied: "Well, the situation was not free from Lees. Then we went our ways." I asked: "What happened afterward?" He answered: "An hour had passed before I saw my friend facing me. He took me by surprise as he fell into my arms saying, 'Forgive me.'" I responded: "Thanks be to God who moved his heart. What, then, is making you weep?" He said: "I feel as if I was robbed! As if someone had taken my Crown!"

That was one of the rare occasions throughout his life when someone preceded him with humility and apology! It was customary for him to hasten in humbling himself before the other person regardless of the cost. And every time, he reaps divine joy and peace that fills his entire being. I told him: "My brother, don't be greedy ... If your brother (Friend) has gained a virtue as such, you ought to rejoice because he rejoiced the heart of Christ."

As such, that brother lived his life, experiencing the power of his Savior's commandment. Thus, he loved it with complete conviction and realized it was the only way to the Kingdom of Christ.

On the contrary, throughout my ministry, I encountered souls becoming hardened. Thus, breaking the bonds of love without deterrent and holding on to hostility until death… This is a sad state for the soul that deprives man of Christ because he who abides in love abides in God. Therefore, he who deprives himself of love, how can the love of God abide in him?

I know a man who acquired a lifelong friend … Their love for one another was the perfect example. When an issue occurred between them about which they disagreed, each believed they were faultless …. Animosity and division widened between them. Then, one of them departed from this world. Years later, a group of friends was browsing a photo album that contained an old photo of those two friends. When the friend saw the picture of himself and his departed friend, he told the album's owner, "Remove this picture and get rid of it."

I was appalled, felt sorry in my heart, and asked myself, "Does enmity remain even after death?"

The departed Hegumen Maximus of El Maragha[236] Was a simple man and kind-hearted. While imprisoned at E Marg prison, he told me some anecdotes he had encountered. One of the hilarious yet sorrowful accounts he told me was about two men in the Church he served who were constantly at odds. There was a rift between them and a lack of peace. When one of them departed, the other was present for the funeral prayer. However, enmity prevailed fully over his heart.

Abouna Maximus said: "While I was praying and uttering, 'this very soul for whom we are gathered, O Lord, repose him in the kingdom of the heaven. Open unto him, O Lord, the gate of Paradise ….The gates of rest ….' The friend, behind me, was saying with his Upper Egyptian accent, 'Don't follow him O Lord.' Meaning: Don't listen to the priest's prayer seeking mercy!"

I was astonished by what I had heard, and I thought saying: "It is to such an extent, that once Satan reigns over the human heart by enmity, he descends to the lowest levels."

---

[236] It is a city in the Sohag Governorate in Upper Egypt. It is located on the west bank of the Nile River.

"Do everything as if He [Christ]
were dwelling in us. Thus we shall be
His temples and He will be
within us as our God."

– St. Ignatius of Antioch, Epistle to the Philadelphians

74

Memory That Was Engraved so Profoundly

Mr. Hafez Zaki ....A vitreous man who was contemporary to the early days of the birth of the Church named after the great martyr St. George at Sporting. He and his family were among the people dearest to the heart of Abouna Bishoy Kamel. He was one of those servants who devoted themselves to servicing the Church since her inception. The man had an Angelic nature…His body was weak, as he was born with a defect in the spine. Thus, he was short due to this birth defect. Yet was pleasant to everyone, gentle and courteous. He was abundant in prayer, loving Christ, and adhering to His Commandments. He was, indeed, the epitome of "Perfect Christianity" in his generation.

He was well-spoken of, at his place of work, by the non-Christians. At the Church, he was adored by all the brethren without exception. He regularly attended Church from 1959 until he was severely ill toward the end of the nineties (1999). It was never reported that anyone had ever seen him agitated or angry. He was meek like His Master[237]. No one had ever heard him shouting. Throughout his years working on the church committee, it was never reported that he had a conflict with anyone over any issue. That was truly marvelous!

The man maintained the meekness of Christ, and by his fantastic humility, he disparaged himself before everyone….Thus, everyone loved him. Moreover,

---
[237] Our Lord and Savior Jesus Christ.

in his astonishing humility, he was exalted in the sight of the Fathers and the brethren.

During his last years, his memory was completely diminished. He could no longer recognize anyone, including his children and even himself, he couldn't recognize in the photos. Old age had completely eradicated his memory. Several months before his death, during my visit to Alexandria, I visited him at his home. The man was very dear to my heart, and we have lived for many years in sincere love and holy Christian affection. His home was to the Fathers, Abouna Bishoy, Abouna Tadros, and I, like the house of Bethany[238]. During the days of service at St. George's Church, any of us would go to his house, as well as many of our beloveds' homes, to eat, drink, and rest for a little while. Many houses were wide open for us. We felt those were our homes, for the love bestowed upon us was tremendous and sacred.

I arrived at Mr. Hafez's house. I had not seen him for years, and I couldn't bear to see my loved ones in such a condition. I preferred to preserve their bright image as I knew it, away from the frailty of the flesh or the symptoms of death.

I found the man in a condition I never wished to see him in, but I forced myself… He saw me …. He burst into weeping …. I greeted him with a holy kiss, and he kissed my hand. His daughter was astonished when she saw that. I asked him, "How are you doing, Mr. Hafez?" I tried to say more …However, the man was looking at me without focusing or responding to anything. My heart was crushed. It was painful!

Then, without realizing it, I asked him: "Do you remember Abouna Bishoy?" It was as if I had detonated a bomb! The man started shouting and saying: "Abouna Bishoy …. Abouna Bishoy … Brother, how could you talk as such … Do I know Him? Of course, I know him … Abouna Bishoy, Abouna Tadros, and Abouna Loka … They are my beloved ones, my brother … How is it possible not to know them?" Then he fixed his gaze on me and said: "It is interesting, my brother, that your eyes are like the eyes of Abouna Loka!"

---

[238] The house frequented by our Lord Jesus Christ.

I was greatly affected. The memory of Abouna Bishoy was deeply engraved in the man's soul, too deep to be erased by illness, old age, or time. I realized the inward spirit is renewed even if the outward man perishes[239].

---

[239] II Corinthians 4:16

75

The Fervent Prayer

Truly, indeed, it had been given to us, the Christians who believe in the Son of God, as a great treasure: "Prayer," provided that we offer it to Christ our God with undoubting faith. The Lord has shown us prayer through His Divine words when he said: "You ought always to pray and not lose heart[240]....Whatever things you ask in prayer believing, you will receive[241] ... If you have faith as a mustard seed, you will say to this mountain, move from here to there, and it will move[242] ....All things are possible to him who believes[243]."

Our Forefathers experienced and lived, by faith, the "Life of Prayer." Thus, the mountains obeyed them according to the Lord's faithful saying. They healed the sick, raised the dead, cast out demons, and performed miracles and wonders by the power of the "Fervent Prayer."

In the book "The Paradise of the Monks," I read an account concerning a group of monks who lived in the wilderness of Sinai. At a certain point in time, the rain ceased for an extended period. Drought threatened their lives. One of those monks was walking in the desert and met with a hermit, and he said to him, "My father, the absence of rain for a long time threatens our lives." The hermit responded to him by saying, "Pray." The monk said, "Father, we have prolonged the prayer and made many supplications, but nothing happened." The hermit said to him, "My brother, I perceive that you didn't pray." Then he raised

---

[240] Luke 18:1
[241] Matthew 21:22
[242] Matthew 17:20
[243] Mark 9:23

his hand toward heaven and prayed, and it rained immediately. The monk went back to the fathers and informed them of what transpired.

We need to realize, then, that we haven't yet reached the magnitude of prayer as it ought to be—not as a superficial practice or repetitive routine that makes prayer lose its effectiveness, but rather as the prayer of the pure heart, because the effectual, fervent prayer of a righteous man avails much[244].

In the late fifties of the past century, I knew a servant. The Lord had bestowed that servant a simple, pure, and humble heart. Prayer was his only support and refuge in every work and every service. I remember that he was ministering among some laborers. Most of them were peddlers who resided close to each other in the neighborhood of Rawd al-Farag in Cairo and next to the wholesale market for vegetables and fruits. They were simple people in terms of education and knowledge and had their customs, methods of living, and rationalization. They had problems and altercations within their milieu under the norms and values of their society, their language, and how they perceived their surroundings.

That good servant entered into the midst of those groups of people. They were numerous families, some of whom were relatives, and most came from Upper Egypt. They had many children of various ages. He was visiting them at their homes, spending time with them, and sharing their livelihood. Teaching the children a simple hymn or parts of the Liturgy Responses. And help them memorize, "We exalt you, the Mother of the true Light." Or the "Creed" with patience and astonishing perseverance. And he was talking to the adults with the words of the Bible in a simple, exciting form.

Everyone loved Mr. Michel[245]. Amin, along with his pleasant smile and gentle voice. Because, truly indeed, the grace of God was upon him due to the humility of his heart. As their relationships with him strengthened, they began to seek his help with their problems, which were many, concerning their daily dealings and their finances. Brother Michel had a peculiar approach to solving their issues. He didn't present himself as a judge or even as a listener to their reproach of one another. He did not permit himself to hear the sounds of altercations or the exchange of vulgar expressions. He resorted to prayer by asking them, "Would you like to pray first? Let us pray, 'Our Father who art in heaven....'"

---

[244] James 5:16
[245] Michael.

The Fervent Prayer

As they stood up for prayer, he would lift his heart to Christ, whom he loved, entreating Him with all his soul in such fantastic sincerity and without embellishing words. Rather, with a simple heart, he would present the matter before Christ. While praying, he would recite parts of the Psalms several times, asking the Holy Virgin to look upon her children as a mother and grant them love for one another. As soon as he concluded his prayer, the disputants hugged each other. Truly, the fervent prayer avails much.

One day, a severe altercation occurred between two relatives; they exchanged accusations and insults. Then, they became engaged in a physical fight. The ambiance was saturated with copious talks and quarrels. When Brother Michel found out, he rushed to the home of one of two relatives, for he exhibited significant influence on everyone and talked to him with soft and meek words that turned away wrath, and he prayed with him. Then he visited the other and did the same thing. He asked each of them, "Are you forgetting that today is the eve of the Feast of the Cross? Let us go to Church. Do not let any affair of the secular world prevent us from celebrating the Cross. The Cross by which Christ reconciled the heavenly with the earthly and abolished enmity."

They both went separately as he, Mr. Michel, stood at the Church's gate. When the first relative arrived, he asked, "Is your heart clear regarding your relative?" He answered, "Truthfully, my heart is still not free from Lees." So he led him into a room at the entrance of the Church and said to him, "Pray before you enter the Church and appear before God while you still remembering the vice because Jesus said, 'Therefore, if you bring your gift to the altar, and there remember that your brother has something against you, leave your gift there before the altar, and go your way. First, be reconciled to your brother[246]."

Then he stood by the gate, waiting for the other relative, and when he came, he greeted him, saying, "How are you doing? Has your heart forgiven your relative?" He said, "Truthfully, no." So he informed him, "Do you believe it? He is praying for you wholeheartedly, seeking a blessing and grace for you." The man exclaimed, "Is this true?" So he pointed to his relative and saw him standing with his hand raised before God. Brother Michel said to him, "Let us pray together."

They stood next to the first relative, and Brother Michel prayed fervent supplications and humility before God. He spent a long time, and when he concluded his prayer, he turned around ... Behold, they were hugging each other, weeping and saying to one another, "It is me who is at fault; you are more righteous than me."

---

[246] Matthew 5:23-24

Brother Michel brought them both into the Church, where they honestly and sincerely celebrated the Feast of the Cross. Then they met with Abouna Mikhael, who was a good and holy priest. They asked him, "Can we confess?" He responded, "With joy." One of the two relatives said, "Can we confess together so that you absolve us and recite, for us, the absolution." Abouna responded, "Each one in turn." They both said, "Please allow us." Each of them was swift to admit fault. The Holy Priest marveled; he prayed for them and blessed them.

Brother Michel stood afar, with his head bowed, while his heart rejoiced at the fruit of fervent prayer.

76

The Zeal for Your House Has Eaten Me Up

The Psalmist says: "Lord, I have loved the habitation of Your house, and the place where Your glory dwells[247]".And he says: "How lovely is Your tabernacle, O Lord of hosts[248]!"

We have learned, as it was delivered to us, from a very early age how to love the Church and sanctify her; we long for her like dear pants for the water brooks[249]. ….. "My longs, yes, even faints for the courts of the Lord[250]."Spiritual longing for the Church—the house of the Lord—is a feeling that cannot be expressed in words. The presence in the Church is Joy, safety, and peace. Is she not the gate of Heaven?

I have encountered many whose hearts were attached to the Church; thus, she became everything to them.They lived in the Church day after day and served her till the last breath.One of my beloved ones (Shehata Mahrous) worked in forensic medicine in Alexandria … When we began building the Church of the Lady Virgin Mary at Cleopatra[251]., he found what he had always sought in that new Church! And he became as if he were one of her stones.

---

[247] Psalm 26:8
[248] Psalm 84:1
[249] Psalm 42
[250] Psalm 84:2
[251] A neighborhood in Alexandria, Egypt.

He was always present, always active in all the tasks entrusted to him, and he had a zeal for everything that belonged to her.

When we faced resistance from the outside[252], he became filled with zeal. We pitied him and assured him that the owner and the Lord of the Church were responsible for her safety and that she could not obtain peace from the trust in men. And so it was, through his submission and love, he calmed himself down. We transformed all that[253]. Into more prayers and self-sanctification.

That brother was devoting all his time to working in the Church. We were building the east side of the Church in haste but with great joy. It occurred to Brother Shehata to whitewash and paint the newly constructed walls. He did not hire a painter but decided to do that work himself. He purchased the paint and all materials required for such work.

Upon returning from his job, he would remove his professional clothes, put on the painting ones, and start painting the walls. While he was painting, he immersed himself in praises and glorifications. His voice was ecclesiastical and comforting.

One of those days, and before the work was completed, he came to the Church as usual, changed into painting clothes, and immersed himself in the work. His hand is holding the brush, and his sweet voice utters praise. Next to him were young lads who loved his spirit, compassion, and attachment to the Church. Suddenly, they realized that he had ceased to praise. His sweet voice fell silent. They turned to him ... Behold, he was lying on the Altar's floor ... in a fleeting moment, the voice ceased on earth to resume the new hymn in heaven! From the visible Altar to the heavenly Altar ... His departure was mesmerizing .... Blessed is he ....

+ At the same Church, one of her committee members (Mr. Milad Aziz).... a pious and humble man. God had bestowed him with a simple heart full of love. Upon his retirement, he found his place of rest in the Church; he spent most of his day there. He was very affectionate towards the poor ... So they loved him, not only because he honored them and was generous but also because of his kind treatment and the humility of his soul.

That man, also, departed to Paradise a few minutes after leaving the Church....He was adorned with every spiritual adornment, pious life, and unceasing prayers. His departure brought forth sorrow within the souls, but

---

[252] From the Egyptian government concerning building permits.
[253] Obstacles.

the poor missed him the most as their supporter who bears their burden upon himself.

77

Your Word Is a Lamp to My Feet

I know a lady, in Christ, who began the journey of life, being the only child of her parents, in one of the villages of Upper Egypt. From a very early age, her insight was opened to the enlightenment of life in Christ. Her father was a pious, God-fearing man and a devout deacon. He was merciful to the poor and had tender feelings toward his only daughter. That young girl was raised in the bosom of the small village Church. She had no comfort except in the Holy Bible, reading it with passion. Thus, it was imprinted in her pure memory and engraved in her depths. That life of purity enabled her to comprehend the Holy Books with a scarcely unparalleled understanding. She memorized many books by heart as a person who ruminates life and meditates in the "Law of the Lord," by which she was delighted day and night.

Once her life became permeated with the Living Bible, she began to draw more from its fountain over a period of nineteen years, during which she had memorized many of the books of the New Testament such as The Epistle of St. James, First Epistle of St. Peter, the majority of the Gospel according to St. John, and the Sermon on the Mount. From the Old Testament: Most of the Psalms, many Chapters from the Book of Isaiah …. Etc. Add to that her mental and spiritual understanding of the entire Bible. You may even be surprised to know that the vintage names, all the circumstances, all accounts, and all that is mentioned in the Holy Bible were imprinted and perpetually present in her heart and her pure memory.

One of the interesting facts is that she did not know how to read except for the Holy Bible. Only through the bible, and by the Bible, she learned how to read. For she was never enrolled in the secular schools, nor did she obtain any knowledge of the science of this world.

Her father married her off to his sister's son[254]. He was also a simple man in the prime of his life, a loving man of Christ, living a simple rural life according to the traditions of his generation, possessing dignity despite his young age, strict, and wise. He also did not obtain any form of education. He was illiterate yet rejoiced in his love for Christ and the Church. While still a young lad, he was one of those enthusiastic and eager people to build a Church in his village. Thus, he participated with all his effort and time in doing so. As he and the others were digging the foundation for the Church, they discovered a vintage censor buried. Even though the land they had chosen to build the Church on was part of a farm, therefore, they rejoiced and strengthened their hands for work.

Once he was joined to his wife by the bond of Holy Matrimony, the pious life she was living and the Biblical knowledge she enjoyed evoked, in him, the "Holy Zeal." Thus, he requested that she teach him how to read the Holy Bible. She did. He became happy and joyful by that grace, and he began to draw, for himself, from the "Fountain of Life." Until he transcended above and beyond those who studied and learned so that he was, many years before his departure, reading the Holy Bible regularly, both testaments, two times a year. Such reading added, to him, virtue and love for ministry. Hence, he was serving, within the scope of his influence, every soul that came in contact with him. Strived as an ambassador, reconciling people to God and reconciling people with each other, and showing them the way to their salvation. He left behind a unique life of pure love, humility, sufficiency, and spiritual satiation, even though his portion from the ruins of this fleeting world did not exceed the "Sufficiency in everything[255]."

Rural life became unprofitable for that good man and his virtuous wife. So they relocated to Cairo, settled there for several years then moved to one of the cities of Lower Egypt. The man was struggling, as a laborer, to support his family and could barely obtain the necessities. However, joy and thanksgiving did not depart from his life, and his tongue was gushing with praise for the

---

[254] Acceptable marriage by the Church and by the people according to the values and traditions of that era.
[255] Bare minimum.

blessings bestowed upon him by the Lord. Thus, he was happy with the "Few" to the highest extent of happiness. Perhaps that spiritual behavior, which convicts thousands of families who own everything but have neither gratitude nor joy, was due to the contentment of the wife, who was relying on God and not greedy in anything. Rather, she offered alms from the "Few" to those most in need.

Due to their low income and distressed situation, that simple family lived in one of the impoverished neighborhoods on the city's outskirts. In one of the alleys of that neighborhood, they rented a small house. None of the Christians resided in that area because of the harsh, unfavorable environment concerning customs, norms, and behaviors. Not to mention shouting, altercations, and unceasing vulgar expressions. The language and behavior of people in such destitute neighborhoods are unbearable.

But just as the righteous Lot, who dwelt in the city of the wicked, was protected by Divine power, the Angel of the Lord also became a guardian to that family. Therefore, that unfavorable environment didn't affect the healthy mental state of the wife or the good husband. On the contrary, they preserved their children from mingling with the evil company. The mother was abundant in prayers, praises, and sowing, in her little children, the seeds of the "Life with God." Along with her regularity in life with Christ, constant partaking in the mysteries, and conscious reading of the Word of life.

She became a source of blessing even to her non-Christian neighbors. They approached her to hear her words. She was leading them, by her life of humility, to peace. They knew she was holy—body, soul, and spirit—and that her tongue did not utter one obscene word. She also did not like to hear shouting, insults, or idle talk. Therefore, if they convened with her, they took heed not to utter any vulgar word.

They respected and loved her, and there was no dispute or quarrel between her and anyone. Hence, she bore witness to Christ by her life, and they testified that she was not of this world.

That pious woman spent every evening with her little children, closing her door behind her as if she were entirely isolated from the outside world, satiating them with prayers, praises, and Spiritual hymns, for God had bestowed her with a melodious angelic voice. Thus, it was imprinted in the beings of the little ones, the love of Christ, the love of praise, and the life of prayer, in addition to what she had instilled in them a passion for Biblical memorization.

Her children multiplied around her as the Lord bestowed her mercy and bounty. She epitomized what the Palmist said: "Like a fruitful tree .... Her children like olive plants[256]." She cared for them, met their needs, and continually rendered her best efforts. Many times, amidst the busyness of the day and the vast number of requests, she was physically exhausted, and when she felt distressed, she would sit down suddenly and ask one of her sons saying: "Hand me the Bible, my son, for I feel my soul is departing from me." As soon as she opened and read her Bible, she returned to her joy and consolation as if she were recharged to continue the life journey. Her soul was thirsty for the word of God to be quenched, satisfied, and overflowing. For out of her heart, rivers of living water were flowing according to the saying of the Lord Christ[257].

Since she had no relatives or family in that city, she stayed home and only went out once every week on Sunday. She would take her children to Church, partake in the Divine Mysteries, and return home full of grace and peace with them. Her children would notice that her clothes perfumed the entire house and her wardrobe scented incense.... It was as if she was accumulating the scent of incense from the frequent liturgies. In truth, the incense of prayer flowed from her clothes and her entire life.

During the fifties era, she gave birth to a baby girl, the fifth in the order of her children. The child was a miracle of beauty in her creation, with her golden blonde hair, blue eyes, and bright fair skin. The girl's beauty and wit mesmerized all her neighbors and acquaintances. The girl fell ill at the age of two, and the doctors failed to treat her. She was weakening and withering day after day. One afternoon that righteous mother was holding her sick daughter. All of a sudden, her soul departed while in the bosom of her mother, who never had any prior experience with such matters. She placed her daughter's body on the bed and knelt next to her, crying, praying, and saying: "Lord, you know that your maidservant is poor, feeble, and lacking in knowledge. And I have no one but You. She is your daughter, Your Creation, and the works of Your hand. I received her from Your hands, and in Your hands, I submit her. From You and for You are all things[258]. The Lord gave, and the Lord has taken away; Blessed be the name of the Lord[259]."

Her spiritual approach and conduct became a practical sermon to everyone around her.

---

[256] Psalm 128:3
[257] John 7:38
[258] I Chronicles 29:14
[259] Job 1:21

"Filthy talk makes us feel comfortable with filthy action. But the one who knows how to control the tongue is prepared to resist the attacks of lust."

— St. Clement of Alexandria

78

The Ministry of Prayer

At the end of 1979, I went to offer my condolences to an elderly woman upon her husband's departure. That family was one of the Church attendees that, upon establishing the Church of the Angel, became closer to their residences. So she and her husband were accompanied by one of their sons, in his car, to the Church. Also, many times the man and his wife would go, to church, on foot. In his last years, he suffered from paralysis, which prevented him from walking. He was saddened that he could not walk to the Church on his feet. So I used to humor him, saying: "I also do not go to the Church walking on foot; I go by car." We had a pleasant relationship with them …. For they were a religious family who raised their children in the fear of God. I had a strong, loving bond with them. Since one of their sons was a student[260] of mine at the College of Engineering in 1965.

I convened with that honorable lady, talking and contemplating the word of God. We read a chapter from the Gospel, and when we were done, that honorable mother said to me: "My heart aches, and I suffer a lot for the sake of the Americas that are held hostage in Iran[261].!Believe me, because of them, I cannot sleep at night. Thus, I get up several times at night to pray and implore for their sake."

I responded jokingly: "Why? Do you have relatives among those Americans? Or do you know their names? Or maybe one of them was a colleague

---

[260] Abouna Loka was a professor at the university before his ordination.
[261] Iran hostage crisis - WikipediaIran hostage crisis | Definition, Summary, Causes, Significance, & Facts | Britannica

of one of your children?" She said: "None of this, but they are souls in distress, and my heart cannot bear to see anyone in distress or anguish like this."

I truly marveled and said to myself, "This is the Christian heart that reflects Christ's feelings, His goodness, and His compassion and mercy for all creation." I remembered what was written concerning the saintly fathers who were groaning for the sake of everyone afflicted and how they supported the feeble and the destitute with acts of mercy and prayers. And I knew how the fathers, inspired by the Spirit, established prayers[262]. For all distressed souls, the bound, those who are in prisons, the oppressed, the shackled, and the humiliated. So that the priest would lift his heart in prayer and entreat God as an intercessor who shares with all. "Who is weak, and I am not weak[263]?" "Remember the prisoners."

---

[262] **Litany of the Sick.**
[263] II Corinthians 11:28

79

Mothers Sowing Faith

One of my beloveds was a Christ-loving person. He was indescribably attached to Saint George and was confident that St. George, his intercessor, did for him many wonders which were attested, throughout his entire life, by many proofs. That friend of mine, a man whom the Lord opened many doors before him, bestowing him abundant benefits from every direction. When the Lord reached out His hand of grace to him, he became rich in compassion and love. And the grace of our Lord significantly increased, with him, even regarding material matters, was a very generous man who cherished doing acts of goodness. He reached out his hands, with almsgiving, to countless souls. He couldn't bear to see someone in need, distressed, or lacking abilities. He became well-known by this grace and well-spoken by all his acquaintances.

However, I pondered in my heart the secret behind that generosity and that grace of almsgiving he possessed; I wondered who taught him. Who raised him by this virtue? I am aware that in his early upbringing, he was not from a wealthy family with many resources. Rather, he was from a middle-class family. The father was a simple employee, and the mother did not work due to the traditions of society at that time. While I kept pondering those things, we sat once, him and me, talking about the acts of God and the works of mercy that let man inherit the satisfaction of Christ. And it is mercy, an open door in heaven. How wonderful it shall be when we hear Christ's, the just judge, tender saying: "Come, you blessed of My Father, inherit the kingdom prepared for you from the foundation of the world. For I was hungry, and you gave Me food; I was thirsty and you gave Me drink; I was a stranger and you took Me in; I was naked and you clothed Me; I was sick and you visited Me; I was in prison and you came to Me."[264]

As we were talking, the man retrieved, from his desk drawer, an Egyptian pound torn into two halves and said with extreme affection: "Do you see this?" I answered: "Yes." He said: "This[265] is the commandment of my mother; may God have mercy on her. I never loved or sanctified any person in existence as her. Her rank, to me, is after God." He continued saying: "She held this pound, tore it into two halves and said, 'My son, if you only had one single pound throughout all your life, split it with someone in need.'" My friend elaborated: "At that time, I was a young lad, around 16 or 17 years old. And out of my love for my mother and her commandment, I followed her advice to the T. As God honored me with many goods, my mother's commandment continued to be sacred to me. Because it is, in fact, the commandment of Christ by which she thrived despite her inadequate means. Yet, her life was only giving and sacrifice. Therefore, she has lived a life of perpetual joy with an illuminated face all her life. Because 'God loves a cheerful giver[266].' She lived and experienced God's love through the love of the poor … I feel that this is the mystery of blessing in my life."

I continued glorifying God, whom our forefathers worshipped with genuine piety. I followed His holy commandment, which is the gate of heaven, and delivered it to their children as a "Life" and "Applied Practical Experience."

Another wise mother who possessed a strong personality and love for Christ. She spent her life in spiritual and practical endeavors. Her husband died and left behind, under her care, eight kids. Her eldest son was a Sophomore at the time of his father's death[267]. She had no steady income, and it was very little. On the day, her husband died, and while his body was still lying inside the house, she brought her son into the room where the body was and said to the lad, "Listen, my beloved … Your dad did not die, for he was serving Christ by going about, in the cities, doing good … Therefore he didn't die." She placed her hand in her son's hand and said: "You are a man. Your hand is in my hand, and by the grace of Christ, we shall complete the life journey."

That incident and those words were a driving force for her son forever. The Lord supported that young man and he became one of the great men and most beneficial. He entered the life of commerce, trading with few pounds and

---

[264] Matthew 25:34-36
[265] The split Pound.
[266] II Corinthians 9:7
[267] He was about 14 years old.

gaining experience. His mother supported him and taught him to love everyone from the depths of his heart and soul without discrimination. Thus, he became a supporter of the feeble. He squandered his life serving weak people, the poor, and those with special needs. His connections expanded until he became one of the wealthiest merchants in Alexandria. His relationships with everyone were characterized by "Love" and "Service." He rested in love and devoted himself, day and night, to solving people's problems.

He had close ties with the rulers, including policemen, district attorneys, and counselors, which he utilized to bring justice to the weak and helpless. When the people recognized this fantastic great measure of love in him, myriad requests came his way from everyone, Muslims and Christians. Rather, the majority of his beloved ones were Muslims.

He got acquainted with a newly appointed counselor in Alexandria whose name was Sayed El-Ashree. He was a man of good morals and honesty that was rarely encountered. Upon their acquaintance, the counselor told him, "You know, you are the first Christian I have dealt with. I grew up in a village where all its inhabitants are Muslims, and during my college years, I didn't get to know any Christians as well as in my place of work. I did not fully know who the Christians were until I met you."

The pious son introduced me to his friend, the counselor, and we developed a wonderful friendship until his death.

The virtuous lady (the mother) fell ill after years of endeavor and after she raised her children, all of whom became successful and heads of holy houses, possessing a love for Christ and the ministry of Christ. She reposed in the lord after a long struggle with cancer. The crowds of mourners surrounding the house were thousands of people; they refused to let the Gasket be transported by car. They carried it on their shoulder to the Church of St. Mina at Fleming[268]. Many priests gathered as we prayed the funeral prayer. Afterward, I stood up to deliver a word of consolation. I perceived that the Church was overcrowded, most of whom were faces unfamiliar to me. More than 80% of the mourners were non-Christians. I spoke about Baptism for us Christians, which is the second birth. During this, the Church hands the newborn to her mother to raise him. In terms of the first biological birth, she breast-feeds him, supports him, and then helps him walk, talk, and all other things related to bodily matters. Regarding the second birth, she sows in him the Christian spiritual life, such

---

[268] A City in Alexandria named after Alexander Fleming. Both the City of Alexandria and the Scottish physician were named after Alexander the Great.

as Love without hypocrisy, humility, and ministry of washing of the feet, and trains him to live and observe all commandments of Christ.

I said to the crowd, "All that you observed in this friend of mine (The son of the pious woman) is not due to his righteousness. Rather, the credit goes to this righteous woman who fed him, along with regular milk, the milk of faith working through love[269]."

Upon exiting the Church, Counselor Sayeed El-Ashree approached me, hugged me tightly, and swore, "I have never heard in my life words that are as genuine and truthful as I heard today."

In June of 1981 AD, I was at the Church receiving confessions from some young lads. One of them approached me and said: "A foreign lady is requesting to meet with you." I responded: "Let her wait until I am done with confessions." I went to her as soon as I was done; she was standing next to the shrine of Abouna Bishoy Kamel. I greeted her and inquired about her request. She said: "I am a Swiss woman serving in the World Council of Churches, and I am interested in finding the ideal way of worshipping Christ and serving Him. So I thought to myself, 'I will follow the footsteps of the saints wherever I hear about them. So that, if I was assured of their life model, I follow their example and join the Church to which they belonged.' So I heard about saints who were in Russia, so I went there and visited their places, Churches, and Monasteries. I also heard about others in Serbia, in former Yugoslavia, so I went there. I traveled to Greece and Jerusalem. Finally, I heard about Pope Kirollos the Sixth and Abouna Bishoy Kamel, so I came to Cairo. I got to know many Coptic families and visited St. Mina's Monastery. And here I am now at the shrine of Abouna Bishoy. If you are willing, tell me more about him than what I have heard." Then she told me some of the stories she heard from those she had met.

When I sat down with her for a talk, I discovered she had gathered much information from everyone she met, including Church politics. Even problems and disagreements. I asked her: "When did you arrive in Alexandria?" She replied: "This morning." I asked again: "When are you departing?" She answered: "Today at two in the afternoon." The time was nearly noon. I thought, "What shall this sister benefit from so many stories? It's just entertainment and a waste of time. Also, I don't have extra time to waste." When she looked at me while pondering his situation in my heart, she said: "If you have a little time to spare, my traveling could be postponed."

---

[269] Galatians 5:6

Mothers Sowing Faith

I thought to myself:"For the sake of one soul, Christ died. Why should I disappoint her?..... Who knows." So I told her: "Only if you are serious about your request, for I am not the author of my time or soul. Both, in entirety, belong to Christ." Then, I began to speak to her with words of repentance, the return to God, and the sanctification of soul, body, and spirit because I was aware of the living methods of most foreigners and their customs. She responded:"But this is my personal life." I countered:"I specifically mean your personal life. For if you got to know all the saints, even when they were alive in the flesh, and became familiar with their customs and mysteries. Still, you didn't live a life of holiness, prayer, and following the commandments of Christ; how would this information benefit you?" Not everyone who encountered a saint became a saint. Rather, he who lives in the presence of God and keeps His commandments becomes a saint." She said:"Talk and teach me as you see fit."

We read and discussed the Holy Bible. As three p.m. approached, I hosted her at my house .... My wife welcomed her, as did my young little children. My mother, who was living with me then, also greeted her with a smile since she didn't know English.

When I perceived that she received and accepted the word of the Bible with passion and understanding, I gave her time and taught her as much as Grace granted me to utter. She had a notepad documenting every word I had spoken to her. She asked permission to stay with us for a day or two. I said to her, "Gladly."

It was an excellent opportunity for her because she inquired about numerous matters. We gradually talked about faith, then the Orthodox dogma, the history of our Church, and her saints.(Many subjects.) Afterward, I brought her to the bus station so she could safely travel to Cairo. On the way .... I decided to ask her about what she had gained and what affected her the most from all that she had heard and learned ... So I asked her. She rendered me a response that contradicted all expectations. She said: "The thing that I was affected by, took hold of my emotions and moved my spirit was your Mom." I responded as if I had misheard: "What?" She said: "Mom." I replied: "How so? She did not speak one word with you and cannot because she does not know your language." She explained: "It is true that I fully understood all you have spoken to me and documented it in my diary so I won't forget. Indeed, they are valuable words that are beneficial for my soul. However, I was searching for the 'Living Christian Epitome.' Which I found in this lady."

When I searched the memory, I remembered that during the two days, she had been gazing at my mother for a long time, observing her movement, bright smile, her love for the children, and her silence for long periods as if she were in a state of trance within the realm of God. Indeed, my mother, may God repose her soul, had the grace of God upon her. That foreign sister realized it. The Lord gave her the desires of her heart when she searched to see what the life of saints was like, and she found it in that simple lady. This is indescribable, and all the books cannot express it ... It's a life.

80

Always Ought to Pray and Not Lose Heart

The account of the Russian Pilgrim who was preoccupied with the verse that says: "Always ought to Pray and not lose heart[270]." So he began to search everywhere, asking every one of the preachers and scholars and traveling from one country to the other without ceasing. He did not rest until he encountered a hermit living a life of perpetual prayer. Thus, he learned from him how to live a life of prayer without losing heart. Prayer became the provision of life and the breath of life that is indispensable. His heart began meditating with prayer even during his sleep. "I sleep, but my heart is awake[271]." This is said by the Bride in the Book of Songs.

The account of the Russian Pilgrim has a profound impact on the lives of Christians around the world, especially the Orthodox who seek and long for a life of Christian perfection and a life of prayer. The origin of this life of perpetual prayer and its practice was done, in fact, by the early Desert Fathers, such as Saint Anthony, Macarius, Abba Bemwa, and John the Short, whose minds underwent a state of Trance during payer to the point of the unawareness of his surroundings. Abouna Bishoy Kamel was influenced by the life of the Russian Pilgrim and was apprenticed to the Life of the Fathers, and he wished for all his spiritual children to practice it. He often directed them, during confession, to meditate and utter the name of Salvation that belongs

---

[270] Luke 18:1
[271] Songs 5:2

to our Lord Jesus Christ, according to the Tradition of the Fathers, by this short prayer, or as he named it, "The Arrow Prayer": 'O Lord Jesus Christ, have mercy on me.', 'O Lord Jesus Christ, help me.' 'O Lord Jesus Christ, save me.' 'I praise You, O Lord Jesus Christ.'

I recall that in the year 1966 AD, I was traveling from Cairo to Alexandria. The Grace of God arranged that my seat on the train be next to a modest Monk in appearance who did not raise his sight from the floor. I greeted him, sat in my seat, and immediately felt blessed. He did not speak to me, look at me, or be concerned about my presence beside him. A full hour had passed while I noticed his lip-sync occasionally, and I hardly noticed their movement. So I was encouraged and told him, "Father, tell me a 'Word of Profit[272]."He put his hand inside his pocket and brought out a small piece of paper written on it, with a simple handwriting, the following:

"Lord Jesus Christ, have mercy on me."
"Lord Jesus Christ, help me."
"Lord Jesus Christ, save me."
"I praise You, my Lord Jesus Christ."

Remember me in your prayers – Hegumen Angelos El-Suryani[273].

He turned and said to me, "Keep praying this prayer. The more you pray it, the more consolation you will enjoy." Then he turned back as before until we arrived in Alexandria. I greeted him, and everyone went their separate ways.

I found out later that Pope Kirollos, may the Lord repose his soul, had assigned him to serve for some time at the Church of Saint George the Martyr located at Moharam Bek[274]. At the beginning of her founding. (During that time, the Church belonged to the Monastery of the Martyr Saint Mina the Wonderworker at Mariout[275].) There, at the Church, he ministered in serenity, writhing these papers containing the "Perpetual Prayer" and distributing them to everyone, especially young people. This prayer has benefited many of them, and they were encouraged and advanced in their Spiritual lives.

When I was ordained Priest at the Monastery of Saint Mina the Martyr, I encountered Abouna Angelos in his simplicity, humility, and amazing effortless love. How happy was he when he saw me? He offered me compassion, humility, and valuable pieces of advice. We spent several days together at the Monastery. I never perceived him busy on any of those days except with prayer. Prayer poured

---

[272] A Spiritual advice and teaching.
[273] The Syrian Monastery of the Virgin Mary. Egypt.
[274] A neighborhood in Alexandria, Egypt.
[275] Lake Mariout is a brackish lake in northern Egypt near the city of Alexandria.

on him an anointing of holiness, humility, and meekness of the heart. Later, he became the father of confession for the nuns until he departed in peace.

The account of the Russian Pilgrim reminded me of Brother Youssef. A man who lived among us and fell asleep in the Lord in the year 1969 AD. He was a poor man who lived celibacy in a simple, modest room. He had a married sister who supported him. He used to come to our Church of Sporting and spend long hours in a corner of the Church. When he became advanced in days, he continued, despite a bent back and walking in slowness, to come to the Church every day early in the morning holding his Bible and some booklets, tied together in one group, and sit at one of the Church corners—praying, praising, and reading for long hours without talking with people and without mingling with anyone. He had no friends or family and was not busy with anything. Rather, he was consecrated and devoted to prayer. If anyone met him on the road, he would always be in a state of heart-prayer that never ceased. His appearance resembled that of a wilderness hermit. His face was shining with grace. Many of those who came to Church perceived him as a silent worshipper. Thus, they would ask him, saying, "Pray for us, Brother Youssef." He would smile and respond, saying, "It is me who needs prayers."

He fell asleep in the Lord without illness or any other condition while praying and praising God.

Among those whom I encountered, Holding on to the grace of perpetual prayer, was the departed Bishop Anba Bemwa. I have had a strong bond of love with him ever since we met at the Monastery of Anba Bishoy in 1967 AD; at that time, he was seeking the monastic life. The relationship between us became even more vital when we were imprisoned for several months together in 1981 AD. At that time, I got to know him closely. I found him to be a beautiful Icon of the life of prayer, as he didn't talk much with people. Instead, he always prayed diligently, especially the prayer of the heart. He used to tell me that his role model was the departed Pope Kirollos. Even though he never met him in the flesh, the spirit of the "Man of Prayer[276]." was his motive for his life and his endeavor.

Sometimes, he would sit alone, praying parts of the Divine Liturgy. He kept telling me: "The words of the Liturgy are the deepest propound prayer that can be prayed all the time except the Epiclesis.[277]"

---

[276] Pope Kirollos was known by the "Man of Prayer."
[277] Invocation of the Holy Spirit.

He was, during the early days of the fort five days of imprisonment, sharing a cell with Anba Ammonious, Bishop of Luxor. The man was almost silent, and they did not speak together for days. His Grace Anba Bemwa told me regarding that arrangement: "This helped more to enjoy prayer as if I were alone in the wilderness."

The life of prayer was apparent on Anba Bemwa's face, filling him with joy and peace. His face never appeared upset during the months he spent in prison, despite what was unfolding around us and regardless of the pressures that were oppressing every soul.

Thus, prayer was his fortress and refuge in times of distress. That was testified for by the believers imprisoned with him and non-believers alike. When the prison crisis began to ease, I began to ask most of the fathers, priests, and lay brothers …. "Who is the person you were influenced by all this period?" The answer from everyone I asked was: "Anba Bemwa."

The man did not preach or speak much, and he did not have relationships or dealings with many people, but the Mystery of God, in the lives of the righteous, is not hidden from anyone. Rather, it is recognized by anyone who acknowledges it and deals with it.

81

Testimony of Faith

When God convinces the human heart by His presence, His support, and the strength of His arm, it becomes impossible for the forces of Evil, skepticism, and lack of faith to find a way into the heart and mind of man at all. Because faith would have already taken over the heart and settled on his throne as a testimony for the Resurrection of the Lord Christ, which He bestowed upon His pure Holy disciples when they felt Him and touched Him by hand, as they reached with their fingers the print of the nails and put their hands into the area of the penetrating spear, they shouted out the proclamation of the faith. (Which cuts through doubt with the power of certainty.)

A few days ago[278], I was in a meeting with one of my beloveds. We were discussing this, aforementioned "Testimony of Faith" in the life of every one of God's children, and that when this faith becomes vivid in miraculous ways, the way by which God reveals Himself to his loved ones to help their faith, then the soul will have already placed her hope in God, without hesitation, forever. The soul will also have held unto the reliable and firm anchor, which the sea waves of this fleeting world cannot move or destroy.

The conversation concerning the life of faith led us to many actual accounts of the lives of God's children. Then my friend said: "Why should we delve deeper? Let me tell you what happened to me personally. In my early years as a philosophy student, I was passionate about what I was studying and learning more and more. By the arrogance of the youth, I accepted all ideologies of

---

[278] The narrator is Abouna Loka Sidaros.

atheists and existentialists and those who denied the faith without scrutiny. I continued to judge religion according to the views of philosophers and atheists. I became convinced that religion was a retardation and that religious people, indeed, were misguided people who lived in delusion and illusion. In boldness, I began to spread my opinionated ideology and tried with all my might to influence my peers and colleagues by spreading my dogma among them. My persistence in reaching my target was enhanced as my college years passed. In vain were all the efforts of those who tried to separate me from my ideology. In fact, I was mocking all the schools of thought of the religious people.

"Then the unthinkable happened. My class was scheduled to go on a bus trip from Cairo to Alexandria, from Alexandria to Marsa Matruh[279], from Marsa Matruh to Sidi Barrani[280], and finally to Kharga Oasis[281], the students, along with the professors, as a study field trip. Indeed, we traveled and were very happy. Everything was fine except that on our way from Sidi Barrani to the oases, which was an unpaved road, we were following the tire tracks of other vehicles for directions, and we got lost. Subsequently, we lost our water resources because that road has three water wells. Shortly after, we ran out of water. Hours passed, and the bus was not equipped for such a trip. It also happened that there was a leak in the bus's radiator and that it needed constant filling of water; otherwise, the engine would overheat. Thus, the driver screamed and said, 'Reserve every drop of water for the bus. No one drinks.' We were on the verge of losing hope in living, as the bus would stop, and there would be no chance for survival if we remained lost."

My friend said, "Here I found myself, for the first time in years, delving into the depths of my inner self and feeling that I needed prayer and crying out to God."

My friend said: "I didn't know how or what to pray. But I found myself saying to the Lord Jesus, glory be to Him, with simplicity, 'Now is Your time, and this is Your hour in which I can truly acknowledge Your existence, rather Your love for me and your preserving of me despite my ignorance and feebleness. Now, I implore You to do a miracle with Your bondservant to be the cornerstone of my life and the principle of a life of faith in You. Faith that does not tremble or shake. Show mercy, according to Your Word, to the rest of

---

[279] A resort town on Egypt's Mediterranean coast.
[280] A town located 95Km east of the Egypt-Libya border.
[281] Located in the Western Desert.

Testimony of Faith

these souls, those who know You and those who do not. For there were about 15 Christian students, the majority were religious and living a virtuous life."

"O the wonder of wonders …. As soon as I finished that heartfelt prayer, which I sincerely felt for the first time, I spoke with God from the depths of my soul. I also felt with certainty that He heard my prayer and answered my supplication, which lasted several minutes. The bus driver shouted: 'Thanks be to God; we found a water well and are now in the right direction.' Everyone uttered a great shout of joy. As for myself, I was there within the depths of my soul offering my prostration of the heart, my confession of my Savior, and my inexpressible gratitude."

He continued: "Everyone rushed to the well; all were thirsty, but they became disappointed, as there was nothing to draw with! They stood still. Confused. However, I remembered the well of Samaria and I remembered the Lord Jesus, He quenches the thirsty with the 'Water of Life', who had nothing to draw with and the well was deep[282]. He inspired me to a merry method. I collected, from the students, all their neckties and belts … Tied them together, attached a teapot to one end, lowered it into the well, and drew water. I was the first person to drink. The drops of water entering my belly were like the flowing fountain of Living Water that the Lord had given to the Samaritan woman and everyone who believes and loves His Holy Name. I said to myself, 'Truly my Master … You sprung up, in me, the fountain of Living Water that has existed in my inward parts since my Baptism and birth from water and Spirit.' The Living Water was always present within me, and the matter was nothing more than digging up old wells[283] and removing the dust of ignorance and false philosophy."

My friend had reached the zenith of affection as he told me the details of that miracle, even though it had been nearly 45 years. However, Will the light of the Testimony of Faith fade?!

He said, "The lord has sustained my life journey with more testimonies. All of which became deep, solid foundations that I run to and be safe[284] Whenever life's trials storm me, once I get to them, I say: 'I know whom I believed[285]. And I am confident that He who has begun a good work in me will complete it[286].'"

---

[282] John 4:11
[283] Genesis 26:18
[284] Proverbs 18:10
[285] II Timothy 1:12
[286] Philippians 1:6

He continued saying:"Upon my graduation, I was hired.[287] in Aswan[288], as a high school philosophy teacher, despite graduating at the top of my class. At that time, this matter caused sadness for my family, but I accepted it with gratitude and joy. I did not know anyone in Aswan or any location. However, I traveled there by train. Since I am naturally shy, I couldn't eat on the crowded train. So I remained without eating for a long time until the train reached the city of Sohag. At Sohag station, most of the train cabins became vacant. I chose an utterly vacant cabin from passengers, sat down, and unwrapped my food. However, two minutes[289] Before the train left the station, a man and a woman stormed into the cabin and sat down. The man asked me, 'Can we share the cabin with you?' I was distraught, but since I was shy, I said, 'You are welcome to do so.' I could not eat my food, so I rewrapped it, and since it was not suitable for keeping for such a long time, I tossed it out of the window.

"Then, at the next station, upon realizing the situation, the man wanted to buy food from the station vendors. When I tried to pay, he insisted on paying the full price. Then he approached me. I was sitting next to him, and he said, 'Maybe you got upset because we are sharing the cabin with you.' I responded: 'Truthfully, yes.' He explained: 'This lady is not my wife, but she is the widow of my fellow merchant. I am accompanying her to meet the merchants and collect the money they owe her late husband. Since we are from Upper Egypt, I prefer not to be alone in a cabin to preserve the woman's integrity and good reputation. Lest someone from our city sees us and spreads inappropriate rumors.' Then he asked me: 'Where are you heading?' I answered: 'Aswan.' He asked: 'Why?' I replied: 'I am hired as a High School teacher there.' The man retrieved a card from his pocket and said: 'I have a dear friend named Mr. Adel Soreial. I hope that if you were to meet him, give him my best regards.' I took the card and wondered: 'Who is this man? And what is the benefit of greeting him if I ever encountered him?' However, I put the card in my pocket."

"I arrived in Aswan and went to see the Director of the Education District. I was shocked that I had been assigned as a teacher in an institute in Nubia.[290] I had to take a boat to get there because it was the only means of transportation. I refused, and the situation worsened between me and the

---

[287] Executed by the Education District. Their decision is mandatory.
[288] A City in Upper Egypt that is about 1117.3 Km from Alexandria.
[289] Usually the train remains about 10 to 15 minutes in every station. Passengers have amble time to purchase food and refreshments.
[290] **A city in Sudan.**

Director. I left him determined to return to my city, El-Qantara[291]. I said to myself: 'This is more than I can bear.'"

"I sat in a coffee shop to calm down and wait till the arrival time of the train approached. I lifted my heart in prayer, for I was a stranger, and matters were tense and complicated. I prayed the same short prayer derived from the heart, but this time, it was supported by the first testimony. Thus, my life was different, and my prayer was different."

"Behold, I became shocked as I stared at a passerby standing before me. He is a relative of my father whom I haven't seen in 15 years. However, he recognized me, greeted me with hugs, and asked me what had brought me to Aswan. I told him everything. He reassured me, saying: 'I know that the director has a friend named Sheikh[292]. Of the Institute of Religion. We can reach out to him so he can mediate[293]. On our behalf. Take it easy on yourself. However, I need, first, to go to the Credit Bank as I have an errand to run.'"

"We went to the bank together. He asked to meet with the bank manager and was informed that he had stepped out and would return shortly. We waited in his office. I got bored of waiting, so I got up and started pacing in the office. I saw on the Manager's desk a wooden plate with the words 'FEAR NOT, FOR I AM WITH YOU[294]' was written on it. I became so happy when my eyes fell on those words. I felt that the words were crying out to me from the voice of the Eternal One who knows the heart of everyone. I picked up the wooden plate, kissing[295] it while holding it in my hands. I saw on the other side the name of the Bank Manager; it was Mr. Adel Soreial. I thought to myself: 'I heard that name before.' At that moment, I realized that this name was the name of the man written on the card, which was in my pocket, and he was the friend of the person I met on the train. I took out the card. Indeed, it was the same name."

"At that moment, the Bank Manager, Adel Soreial, entered his office and was very friendly with my father's relative. So my relative introduced me to him. I handed him the card, and he was extremely cordial. He said to me: 'How can I help you?' So my father's relative explained the situation, to which he responded: 'My son, wait for me an hour.' After that, he took me in his car to the Education District and entered the Director's office. I perceived that the

---

[291] **About 1034 Km from Aswan.**
[292] A leader in a Muslim community or organization.
[293] Ask a favor from the Director.
[294] Isaiah 41:10
[295] In actuality kissing the Word of God, which is the biblical verse engraved in that wooden plate.

Director honored him very much …. So he, Adel Soreial, said to him: 'Don't you know that (So-and-so)[296] It is my relative.[297]'The Director responded with an oath, 'I didn't know, and he didn't inform me.' He said to him: 'Now you know.'The Director said: 'You give an order, and I comply.' The Bank Manager said: 'Appoint him a teacher at the girls' High School so he can care for my daughter.'The Director responded: 'It shall be as you said.'"

My friend said:"I became certain, from that day, that my simple life was proceeding according to a wonderful and perfect Divine economy, and there was no room for coincidence or circumstances. Do I meet that man on the train by coincidence? Did he give me the Bank's Manager's card by coincidence? Did coincidence lead me to his office, which was the only place I visited in the entire city? Was it a coincidence that he turned out to be a very close friend of the Director of the Education District?"

"Do all these coincidences come together to serve the same purpose? This is IMPOSSIBLE, but it is a perfect Divine Economy. God, who cares for me makes all things work together for good to those who love God[298]. From that time, I trusted the Lord's saying, 'But the very hairs of your head are all numbered[299].'"

---

[296] Abouna Loka's friend.
[297] This was true since we all have one father and one mother, Adam and Eve.
[298] Romans 8:28
[299] Matthew 10:30

82

If Anyone Wants to Take Away Your Tunic, Let Him Your Cloak Also

My father, may the Lord repose his soul, in the early twenties of the last Century, was residing in the village where he was born in Upper Egypt. Piety Christian life was the main characteristic of his generation despite the lack of knowledge and science. Most of the village's residents were illiterate and did not know how to read or write, but they lived in the fear of God, kept His commandments, preserved the love, and perfected the life of holiness. There was nothing of the deeds of defilement between them, and hatred did not have a place among them.

My father told me that one of his loved ones, at that time, was a wealthy farmer who owned a few acres and enjoyed a high social status among the villagers. He was a pious man who feared God and lived a vitreous life. His chaste tongue always uttered words of wisdom and love for all people, whether Christians or Muslims. If people gathered to chat, as per their customs, and El-Megadess Nashed[300] was present in their midst, they revered him and respected his presence. He was a light and salt for the assembly. All were attentive to him, enjoying his pleasant talk and the sweetness of his tenderness.

---

[300] The protagonist of this account is the wealthy farmer. He was given the title "El-Megadess" because he visited the Holy Land.

It happened, one time, that El-Megadess was going to his field, and it was the wheat harvest season. When he drew near, he saw a non-Christian young man from the village who had packed a large sheaf of wheat from his field and was about to steal it. When the young man, taken by surprise, saw the man approaching, he couldn't escape. Rather, he found himself face to face with the owner of the field from which he was stealing. The lad bowed his head and was ashamed when El-Megades greeted him in his usual pleasant manner, saying: "How are you, my son?" The young man said: "Forgive me, Megades Nashed." The man said: "You are determined to take this bundle. Let me help you carry it." The young man responded: "No. Forgive me, Megades Nashed." The man insisted, saying: "You must take it, for you need it." He urged him firmly and helped him carry the bundle he was about to steal.

Days and weeks passed, and no one knew what had taken place. And so it happened that if El-Megadess Nashed approached a gathering of men chatting and joined them, and that young man was present among them, he would hastily get up and leave the place. That situation occurred over and over. The young man could not bear to be in the presence of El-Megadess. Once, El-Megadess Nashed entered a house belonging to one of his loved ones, where an assembly of people was chatting and talking to each other. The Young man was in their midst. When El-Megadess joined them, the young man sat quietly for several minutes. Then he burst into screams, tore his clothes, slapped his face, and said: "O El-Megadess, you are killing me. You killed me! Why did you do this to me?" Everyone was astonished by those words, so they asked: "What happened?" The young man said: "Can you believe it? He caught me stealing his field and did not say anything to me. Rather, he insisted that I take what I intended to steal. I could not sleep, and my mind has not calmed down since that day ... I am tormented." El-Megadess stood up, embraced him, and said, "My son, do not talk as such. You are the same as my son. These are all minute issues. My field is yours, and everything in it is yours. We, all, are one family, and we all are brothers."

So everyone rose to embrace and kiss El-Megadess and bear witness to the fact that he was truly a man of God. The majority of the assembly were Muslim brethren.

This account reminded me of the conduct of St. Makarios the Great toward those who came to rob his cell. When he realized that there were items they left behind, he picked them up and went after them, saying: "Take these also; you forgot about them!"

If Anyone Wants to Take Away Your Tunic, Let Him Your Cloak Also

He was liberated from what people labeled the "Love of Possessions" or "Love of Ownership." He acquired "Christ," and beside him, there was none upon earth that he desired[301].

Also, Saint Gelasius, whose Bible was stolen by some thief, was precious and valuable. When the thief attempted to sell it at the village's marketplace and reached a price agreement with a potential buyer, the buyer kept the Bible and said to him: "Tomorrow, I will render you the money." The buyer took the Bible to Saint Gelasius, seeking his opinion concerning the negotiated price because he knew Saint Gelasius was a highly skilled scriber with excellent knowledge and experience.

When the Holy Father saw the Bible, he realized it was his stolen Bible. However, he did not say a word but asked the buyer: "How much the seller wanted to sell it to you for?" The man informed him of the price. The Father responded: "It is a good price; buy it." When the thief returned and met with the potential buyer, he said to him: "I consulted with Father Gelasius, and he advised that the price is high[302]." The seller responded: "Did he tell you something else?" He said: "No." The thief said: "I no longer want to sell it." The buyer countered, saying: "I will pay you the amount we agreed upon yesterday." The seller responded by saying, "No." Immediately, he retrieved the Bible and brought it back to Saint Gelasius. He wept before him fervently. The saint refused to take back his stolen Bible but told him: "Since you need it, Keep it."

The man continued weeping and begging, so Father Gelasius agreed to take his Holy Book back. As for the man, he left the world and everything in it and completed the days of his repentance as a Monk and a Disciple of Father Gelasius.

O what a wondrous grace of Christ …. O the power of His Holy commandment that can transform even the most hardened sinners and change the stony heart.

---

[301] Psalm 73:25
[302] That was untrue. The Buyer lied to the thief for the sake of lowering the price.

83

Rejoice in the Lord Always

One of the distinctive signs of the "Life in Christ" is the perpetual joy caused by the presence of Christ and the tangible, accurate perception of Him in every place and at all times. Is He not "Emmanuel," which is translated "God with Us?" Isn't He present in every place, at every time, filling all things, and in Him all things exist? Didn't He say: "I am with you always, even to the end of the age[303]." Therefore, "Perpetual Spiritual Joy" became a sign of sound spiritual life and union with God. However, how is it possible for the spiritual life to reconcile repentance, tears, groaning, and sorrow? It is godly sorrow that produces genuine joy.

If the life of every Saintly Father was considered a "Life of Perpetual Repentance," likewise, also is the consideration of the "Life of Joy" through salvation, inexpressible blessings, and enjoyment of all the gifts of the Spirit. With this Joy, believers fulfilled acts of repentance, prayers, vigil, fasting, and all acts of mortification. With this Joy, they overcame persecution and insults. With this Joy, Martyrs triumphed over the pains of torture until death. With this Joy, Fathers[304] dwelt in the deserts and made the caves of the earth bring forth the same joy as the heavens. The lives of the righteous, in every generation, were distinguished by this blessing, and it supplemented their facial countenance with some sort of cheerfulness. Hence, their faces became luminous with a special touch and grace that cannot go unnoticed by the onlooker, and he finds, by looking at their beautiful faces, comfort and peace that surpass all

---

[303] Matthew 28:20
[304] Monks and Hermits.

understanding[305]. He who was seeing the face of Saint Anthony was seeing the Grace of God. Many of the Saintly Fathers were known as; "Those who are clothed with the Spirit." Because the invisible Spirit became visible in the features of their faces. The Spirit exuded, on their bodies, the unction of peace and joy which the world does not know.

I used to visit one of my loved ones residing in the "Ghobrial" neighborhood. The majority of the residents of this area were from Upper Egypt, and most of them were from poor families. I had distant family ties with that man. He was poor and almost destitute. He did not possess anything from the ruins of this world[306]. He had a wife and three sons. His wife passed away years ago, and then the Lord visited[307] his three sons. One of whom was conscripted into the army and was brought back in a coffin, and he knew nothing about what transpired with him. The second one fell ill with cancer, and the third suffered a sudden heart attack and died .... All of that was within a few years. The man was left alone by himself after these difficult trials fell upon him.

Occasionally, I would go to him and spend some quality time with him. Many times, I forced myself to visit him ...... What should I say to him? Or How should I console him? However, on the contrary, and despite what was expected, every time I met him, I found grace and magnificent peace manifested emanating from his face. Even during that time, he was overcome with emotions, and tears were running down, yet his face was shining with wondrous peace. He was always amazingly thankful. I would ask him: "How are you doing, Mr. Azer? He would always answer: "Thanks be God, Abouna. His goodness toward me is abundant. If I could, I would kiss Him."

(That man reminded me of what is written in the "Paradise of the Monks[308]" and narrated by Saint "John the Short " that on one occasion, upon coming down from the Monastery into the world to fulfill some basic needs, he spent his night in a house for hosting strangers. Among the guests was a destitute person whose rags barely covered his body.

When Saint John stepped out, at midnight, from the house into the open space to praise and pray, as per the customs of the Monks, he saw, in the

---

[305] Philippians 4:7
[306] The fleeting World.
[307] The Lord reposed their souls.
[308] The Book of Paradise, being the histories and sayings of the monks and ascetics of the Egyptian desert : Budge, E. A. Wallis (Ernest Alfred Wallis), Sir, 1857-1934 : Free Download, Borrow, and Streaming : Internet Archive

darkness, a silhouette of a man praying. When he drew near to investigate, he was astonished by what he encountered. He saw that destitute man immersed in thanksgiving and praises, as he was numerating, before God, the blessings He bestowed upon him, such as the blessing of sight, a healthy body, and the ability to raise the arms and stand on the feet. At the same time, thousands of people are deprived of these blessings, even if they are wealthy. Saint John returned to his Monastery and told the brethren how a poor person found reasons for thanksgiving and praise.)

Thus, that poor man, Mr. Azer, every time I visited him, convicted me with his abundance of thanksgiving to Christ despite the many bitter trials he endured. He was saying: "His trials are good, my father." He also said: "God cannot be tempted by evil, nor does He Himself tempt anyone[309]." However, it was confident in the life of that pious poor man that he was seeking what was from above. He thought a lot about the heavenly things and their glory. He would ask inquiringly, "I wonder how much they, in heaven with the saints, are joyful? Who taught them the praises of the Angels?"

His only refuge was prayer. Despite his simple knowledge, he memorized the Psalms by heart …… Most of the Agpya Psalm … He did not cease praying.

As far as his loved ones were concerned, he was an example of "Practical Living Faith." He did not cease to remember them in prayer. Thus, he was always consoled, saying: "I am confident that I am propped by their prayers, for they remember me as I remember them. Rather, they are better than me." Amazingly, the Lord permitted him, from time to time, to have consoling visions.

He would place pictures of his loved ones side by side next to images of the Saints with whom he was closely bonded with affection and love. He used to say to me, "This is my heaven. Whenever I look at them, I feel that they are my life support… I shall go to them."

I saw this conduct in the departed Mr. Philip Attala, the brother of Dr. Fahmy Atalla, who was one of the early immigrants to the United States in the early Fifties of the past Century.

Mr. Philip was celibate his entire life and a meek deacon. I was visiting him in his room in an apartment building owned by his brother in Los Angeles, where Abouna Bishoy Kamel resided during his early ministry days in Los Angeles. I could not see an inch of the walls of Mr. Philip's room as he had uniquely covered them with pictures of the Saints. He used to say: "This is my family …Everyone has a wife and a child or two, and I have a huge family …

---

[309] James 1:13

I arouse from sleep and greet them all and enjoy my company in their midst. These are not pictures on the wall, but rather, they are living, glorified persons. I see their glory and revere them as much as I can."

Thus, the Pious Man continued to live in the shadow of the "Cloud of Witnesses" that surrounded him until he joined them with the Joy and comfort of the Holy Spirit.

84

Harmless as Doves

It is narrated about Saint Abba Abram, Bishop of Fayoum, that one of his congregation came to him. He was a married man. Due to the circumstances of his work, he traveled abroad for a year or more. When he returned home, he learned that his wife was pregnant with a child. The man went crazy and could not find a door before him to knock on and enter except Saint Abba Abram.

The man brought his wife and came crying before Abba Abram. When the Saint asked him: "What is the matter, my Son?" The man answered: "I was traveling abroad, and when I returned, I found my wife pregnant." So the Saint responded with the simplicity of children and purity of a Holy mind: "What is the problem, my son? She is pregnant and shall give birth to you a son who shall be a help to you and in whom you will be pleased." The man tried to explain the matter once and twice, taking heed not to explain it with a scandalous or obscene word. When he failed to do so, he said explicitly to the Saint: "My father, this pregnancy is from sin."

At that moment, the saint was struck with a sort of sadness he couldn't conceal, and he cursed the days in which these words and those actions took place. He said to the man: "Go. If this is from God, it shall be confirmed. If not, then it will not be confirmed."

The account states that the wife miscarried her fetus before exiting the gate of the archdiocese.

(In such a manner, the fathers lived with astonishing purity and chastity of mind. Even though they were in the wisdom of the Holy Spirit, a state of sound mind, and perfect spiritual awareness. However, by the realm of the mind, they lived as simply as our Father Adam before he got attacked by the death of sin. They, by this life, proved that they became, truly, a new creation born from God, created in His likeness of righteousness and holiness of the truth. It was, and still is, many of those who are living by the Spirit enjoy this grace, which is the purity of the heart from the filth of sins, and there is not a word, in the dictionary of their minds, of idleness nor malicious thought.

As we contemplate this matter, we observe the new generations and how the tyranny of the world and its defiled ideology conquered the whole world with all that is repugnant of expressions and actions. Satan has put his finger in the "Media" to spread, with a fantastic speed, to every house and every soul, all that is anti-holiness, humility, and purity of the heart. To the point that young children, at the young age of seven or eight years, became devoid of simplicity, for their eyes were opened to evil, evildoers, and reprehensible actions from such an early age. Unfortunately, we say that the kids have lost the children's simplicity, children's naivety, purity, and childhood innocence.

I have dealt with numerous people, unnumbered, of those who preserved the purity of the heart and its simplicity despite being advanced in age. They lived in the world, but, indeed, they were not of this world. Rather, Christ kept them from the evil one according to His faithful promise.)

I knew a lady in Christ. She was a mother of many children; she raised the children in the fear of God. She lived for tens of years, as a wife and mother, but the purity of her heart was not scratched by the world. Also, despite being a wise woman who managed her home, moved between many countries, and lived and dealt with many types of people, she did not know cunning talk, misinterpretation, going in circles, or lying. Contrary to the popular, none of her neighbors or relatives were able to utter an obscene word in her presence. Thus, her mind became pure and chaste.

An example of the simplicity and purity of childhood is what we perceived in the departed Anba Maksimous, Bishop of Qalioubia. God had bestowed him with this innocent, childish heart. He preserved this heart even though he became advanced in years and was a scholar. As such, ought the pure heart be, does not retain the remembrance of evil or abuses. But shall be like His Master, very forgiving and very forgetful. "Cleanse us from the remembrance of evil entailing death." As such, we implore in the prayers of the Liturgy.

Forgetfulness is a blessing. Not remembering what others had done is a blessing. Let the mention of the brethren be sweet in your mouth[310].

The pleasant people died graciously[311] …. When Saint Macari was unjustly wronged and humiliated for a sinful act he did not commit, did he hold grudges against his oppressors? Or when his oppressors discovered the truth and came to him to apologize for their wicked deeds, didn't he flee? He accepted being insulted, but he couldn't endure being honored!

El-Megadess Ibrahim Gerges was a righteous man who lived with purity of heart and maintained love. Love was his treasure. He had many siblings, and their business interests were intertwined. In such circumstances and with financial transactions, love among brothers usually corrupts. However, in spiritual wisdom and simplicity of heart, the man advised his children, especially his eldest son, to preserve love. When his departure from the world was near, he summoned the eldest son and urged him, saying, "The greatest treasure you can acquire is love. Your uncle, so-and-so, may covet material things. Lose the material things, and do not lose love. Your brothers are your responsibility. Strengthen the bonds of love. Take heed not to lose love."

---

[310] Talk nicely about them.
[311] Egyptian Proverb meaning that humble people received honor even on their deathbeds.

85

Examples of "Giving" with Liberality

Apostle Paul said, "He who gives with liberality[312]."

He also said, "Command those who are rich in this present age not to be haughty, nor to trust in uncertain riches but in the living God, who gives us richly all things to enjoy.Let them do good, that they be rich in good works, ready to give, willing to share[313]."

The abundance of Christian life stems from the heart. It comes from our new creation by the Holy Spirit in the likeness and image of Christ, to whom glory is due. Also, it acquires its existence and continuity from Him, and by the Spirit, it brings forth its fruit.Among the most delicious fruits of the spiritual person is giving with liberality and generosity in distribution. Contemporary Church History recorded, for us, the biography of St. Abram, Bishop of Fayoum, whose reputation for this virtue grew beyond all people's customs and the standards of logic.He kept giving all he possessed without distinction or discrimination between what he received and what he donated according to his ability.Sometimes, even beyond his ability!He became famous in his contemporary generation and those (Generations)not contemporary to him.This is the horn of the "Truth."It is not confined by time.

The More Anba Abram gave liberally, the more God provided him with rivers of blessings, to the point that the post office of Fayoum allocated a

---
[312] Romans 12:8
[313] I Timothy 6:17-18

particular branch for Abba Abram's daily incoming mail, including gifts and money orders, as well as letters depicting peoples' pains and requests sent- by them- to that generous man who was more delighted in giving than receiving[314].

Moreover, concerning this virtue, we encountered witnesses to the Lord's grace and abundant benevolence in all types of believers. The virtue of giving is not limited to one group or another, and "Almsgiving" is not restricted to the rich and able. Rather, there are those who give out of their poverty and those who give their whole livelihood. This is AMAZING.

I knew a wealthy person in Christ, and the Lord bestowed upon him great wealth. He obtained this grace, the grace of almsgiving. However, he was hindered by the fact that people knew that he was wealthy, and he gave without measure. Thus, he believed that people's knowledge of his charity was considered an earthly reward, and it became difficult for him to offer charitable deeds in secret.

One time, his Church needed a large sum of money. The Church committee convened - of which he was one of its members- and presented the matter of concern. Each of those present donated a sum of money toward that project. When it was the man's turn, he donated a small amount of money and apologized for being unable to pay more due to personal circumstances, which he didn't mention. (He purposed in his heart not to receive glory from people. He did not want praise from anyone.) The meeting was adjourned, and most of the members were perplexed.

The man secretly deposited large sums of money in the church's donation boxes. He disturbed them among the boxes on several consecutive days, satisfying the amount needed for the project.

The brothers in charge of that project were amazed at the money they retrieved from the Church donation boxes. They glorified God, who was working in His Church.

---

[314] Acts 20:35

Another example of the love of Almsgiving:

Upon our release from prison during Sadat's presidency, a loved one adhered to me with a unique spiritual bond. The Word of God drew him, so he attended the liturgies regularly. The Word of God became his comfort. He loved it passionately; thus, his spiritual awareness was opened to prayer and enjoyment of authentic and genuine communion with Christ. Although he grew up in a good family, he lacked deep knowledge and understanding of spiritual life.

As our spiritual bond strengthened, he became more passionate and keener to draw more from the fountains of the Spirit. He was racing on the path to eternal life without laziness. He experienced the blessing of giving abundantly to everyone who asked of him. The Lord multiplied his wealth exponentially. He told me, "I know how to deal with God! The more I give, the more God gives me. Sometimes, I give not only from my profit but also from the capital, and I am confident in the saying of Christ, 'Give, and it will be given to you[315].'"

According to the Lord's commandment, He did not send anyone away empty-handed. He told me, "Do you know the colloquial proverb used by amateur pigeon breeders? 'If you let your pigeons fly away, they will return to you.[316]' This proverb is one hundred percent true."

I learned from him how a person can be generous without limits, so he was always happy and consoled.

He was afflicted with unique illnesses that amazed the doctors. He was not able to fall asleep, his body swelled by allergies. He would take his sleeping bag and go to the church at midnight. He only found comfort and help there; the Lord consoled him with visions and tangible consolations and did not abandon him during his tribulation. Indeed: "Blessed is he who considers the poor; the Lord will deliver him in time of trouble[317]."

He lived many years increasing in grace; then the Lord granted him the illness of Paradise[318]. For several months, his faith was approved, and his life was purified. Then he departed in peace to eternal tabernacles to meet his many friends whom he made by unrighteous mammon[319].

---

[315] Luke 6:38
[316] **If a person squanders all his money on almsgiving, he will gain all his money back.**
[317] Psalm 41:1
[318] This phrase was coined by Abouna Bishoy Kamel regarding Cancer.
[319] Luke 16:1-13

86

Confess to the Last Breath

The hour of the soul's departure from the body is the most critical hour and most dangerous moment that a person faces during his life on earth. We heard about the departure of the saintly fathers and their fantastic preparation for these moments wherever they were during their existence on Earth. They departed from this world while holding the flag of triumph over the world, the flesh, and Satan.

There is no doubt that Satan, the enemy, monitors our movements and walks about like a roaring lion, seeking whom he may devour[320]. Undoubtedly, until the last breath of our lives, he throws his darts and tries his final attempt. However, those who were accustomed to defeating him through the blood of Christ and the Word of His testimony, that is, the Gospel that they submitted to and lived, were the ones who humiliated his pride and resisted him. So he fled from them. Those people depart the flesh holding in their hands the testimony of their "Adherence to Christ," like palm branches, and their tongues utter the first word of the "New Hymn." Although the human body is subject to the power of death, and all the organs collapse and deteriorate, the spirit encompassed by Christ does not perish and cannot be overcome by death.

I have seen many righteous people in the moments of their departure from this fleeting world. I remember the day of Abouna Bishoy Kamel's father's departure. He was a perfect man according to the generation in which he existed. He was a virtuous man who lived seriously and refrained from zaniness. When he fell ill due to old age and the day of his departure drew

---

[320] I Peter 5:8

near, his children and grandchildren came to him on that day. His death throes were like the gradual absence of the sun in the moments of sunset. During the last hours, Abouna Bishoy Kamel sat on his bed and rested his father's head on his knee while reciting the Psalms. With faith and steadfastness, he uttered repeatedly the name of salvation that belongs to our Lord Jesus Christ and said with a tender voice, "Dad. Say, 'O Jesus.'" Whenever the man regained consciousness, he uttered in a low, confident voice, "O Jesus." He continued striving in the last moments as such until he departed, and the last word he uttered was the precious name of our Good Savior.

Abouna Bishoy said as he entrusted his father's spirit into the hands of Christ, "Into your hands I commit My spirit[321]." He also said, "My father is being comforted in the bosom of the One who said …. 'Come to Me, and I will give you rest[322].'"

The Virgin the Helper:

In the Vespers Litany, we pray, "And when my soul departs my body, attend to me, and defeat the conspiracy of the enemies." It is known that Saint Mary is the tender, helpful, and merciful Mother of God[323]. She accompanies us during our journey on Earth and surrounds us with inexpressible mother's love. Upon our departure from the flesh, she is by our side, supporting us with her passion and encouraging us as a mother who desires the salvation of her children. Thus, presenting them to her Son and God as faithful children preserved the faith, kept the covenant, succeeded in their endeavor, and completed the race.

The account of Saint Sidhom Bishay's martyrdom mentions that Saint Mary did not depart from him throughout his endeavor until the last breath. He told those around him, "Bring a chair for the lady so she can rest because she struggled with me all the time."

The book "Paradise of the Monks" mentions an account that manifests the power of the Saints' souls at the moment of their departure despite the

---

[321] Luke 23:46
[322] Matthew 11:28
[323] Saint Mary gave birth to God incarnate. She is rightfully and theologically called "Theotokos." St. Paul says, "Beware lest anyone cheat you through philosophy and empty deceit, according to the tradition of men, according to the basic principles of the world, and not according to Christ. For in Him dwells all the fulness of the Godhead bodily." Colossians 2:8-9 The ecumenical council of Ephesus condemned Nestorius the heretic for calling the Virgin Mary "Christokos." That is the mother of Christ and not the mother of God.

feebleness of the body and its imminent death. The book states that when the departure hour of one of the righteous fathers drew near, the monks gathered with him to receive a blessing. Satan appeared to him as a dog and sat next to the cell's window. When that righteous father saw him, he said to his disciple, "Hand me the Crutch, lest Satan thinks I am weak." When he handed him the Cross[324] in his hand, Satan fled away." The monks saw and marveled.

If our outward man is perishing, corrupted, and delivered to death, yet our inward man is being renewed day by day[325] And is clothed by the life in Christ.

I sat next to the bed of a righteous woman during her final moments. She was in a total coma. We were praying the Psalms; at other times, they brought a cassette player broadcasting prayers of the Divine Liturgy. Her face emanated beautiful peace, and her countenance appeared relaxed and radiated in a manner I had never seen. I drew near her and said the intro of the Psalm, "I will extol You, O Lord, for You have lifted me Up.[326]"O, the amazement and astonishment that took hold of everyone. The righteous lady- who spent her life enjoying fellowship with Christ in prayer and observing His commandment - opened her mouth and said, "And have not let my foes rejoice over me."

Truly indeed, He lifted her up and ashamed the enemies who accused her[327]. She reposed in the Lord crowned with glory.

One of my loved ones approached me while I was serving at the Church of Saint Abo Sefein[328] and Saint Anba Abram in Torrance – California. He informed me that one of his relatives- who lives in a city about a two-hour drive from our Church- has been admitted to the hospital and diagnosed with late-stage cancer and wishes to see me. I asked, "Does the man know me?" He replied, "No. He never met you before, but this is his request." I said, "I shall go to him." The brother gave me a ride, and we went to the hospital. The patient was a man in his fifties, lying weak but fully conscious. He rejoiced when he saw me and apologized for the hardships I endured during the trip to the hospital. I told him, "No, my brother, don't say this. I receive a blessing when I visit you." We spoke a few words concerning some Biblical verses we read; I prayed for him, anointed him with oil, and got ready to leave. The patient said

---

[324] The crutch has a cross on top of it.
[325] II Corinthians 4:16
[326] Psalm 30:1
[327] Revelation 12:10
[328] **Saint Philopateer Mercurius.**

to me, "May I ask your permission for a few minutes to talk to you privately." I replied, "I shall receive a blessing[329]."

Everyone stepped out, and we left by ourselves. This brother said, "I love my Lord Jesus with all my heart, and I long for the hour of my departure from this body. Indeed, my wife and children are in a state of sadness and are shedding tears. I pity and love them, but my love for Jesus dominates my thoughts and feelings. Naturally, any person fears death, but believe me, I am not afraid at all. Fear is not a concern to me. Please pray for my wife and children and implore God so that Christ may complete my hours for me in peace."

As the man spoke to me, the grace of God was upon him, and his face was like the face of an Angel. I glorified Christ for his grace that sustains our weakness. I was happy about that righteous man whose love for Jesus -His Savior—reigned over his heart above and beyond all love. I left profoundly affected and feeling sorry for myself. It was only a matter of hours before that righteous man departed to embrace whom he loved until the end and enjoy eternal life with Him.

---

[329] A humble response equivalent to "Yes, of course."

Epilogue

Now that we have presented this bouquet of contemporary righteous whose lives exuded an aroma of sweet fragrance like the precious oil upon the head of Christ in His Church, He who anoints the elderly, the young men, the virgins, and the married people alike …. Scenting all the parts of the Church at all times, even spreading the hint of His fragrance to the ends of the earth.

You see, my beloved, that the life of holiness is the life of being with God and keeping His commandments. It is not limited to anyone or a particular category of people destined to be saints!!

Rather, Christ's door is open to everyone, and He promised beforehand that whoever comes to Him, He by no means cast out. Also, His arms are extended towards us as He hangs on the Cross. And He provided us, generously, the entrance into His heavenly kingdom. To the point that the thief was the first to enter, thus encouraging us to enter regardless of the magnitude of our sins.

- We can realize a great fact from the lives of those righteous people: the yoke of Christ is sweet, and the burden of Christ is light compared to the bitter and cruel yolk of the world and the unmerciful murdering yolk of sin. Let us embrace the Cross and holdfast to the noble name which is called upon us, being worthy of the calling with which we are called.

- Let us keep the love, which is the first and great commandment, together. Let us delight Christ's heart with our steadfastness in the law of practical love throughout our lives. No more enmity, blemishing affections of love, condemnation, gossiping, quarreling, and any more negatives that quench the Spirit and permit the enemy to covet us. Let us love, not by words of tongue, but by deeds and truth, by offering ourselves with all generosity, giving preference to one another in honor, and a sacrifice that reaches the level of laying down oneself as the example of Christ .... Let us lay down ourselves for the sake of the love of our brethren, and for the honor of He who sacrificed Himself on our behalf.

- Let us pursue holiness and holdfast of it because, without it, no one will see the Lord. Everyone should know how to possess his own vessel in sanctification and honor in accordance with the Holy One who called us. The soul, the body, and the spirit are for Christ. The body is not for sexual immorality but for the Lord, for we were bought by precious blood as of a lamb without blemish .... The Blood of Christ. Our bodies became members of Him who bought us.... Therefore, glorify God in your body and spirit, which are God's. We became the temple of God .... If anyone defiles the temple of God, God will destroy him ... For the temple of God is holy.

- Let us put off the corrupt old man every day, denounce all his former conduct, and cast it away from us by genuine repentance, tearful prayer, and confession with pure intention. Let us put on the new man by our worthy partaking of the mysteries and perpetual thanksgiving as a person offering a sacrifice of praise.

- Let our conduct be free of the love of money and without covetousness, for one's life does not consist in abundance of the things he possesses.

- Let your prayers be a sweet aroma set as incense from a pure heart, with perfect humility and without deceitful lips. May our entrance into the Church and the sanctuary be with the utmost dignity and modesty and with all understanding and spiritual wisdom lest we receive the judgment of those who made the Lord's house a den of thieves. They grieved His heart by being distracted from Him, and everyone turned to his own way.

Epilogue

- Let us strive with patience in fasting and prayer. There is no despair with Christ because He is the Savior of sinners. Sin has no power because the blood of Christ cleanses from all sin. Even death, Christ abolished death by His death. And He had risen Lazarus after four days.

- Also, avoid putting trust in oneself. Many had begun in the Spirit and made perfect by the flesh. Christ won't be deceived nor mocked, for He searches the heart and test the mind and all things.

Therefore, let him who thinks he stands take heed lest he fall.

Remember the Lord Jesus' saying, "Be Holy."

Hegumen Loka Sidaros

Scan the QR code to go to our website where you will find

- Book reviews

- Great deals

- Our full library of books

www.ingramcontent.com/pod-product-compliance
Lightning Source LLC
Chambersburg PA
CBHW031844220426
43663CB00006B/491